THE SHINING BEACON
OF SOCIALISM IN EUROPE

JAGIELLONIAN STUDIES IN HISTORY

Editor in chief
Jan Jacek Bruski

Vol. 3

Tadeusz Czekalski

THE SHINING BEACON OF SOCIALISM IN EUROPE

The Albanian State and Society in the Period of Communist Dictatorship 1944–1992

The publication of this volume was financed by the Jagiellonian University – Faculty of History

REVIEWER
Andrzej Chwalba

SERIES COVER DESIGN
Jan Jacek Bruski

COVER DESIGN
Agnieszka Winciorek
Cover photography: Albanian youth work brigade, 1946

Translated from the Polish by Ian Corkill

ISBN 978-83-233-3515-3
ISSN 2299-758X

WYDAWNICTWO UNIWERSYTETU JAGIELLOŃSKIEGO
www.wuj.pl

Jagiellonian University Press
Editorial Offices: Michałowskiego St. 9/2, 31-126 Cracow
Phone: +48 12 631 18 81, +48 12 631 18 82, Fax: +48 12 631 18 83
Distribution: Phone: +48 12 631 01 97, Fax: +48 12 631 01 98
Cell Phone: + 48 506006 674, e-mail: sprzedaz@wuj.pl
Bank: PEKAO SA, IBAN PL80 1240 4722 1111 0000 4856 3325

Contents

Index of abbreviations

AAOC – Albanian Autocephalous Orthodox Church
AFNCL – Anti-Fascist National Liberation Council
APL – Albanian Party of Labour
ASA – Albanian State's Archive
Comecon – Council for Mutual Economic Assistance
CPA – Communist Party of Albania
CPCh – Communist Party of China
CPSU – Communist Party of Soviet Union
CPY – Communist Party of Yugoslavia
d. – dossier (Alb. dosje)
DPA – Democratic Party of Albania
DPD – Department of People's Defence (Alb. Drejtoria e Mbrojtjes se Popullit)
GDR – German Democratic Republic
HTC – higher type cooperatives
LNÇ – National Liberation Movement (Alb. Levizja Nacionalçlirimtarë)
PASOK – Panhellenic Socialist Movement (Greek Πανελλήνιο Σοσιαλιστικό Κίνημα)
PUWP – Polish United Workers' Party
UDBA – State Security Administration (Serbocroat. *Uprava državne bezbednosti*)
UN – United Nations
USSR – The Union of Soviet Socialist Republics

Albania is the shining beacon of Socialism in Europe

(Mao Zedong in his message of greetings to the Fifth Albanian Party of Labour Congress in November 1966)

Introduction

The works dedicated to European communist dictatorships represent, in modern history writing, a rich and varied collection, analysing a wide range of appearances identified with communism – from political-ideological matters to the rituals of daily life. In the wealth of literature, the case of Albania seems to be clearly marginalized. Covering an area of less than 29 thousand square kilometres, Albania belongs to the smallest European states, but its strategic location in the Mediterranean Sea basin has long given this country a greater significance than a country of its size and population would normally warrant.

Recalling the communist period of Albanian history shows a range of phenomena, which give base to the special treatment of this country against the background of other countries with similar ideology, or, in actual fact, its treatment as the totally separate "Albanian case." Attempts to define the specifics of the rule of Enver Hoxha inclines critics of the system to use the description of crazy or irrational dictatorship, built upon a picture of the hundreds of thousands bunkers which cover the country. Other researchers, who are less critical towards Hoxha's regime, provide examples of Albanian rationality, treating it as an example of an exceptionally pragmatic communist dictatorship. In many aspects, the Albanian regime of Enver Hoxha operated in a system which seems to be original and unrepeatable. It is suffice to recall the example of an atheist state, which as opposed to other communist countries, brought about the extreme negation of religion and recognized religious activities as a crime. The durability of the socialist-realism cultural model for a period of over forty years and the application of a "people's war" model, which from the 1970s was the doctrine of Albanian national defence, seem to be unprecedented, at least on the continent of Europe.

It is impossible to understand the changes which took place in Albania in the years 1944–1992 without defining the point of entry – a difficult heritage, resulting from a few hundred years of Ottoman rule, less than twenty years of independence and, finally, five years of Italian and German occupation during World War II. Albanian identity was based for centuries on two pillars: language and tribal identity (clans). Albania was the only Balkan state where dependence to a religious group did not define nationality. During the Ottoman rule, the scale of Albanian converts to Islam belonged to the highest in the Balkans and could be compared only with Bosnia. The motive behind converting was often for fiscal reasons, and also the desire to maintain family prestige. At the beginning of the 20th Century, about 70% of society were Muslims, 20% were of the Orthodox faith and 10% were Catholics. The Catholics lived mainly in the north of the country, the Orthodox people dominated in the south, and Islam was popular all over the country, with its greatest influence in the central parts of the country and in Kosovo.

In principle, however, Albanian society was not accustomed to religious conflict. If there was such a thing, it was usually caused by conflicts between the principles of common law and religious beliefs. In 1912, both Catholics and Muslims participated in anti-Ottoman events. Catholics, the Orthodox and Muslim dervishes combined to fight for the creation of a national school. To avoid accusations of religious conflicts, the majority of nationalist movement documents contained approval of their contents by the most important religious communities. Similarly, when creating associations, the principle of religious equality among delegates was usually set.

Religion to only a small degree designated ethical principles, losing out to common law (*kanun*), which had its origins reaching back to the pre-Ottoman times. The Ottomans did not destroy common law, just as they did not destroy the tribal organisations. The basic element of internal social organisation in Albania was the tribe (*fis*). Because of the declared blood relations between members, the idea of *fis* is also translated as "clan." The division of clans was also overlapped by ethnic and language differences. The north of the country was the home of the Gegs – an Albanian ethnic group using the Geg dialect. The main occupation of Gegs was shepherding, and the clan-tribal structures were exceptionally strong, as was the awareness of autonomy and individual character, formed during the Ottoman times. The Tosks lived in the south of the country – they were generally farmers and, to a much smaller extent, followed the rules of common law. Local identity and family relations (clan) created the identity of Albanians to a significantly larger extent than abstract wider ideas, connected with the state and its institutions. The small state-creating elite was not able to form a feeling of responsibility for, and identity with, the state in pre-communist Albanian society.

The correct starting point for analysis of the Albanian communist system seems to be the period after the end of World War II. In this time, Albania belonged to the most backward and under developed countries in Europe. This can be seen by the data concerning the levels of illiteracy, economic development, health care, and the standard of living. If we accept this as a starting point for reflecting on the communist legacy, we can get the impression that it was communism that led to the modernization and development of an under developed country once known as "the Bangladesh of Europe." When, however, we compare Albanian communism, with its political isolation and the cruelty of its system of repression, with other European communist countries, the results of forty years of Enver Hoxha's rule should be viewed as in the category of regression and destruction. The death of the dictator in 1985 did not come with a fundamental breakthrough, but the gradual movement away from the isolation turned out to be painful and long-lasting. The delayed transformation processes which Albania experienced in the 1990s led to its description in the European press as the "last island" of communism or the "final domino." When discussing the genesis of the social-economic crisis that modern Albanians are the victims of, questions concerning the communist history of the country can not be avoided.

This book represents a summary of many years of research carried out by the author in Albania. This work wouldn't have its current form if it hadn't been for the help of many friends, both in Albania and in Poland, whose reflections and thoughts have provided priceless help for a researcher of a country with such a distinct culture. I would particularly like to thank Professor Andrzej Chwalba, who was the first reader of the draft version of this book, and whose comments enriched its contents, as well as providing encouragement to the author. I would also like to thank the directors of the Jagiellonian's University Institute of History for their financial support, which has made it possible for the book to be published.

Chapter I: The road to power

The child born in Tirana on 8 November 1941 did not wait even a day among the nation, but lifting its iron hand, began to give ruthless blows to fascists and traitors.[1]

The turning point of modern Albanian history is considered to be November 28, 1912, when a group of nationalist activists who had gathered in Vlore announced the independence of Albanian land, declaring the breakage of almost 500-year-old ties with the Ottoman Empire. The declaration of independence issued during the First Balkan War was a reply to the threat of the land inhabited by Albanians being divided among the Balkan states. The drive towards independence was supported in Rome and Vienna, where a plan to create an autonomic Albanian principality with limited sovereignty was formed. The formal ruler of the new state was Wilhelm von Wied, from the Hohenzollern-Sigmaringen family. After the outbreak of World War I, when Greeks and Serbs crossed the border into Albanian land, in September 1914 Wilhelm von Wied fled from Durrës – the capital of the country he ruled. For the next four years the territory of Albania was occupied by the Austrian, Montenegro, French, Greek, Serbian and Italian armies. The idea of constructing a fully-independent Albanian state was the guiding principle for a group of nationalist activists, who in 1920 gathered at the congress in Lushnje. Albania's change in status to a fully-independent country was confirmed by its acceptance into the League of Nations (December 17, 1920).

Deprived of protection from a foreign power, the country experienced a few years of political instability, struggling with separatist tendencies (most frequently of a clan or religious basis). The beginning of the 1920s represented an attempt to apply the Western European model of parliamentary democracy to Albanian conditions and the creation of a political scene, and, as a result, the first political parties. The attempt to create political parties, formed on the basis of a program or representing a defined social environment, ended in failure after a few years. The political formations active in Albania between the wars were based most frequently on family ties, without forming any political programs which could unite politicians from various parts of the country. The majority of society had little understanding of the concept of democracy, and a painful inheritance of the Ottoman Empire was not

1 *Report Concerning the Activity of the Albanian Labour Party Central Committee Announced at the IV APL Congress by Enver Hoxha on 13 February 1961* (Tirana: Shtëpia Botuese Naim Frashëri, 1961), 4.

only the low level of literacy, but also the aversion to any state institution and hostility to state law.[2] In reality, in daily life state legislation lost out to common law, which was anti-state in its substance. The state was dominated by a small group of landowners, who also formed the nation's financial elite. Being jealous and protective of their own privileges and social position, they tried to monopolize state agencies and local governments, allowing only a few representatives of the middle class or intelligentsia, educated in European universities, to enter. Those who treated education as a pass to a career generally met with disappointment, and as a result emigration or political radicalism.

Albania was the only Balkan state in which, during the inter-war period, no communist party was created. This happened despite visible signs of sympathy towards Russia, as well as towards the Bolshevik revolution, which could already be seen in the press in 1917. Albanians wrote about the Maximalists, (as the Bolsheviks were described in Albania) with sympathy especially when the contents of the London Treaty of 1915, which predicted the division of Albanian territory, were revealed in Moscow.[3]

The first Albanian communist is believed to be Kostandin Boshnjaku, a merchant from Odessa, who was a direct witness of the events taking place in Russia. After arriving in Albania in 1923, Boshnjaku tried to find followers among the radical youth organization Bashkimi, but in vain.[4] In the same year, Dimitrii Penchev arrived in Tirana. He described himself as a representative of the Soviet Red Cross, and tried to convince a group of Albanian politicians to apply communist ideas in Albania.

A threat to the radical change in the political mood in Albania was created by an event which took place in June 1924. The deepening political crisis led to a coup d'etat, described in Albanian history as "the bourgeois – democratic revolution." The ambitious social-economic reform program presented by the government led by Fan Noli were unlikely to succeed without significant foreign help. None of the European powers was inclined to help the government which came into power after a coup d'etat. The international position of Noli's government worsened, when he pushed forward the proposition of entering into diplomatic relations with the USSR.[5] On December 16, 1924, the Soviet representative in Athens, Arkadii Krakovetskii, travelled to Tirana in order to initiate diplomatic relations. Due to internal pressure on the Albanian leaders and the unstable situation in the country, he left Albania after a few days.[6] Formally, diplomatic relations were entered into in 1934,

---

2 Tadeusz Czekalski, *Albania w latach 1920–1924 – aparat państwowy i jego funkcjonowanie* (Katowice: Śląska Agencja Prasowa, 1998), 132–164.

3 *Mbi influencën e Revolucionit të Madh Socialist të Tetorit ne Shqipëri (1917–1924): përmbledhje dokumentash e materialesh kushtuar 40 vjetorit të Revolucionit të Madh Socialist të Tetorit* (Tirana: Universiteti Shtetëror i Tiranës, Instituti i Historisë e Gjuhësisë / Instituti i Historisë së Partisë pranë K.Q. të P.P.Sh, 1957), 15, 21.

4 Nicholas Pano, *The People's Republic of Albania* (Baltimore: Johns Hopkins Press, 1968), 28.

5 Chicherin to Politbureau RCP(b), July 18, 1924, in *Natsional'nyi vopros na Balkanakh cherez prizmu mirovoi revoliucii: v dokumentakh tsentral'nykh rossiiskikh arkhivov nachala – serediny 1920-kh godov*, ed. Ritta Grishina, vol. 2 (Moscow: ROSSPÉN, 2003), 88.

6 Chicherin to Stalin, Dec 6, 1924, in *Natsional'nyi vopros*, 286.

after a Soviet initiative. The Soviets were represented in Albania by a representative residing in Athens.[7]

In December 1924, Fan Noli's government was overthrown by forces loyal to Ahmed Zog, supported by the Kingdom of Serbs, Croats and Slovenes. Politicians who were connected with the overthrown "revolutionary government" mainly fled the country. In March 1925 in Vienna, the National Revolutionary Committee (KONARE), led by Fan Noli, was established. This organization was founded to prepare for the overthrow of the dictatorship of Ahmed Zog and restore a democratic governmental structure in Albania. KONARE had contacts with communist organisations, including the Balkan Communist Federation, active from 1920 in Vienna. The appearance of increasing Albanian interest in Bolshevik Russia could be seen when fourteen young KONARE activists were sent to Moscow, so they could study in Comintern schools. This group included the future leaders of the communist movement: Ali Kelmendi and Sejfulla Maleshova[8].

The first Albanian communist group (Grupi Komunist Shqiptar) was formed on August 28, 1927 in Moscow, and consisted of twelve Albanian students.[9] After finishing their studies, in 1930 some of the Moscow group moved to France, and some returned to Albania. Ali Kelmendi played a leading role in the second group. Originally from Kosovo, Kelmendi studied in Leningrad. After returning to Albania he managed to start cooperation with a group of workers previously connected with the syndicalistic organisation Puna (Labour). They created the first communist group on Albanian soil in Kortcha (Korçë).[10]

The most important role in Kelmendi's plans was played by Tirana. Kelmendi met young workers, and tried to reach young scholars, in the capital's cafe "Elbasan." The widening of contacts was helped by his acquaintances among the Kosovan population living in Albania, as well as the help of his brother who worked in the police force. Kelmendi's activity did not lead to the unification of the Albanian communist environment in one party. He was arrested a few times for his activities, and finally in November 1935, after his release from prison, he fled to Greece. When he tried to return to Albania in 1936 he was again arrested and expelled from the country.[11]

---

7 The accreditation of the Soviet representative in Tirana, Mikhial Kobetskii, took place on January 30, 1935 – Albanian State's Archive (ASA), Ministry of Foreign Affairs, d. 417, 1935. The establishment of diplomatic relations was purely formal, as the two countries did not maintain any political or economic ties.

8 In 1928 the activity of KONARE was suspended due to financial reasons. Some of its activists, cooperating with Comintern, changed the organization's name to National Liberation (Çlirimi Nacional), and its representatives were called clirimists (liberators) – Pano, *People's Republic of Albania*, 32.

9 Kristo Frasheri, *Historia e levizjes se majte ne Shqiperi dhe e themelimit te PKSh-se 1878–1941 (veshtrim historik me nje shtojce dokumentare)* (Tirana: Akademia e Shkencave e Shqiperise, 2006), 37.

10 Krsta Aleksić, *Ali Kelmendi* (Prishtina: Rilindja, 1970), 67.

11 Kelmendi did not return to Albania. At the end of his life, he suffered from tuberculosis. After an operation in a hospital in Paris he died on February 11, 1939 as a result of post-operation complications – Aleksić, *Ali Kelmendi*, 146.

In the mid 1930s, a few communist groups were active in Albania. Left-wing organisations among the youth were most frequently connected with the radical youth organisation, Bashkimi, which was active in the 1920s. In Tirana in 1936, a communist group established by Atanas Qendro, who had earlier left the Kortchan group. At the end of the 1930s, a group of Albanians educated in Moscow gathered in Paris, where they published the *Sazani* magazine. Some of them participated in the civil war in Spain, in the International Brigades.[12] At the end of the thirties, communist activists smuggled translations of Marxist literature, and that of well-known Soviet writers, into Albania (Maksim Gorkii). The quantity was so significant that, in 1936, the Albanian government decided to act to limit the import of books and magazines.[13] The Kortchan group seemed to be the most active group. In Kortcha, there was a French-language school, whose teachers were known for their radical views and could tolerate, or even support, a new political environment. From 1936, the Kortchan communist group illegally published the bi-monthly magazine *Bota e Re* (New World), and from 1938 the *Perpara* (Forward) magazine. Before the outbreak of World War II the number of members never exceeded 70 people.[14] In April 1937, a poster appeared on a few buildings in Kortcha with the phrase Rrofte Bolshevizmi (Long live Bolshevism). The Albanian state, which in 1928 took the name of the Kingdom of Albania, treated the activity of communist groups as a real threat to public order and safety.[15] The poster campaign created great anxiety in the government and instigated surveillance of the youth.[16]

On April 7, 1939, sections of the Italian army landed on the coast of Albania, and in a few days had taken control of the whole country, ruled by Zog I. On April 12, the Albanian parliament met in Tirana, and under Italian pressure decided to dethrone King Zog I and give the crown to the King of Italy – Victor Emmanuel III. After this Italian aggression, a large group of political emigrants, some of whom were connected with the communist movement, returned to Albania. In September 1939, the Secretary of the regional committee of the CPY (Communist Party of Yugoslavia) in Kosovo – Miladin Popović, arrived in Tirana. His aim was to persuade the

---

12 Skender Luarasi, *Ne Brigadat Internacionale ne Spanje* (Tirana: Toena, 1996).

13 In 1936, the local government leader in Kortcha mentioned the appearance of communist brochures in Greek, including the works of Lenin. In the same year, the local leader in Durrës reported the confiscation of two copies of *Capital* by Marx in French – Veli Dedi et al., eds., *Dokumenta e materiale historike nga lufta e popullit shqiptar për liri e demokraci 1917–1941* (Tirana: Botim i Drejtorisë së Arkivave Shtetërore të R.P.Sh, 1959), 366, 369, 378.

14 In 1939, the head of the Kortchan group was Zef Mala, after his arrest by the Italian occupiers his place was taken by Vasil Shanto – Nina D. Smirnova, *Istoriia Albanii v XX veke* (Moscow: Nauka, 2003), 190.

15 Based on the constitution of September 1928, the Albanian state became a "democratic, parliamentary and hereditary monarchy," and Ahmet Zog was announced as the king, accepting the name of Zog I. (Tadeusz Czekalski, *Albania 1920–1939. Państwo – gospodarka – kultura* (Kraków: Historia Iagellonica, 1996), 25.

16 Dedi et al., *Dokumenta e materiale*, 397–399.

Albanian communists to create a united party. This unsuccessful attempt to unite the groups finished in his arrest and internment by the Italians. At the end of 1939, talks took place between representatives of the two strongest communist groups. The result was the creation of a joint Central Committee, which was responsible for organizing anti-fascist demonstrations. However, unification of the parties didn't take place, moreover – in February 1940 a "young group," led by Anastas Lulo, split away from the Kortchan group.[17]

The next phase of activity towards unification of the groups were talks that took place on October 11–12, 1941, in Vitomirica near Peć. The meeting was chaired by the Secretary of the CPY in Kosovo – Boris Vukmirović, and from the Albanian side Koço Tashko, Xhevdet Doda and Fadil Hoxha participated. The participants unanimously agreed that the most important task facing them in the near future was the creation of an Albanian party. It was intended to exclude the current leaders of communist groups from the party rulers, as they were burdened with responsibility for the infighting and organisational problems.[18] The mission of unification was taken on by two the CPY activists – Dušan Mugoša and Miladin Popović. After arriving in Tirana, they entered into talks with representatives of communist groups. The reports written by Mugoša were quite pessimistic when evaluating the activity of the three largest groups. The Kortchan group's activity, he wrote, was limited to making speeches and lengthy discussion, far from any attempt to organize an effective resistance movement against the occupying powers. The second group (Shkodran), which began its activity in 1938, held the view that Italian imperialistic aggression in Albania was necessary to create a working class and proletariat. Investment of foreign capital would help to spread the ideas of communism. The third group, which Mugoša described as a youth group met mainly to compete with other by mutually pointing out the lower middle-class faults of their families and verbally argue about the existing social order. Relations between the groups were dominated by distrust, and even jealousy.[19]

On November 8, 1941 in Tirana, in a house belonging to the communist supporter Xhemal Cami, there was a meeting of representatives of three groups: Kortchan, Shkodran and the so-called young group.[20] Miladin Popović began the meeting and, in a speech delivered in Serbian, outlined the international situation and the necessity to eliminate separatism on behalf of unity.[21] The result of the meeting was the establishment of the Communist Party of Albania (Partia Komuniste Shqiptare,

---

17 Smirnova, *Istoriia Albanii*, 191.

18 Frasheri, *Historia e levizjes*, 212.

19 Henry Hamm, *Albania – China's Beachhead in Europe* (New York: Praeger, 1963), 85.

20 Frasheri, *Historia e levizjes*, 229–230. The proceedings were not attended by members of the *Fire* (Zjarri) group, founded around 1940 in Athens by Albanian students. The group was led by Andrea Zisi, who Enver Hoxha described as a Trotskyite – *Kongresi i I-re i Partise Komuniste te Shqiperise (8–22 nentor 1948)* (Tirana: Shtëpia Botuese Naim Frashëri, 1950), 56.

21 Frasheri, *Historia e levizjes*, 232.

CPA). The leaders of the party consisted of seven representatives of the Kortchan and Shkodran groups.[22] Enver Hoxha was chosen as the General Secretary of the Temporary Central Committee. The new party issued a proclamation, calling the Albanian nation to stop paying taxes to the occupying powers and to fight against the Italians. Members of the first Central Commitee divided tasks which they would perform in the near future among themselves. Political issues were to be undertaken by Tuk Jakova, organisational matters by Koçi Xoxe, work among youths – Qemal Stafa, and Enver Hoxha would be responsible for party finances.[23] Despite the protests of some CPA activists, Yugoslav delegates decided to continue directing the work of the party so that its structure would be formed properly.

The party leader, Enver Hoxha, came from a well-heeled Muslim family from Gjirokastra. After finishing middle school in Kortcha in 1930, he was awarded a scholarship to study law at the University of Montpellier. There, however, he was more interested in politics than education and soon lost his scholarship because of his poor academic results. From Montpellier, he travelled to Paris, where he met the publisher of the communist *L'Humanite* – Vaillant Couturier, as well as a rich emigrant with left-wing views – Llazar Fundo. They led the young Hoxha into the world of Parisian lovers of communist ideas.[24] A lack of money forced him to travel to Brussels, where the Honorary Consul of Albania offered him work as a private secretary. In his free time, Hoxha studied law, but never finished those studies. After six years in Western Europe, he returned to Albania in 1936. For the next three years, he was not connected with any of the Albanian communist groups.[25] The Italian invasion of 1939 took place while Hoxha was working as a teacher in a high school in Kortcha. In 1940 he moved from Kortcha to Tirana, where his sister Fahrije lived. In the capital, he came into contact with Mustafa Gjinishi and Ymer Dishnica, who were active in the Kortchan group and introduced Hoxha to the organisation.[26] Hoxha did not command authority among the communist group activists, but the conflicts within the communist environment were foreign to him and he set about unifying the party, which gained the approval of the Yugoslav delegates.

The creation of the first party structure took place "under the direction" of the Yugoslavs. Mugoša and Popović prepared the first CPA documents and paid attention to party discipline. Albanian activists were still not familiar with such basic ideas as a political bureau or plenum. The basic theoretical literature was *The History of the All-Union Communist Party (Bolsheviks): Short Course*, but only in a poorly

22 The party Central Commitee included: Enver Hoxha and Koçi Xoxe (Kortchan group), Tuk Jakova, Qemal Stafa and Kristo Themelko (Shkodran group) and Gjin Marku and Ramadan Citaku (youth group) – Arshi Pipa, *Albanian Stalinism: Ideo-Political Aspects* (Boulder, CO: East European Monographs, 1990), 56.

23 Smirnova, *Istoriia Albanii*, 194.

24 Hamm, *Albania*, 80.

25 Frasheri, *Historia e levizjes*, 225.

26 Smirnova, *Istoriia Albanii*, 195.

translated Serbo-Croatian version. In the years 1942–1943, while still under conspirational conditions, the first purge in the party took place. Its victims were the excessively ambitious activists, who were not selected to the group of party leaders in 1941 (Anastas Lulo and Sadik Premte), and later those suspected of close cooperation with the British mission active in Albania (Mustafa Gjinishi and Lazar Fundo). In March 1942, the CPA Central Committee created a directive concerning the creation of national independence and partisan group councils by communists and sent it to all local committees.[27] The lengthy and dull ideological discussions were replaced more and more frequently by issues of increased political and organisational activity.

From its beginning, the communist party leadership dreamt of large and well-organized partisan groups, which would be permanently active. A limited form of resistance activity could be observed in Albania from the start of the Italian occupation. In the first years it could hardly be called a permanent partisan unit, but more like a group of armed boys, subordinate to local leaders. They were generally created by former officers, radical intelligentsia, and in the north by clan leaders. Such groups were able to carry out acts of sabotage or engage in short battles with the enemy, but later the "partisans" returned to their daily work. A model for the Albanian communists was the creation of the Headquarters of Yugoslav Partisans in June 1941. This organisation, which was controlled by communists, was given the pleasant-sounding name of the national independence movement and attracted representatives of various groups who were against the Italian occupation. Tito and Hoxha were in agreement as to the necessity of creating a unified leadership, which was to be in the hands of party leaders. That's why E. Hoxha took control of the National Independence Movement, and also became the leader of the growing partisan army.

The first armed groups subordinate to the CPA Central Committee were established at the beginning of 1942, and the first acts of sabotage were carried out in July 1942. With time, larger permanent structures were formed, consisting of 80–100 people.[28] The growing activity of such groups was highlighted by the action carried out on the night of 24/25 July 1942, when telephone connections throughout Albania were successfully cut.[29] These first successes encouraged the leadership of the CPA to create a unified nationwide resistance movement. In September 1942, the most well-known leaders of partisan and political groups from the inter-war years were invited to the village of Peze. The communists were the only organized political power present at the meeting. The result of the meeting was the establishment of the National Liberation Movement (Levizja Nacionalçlirimtarë, LNÇ). Leadership of the Movement was taken by a seven-person General Council, which consisted of

[27] Owen Pearson, *Albania in the Twentieth Century*, vol. 2: *Albania in Occupation and War: From Fascism to Communism 1940–1945* (London: Centre for Albanian Studies / I.B. Tauris, 2005), 175.

[28] Proleter Hasani, *Histori i pashkruar: Historia e organizimit te UNCSh-se* (Tirana: Fllad, 1999), 17.

[29] *Kongresi i Ire*, 72.

well-known partisans without political experience alongside the communists.[30] The local councils created in regions were supposed to form a real structure for an underground state, responsible for conducting armed fighting as well as for supplying people, justice and even for education. There was also an acceleration in the formation of armed divisions, in which communists generally held political positions, and less frequently the position of leaders.[31]

The significant increase in the popularity of the communist movement was connected with the effectiveness and intensity of propaganda. From 1942, the newspaper *Zëri i Popullit* (Voice of the People) was published. This relayed the course of armed fights in the territory of Albania. The magazine *Kushtrimi i lirise* (Call of Freedom) was directed at the youth.[32] The growth in sympathy towards the communists was helped by the worsening supply situation in south Albania. After the end of the Italian-Greek War in April 1941, the Italians stopped investment in this area, which led to a growth in unemployment and poverty.

At the beginning of 1943, a significant part of the south found itself under partisan control. The formation of larger resistance movement structures, battalions, coincided with the first regular battles with Italian army divisions. In May 1943 over 300 partisans attacked an Italian garrison in Leskovik, inflicting heavy losses.[33] In the middle of 1943, divisions subordinate to the LNÇ (numbering over 10 thousand) took the name of the National Independence Army. The LNÇ Council placed control over them into the hands of the General Headquarters, which was controlled by communists. The military leader was Spiro Moissiu, and the political comissary was Enver Hoxha.[34]

An alternative to the National Independence Movement was the organisation called the National Front (Balli Kombetar) established in November 1942. This was based around pre-war politicians who had not been interned by the Italians, a group of intellectuals discouraged by the politics of the Italian occupants, as well as pro-British politicians who despised Italian fascism. The leader of the organisation was Mithat Frashëri. Its program (the Decalogue) declared "activity towards a free, ethnic and democratic Albania, with a modern social base," allowing free development of national culture, punishment of those who acted against national interests, and also unification of the nation in the fight against the occupants.[35] Compared with the

---

30 The council leader was chosen as Kamber Qafmolla, who had not arrived in Peza and in reality did not take control of the organisation – Kastriot Dervishi, *Historia e shtetit shqiptar 1912–2005: organizimi shtetëror, jeta politike, ngjarjet kryesore, të gjithë ligjvënësit, ministrat dhe kryetarët e shtetit shqiptar në historinë 93-vjeçare të tij* (Tirana: Shtëpia Botuese 55, 2006), 466.

31 Stavro Skendi, *Albania* (New York: Free Europe Committee, 1956), 19.

32 Blendi Fevziu, *Histori e shtypit shqiptar 1848–1996* (Tirana: Grupimi Brezi 22 / Shtëpia Botuese Marin Barleti, 1996), 66.

33 Ndreçi Plasari, "Krijimi and Ushtrise Nacional-çlirimtare shqiptare (1941–1943)," *Buletin i Universitetit Shteteror te Tiranes. Seria Shkencat Shoqerore* 4 (1958): 21–23.

34 Hasani, *Histori e pashkruar*, 41.

35 Dervishi, *Historia e shtetit*, 468.

LNÇ program, the National Front's offer was unattractive and incomprehensible for the majority of society.

The increasing activity of the Albanian resistance movement did not go unnoticed by the British intelligence services active in the Balkans. It was in British interest to merge the various Albanian resistance movement groups. British pressure led to a meeting, which took place on August 1–2, 1943 in Mukaj near Kruje, with the participation of representatives of the largest groups. The meeting was intended to be a turning point in the creation of a new, democratic and united Albania. The gathered delegates annulled the decision of the National Assembly from April 1939 and declared its willingness to fight for full independence. The signed agreement foresaw the creation of a joint Committee for the Salvation of Albania, which would direct the whole resistance movement until the formation of a temporary government. The common aim of the communists and *Ballists* was the fight for an "ethnic Albania" together with Kosovo. Yugoslav objections to the understanding from Mukaj and pressure on the leadership of the CPA sealed the fate of the agreement. The CPA leadership considered any cooperation with Balli Kombëtar as unacceptable, and blame for the understanding in Mukaj was placed on the delegates (Mustafa Gjinishi and Ymer Dishnica), who allegedly had acted beyond their competencies.[36]

On July 24, 1943, members of the Great Fascist Council in Italy deprived Benito Mussolini of his power. The new head of the country was Marshall Pietro Badoglio, who on September 8 announced the surrender of his country. This also meant the surrender of Italian units, stationed in Albania, whose number in that period exceeded 130 thousand soldiers. On the day the Italians announced their surrender, the 21st German army left its bases in Montenegro and Greece with the aim of carrying out the Operation Konstantin – to take control of the areas of the Balkans previously occupied by the Italians.[37] The Italian surrender created a chance for the Albanians to acquire a whole arsenal of weapons which had been at the disposal of Italian forces. The LNÇ, for whom the first months of German occupation brought about organisational and armed development, took the greatest advantage of this opportunity.[38]

The Germans occupying Albania tried to create the feeling of "liberating" Albanians from Italian domination. The Germans obtained over a dozen influential politicians who helped them to agree a "non-aggression pact" with some units of the Albanian resistance movement. The II Conference of the National Liberation Movement was held on 4–9 September in Labinot. From September 1943, the only group which continued its active fight with the occupants was the National Independence Army. After the experience of Mukaj, the delegates condemned all attempts to agree

---

36 Miranda Vickers, *Between Serb and Albanian: A History of Kosovo* (New York: Columbia University Press, 1998), 131–132.

37 Bernd J. Fischer, *Albania at War* (London: Hurst, 1999), 161–162.

38 On August 15, 1943 in Vithkuq the 1st Attack Brigade was formed, and within the next few months the majority of partisan units had reformed into brigades.

with nationalist groups, and the National Liberation Movement Council was regarded as the sole true government in the territory of Albania. This meant that the recognition of all other governments was considered as usurpatory and reactive.[39]

After neutralizing part of the Albanian resistance movement, in November 1943 the German military leaders agreed upon a wide ranging operation against the still active partisan units. The German attack, together with the supply crisis during the severe winter of 1943/1944, radically reduced the number of the LNÇ units. They crumbled during battles, as well as because of desertion, which reached the level of even 20–30% per unit. The LNÇ leaders, hiding in the Çermenik mountains near Elbasan lost contact with the majority of its units. The crisis was overcome in March 1944 when the National Liberation Army Leadership began to pay more attention to the training of recruits, there was increased discipline in the units, and the lack of supplies was replenished by British air drops. As the Balli Kombetar units had practically stopped fighting against the Germans, the most desirable partner for the British was the LNÇ. A smaller role was played by Lëvizja e Legalitetit (Legality Movement) – a resistance movement formation created in November 1943 which declared its loyalty to the exiled King Zog I.[40]

On May 24, 1944, the I Congress of the National Liberation Movement was held in Përmet. 188 delegates participated in the Congress, of which almost half were partisans from units located nearby. During the Congress a decision was taken which began the process of the communists gaining power over the country. The delegates closed the road of return to Albania for King Zog I.[41] Only two governmental bodies remained: the Anti-Fascist National Liberation Council (AFCNL) as a legislative body and the twelve-person Committee, which was to act as the government.[42] The Congress finished with success for Enver Hoxha, who acquired two key positions – Committee leader and commander of the armed forces.[43]

The CPA Central Committee Plenum, which took place in Berat (October 20–23, 1944) informed those gathered of the reality of the Albanian party's workings. The party leadership for some time hadn't held regular meetings, and Miladin Popović and three of his most trusted co-workers (E. Hoxha, L. Gega and R. Citaku) had taken full control of the party.[44] In September 1944, after M. Popović had left Albania, his place was taken by Colonel Velimir Stojnić. He also represented the Yugoslav

---

[39] Xhemal Frashëri, *Pushteti popullor ne Vitet e Luftes Antifashiste Nacionalçlirimtare* (Tirana: Akademia e Shkencave e RPS të Shqipërisë, Instituti i Historisë , 1983), 91.

[40] Lëvizja e Legalitetit was founded on November 21, 1943, at the congress in Zall-Herr near Tirana, as a political-military organisation. It was led by a former member of the Liberation Army's General Staff-Abaz Kupi – Dervishi, *Historia e shtetit*, 498–499.

[41] Frasheri, *Pushteti popullor*, 153.

[42] The Council consisted of 121 people, and its leader was Omer Nishani – Ndreci Plasari, "Kongresi Antifashist Nacionalclirimtar i Permetit – Themelimi i Shtetit te ri shqiptar te Demokracise popullore," *Studime Historike* 4 (1975): 32.

[43] Plasari, "Kongresi," 31.

[44] Smirnova, *Istoriia Albanii*, 250.

side during the plenum in Berat and chose a group of his most-trusted people, different from his predecessor's.[45] Speaking at the plenum, E. Hoxha praised the help of J.B. Tito for the Albanian party, but simultaneously blamed Yugoslav delegates for their successes and mistakes.[46] This criticism irritated V. Stojnić, who was clearly closer to the non-critical stance of the party's secretary for organization – Koçi Xoxe. During the Plenum, the Committee was reformed as a Temporary Government. It consisted of 11 members, including 9 representatives of the CPA. The government declared the beginning of preparations for elections to the Constitutional Assembly. The Yugoslav delegate present at the Plenum unscrupulously dictated the most important decisions. The party's new Political Bureau did not include two of Hoxha's closest colleagues – Liri Gega and Ramadan Citaku. The most influential person in the group was one of V. Stojnić's close allies – Koçi Xoxe.[47]

As a result of the Red Army's offensive action in the Balkans in October 1944, German army units began to leave Greece and Albania. From October 1944 in the region of Shkoder there was a concentration of units who were waiting for the expected relief of allied forces, hoping that with their help they could save the town from the communists. When their expectations were not met, the town was approached by the LNÇ partisans, a few thousand activists of a non-communist resistance movement unit looking for a way to escape to Italy. The journey from Shkoder to Bari was made by a large group of ministers from the collaborative government, as well as other politicians who had cooperated with the Germans. The administrative structure created by the Germans stopped working in September 1944. The largest and longest of the battles with the Germans during their evacuation was the Battle of Tirana. The town was captured on November 17, 1944. At the end of November, there were no German units left inside the territory of Albania.

The acquisition of power in 1944 took place through physical fighting. When the first partisan units were formed in Albania, cooperation between them was generally peaceful, regardless of their political views. The joint meetings and friendly discussions finished in 1943. In the autumn of 1943, in the region of Diber, the LNÇ units had the main aim of making the partisan groups compete. On 1 June 1944 units of the I Brigade were sent to the regions of Diber and Mat, with the task of eliminating all the active groups of Balli Kombetar and Legaliteti. Near Shkoder, a few anti-communist groups were formed with representatives of the northern clans. The fate of the civil war was determined by the disproportionate forces. In 1944, partisan forces connected with the LNÇ amounted to about 70 thousand people.[48] Other groups consisted of no more than a few thousand soldiers. An attempt to create an alterna-

45 Miranda Vickers, *The Albanians: A Modern History* (London: I.B. Tauris, 1999), 156.

46 Uran Butka, *Ringjallje* (Tetove: Botues Phoenix, 1996), 35–37.

47 Smirnova, *Istoriia Albanii*, 252.

48 The number of 70 thousand soldiers was given by the official history of the Albanian Labour Party (*Historia e Partisë së Punës të Shqipërisë* [Tirana: Shtëpia Botuese 8 Nëntori 1981], 151). In reality, the whole partisan army in November 1944 consisted of 3 main corpses (in total, 45 thousand

tive political environment was seen at the meeting in Shkoder (October 18, 1944), in which the Temporary Executive Committee was established, with the intention of creating an administrative structure and conducting recruitment for "the troops to defend the country against the threat of communism."[49]

The assumption by the communist party of the slogan of liberating the country from foreign domination by armed activity attracted thousands of people who had no connection with communism. The relatively small social elite from the times of Zog I chose various routes. Some of them officially chose the side of the communists, hoping to make a career which they hadn't experienced earlier or tried to work to rebuild the country regardless of who was in power. The majority of the social elite were against or openly hostile towards the new government, viewing the communists as "people from nowhere," who had taken control of the capital with the support of Yugoslavia. Opponents of the new order decided to flee from the country or hide in the mountains, which had served for centuries as a shelter for outlaws. There were also those who decided on the tactic of waiting until the moment when the communist leaders demobilised their troops and had to face the negative consequences of governing an economically ruined country. All previous experiences led to the assumption that a government which was not connected with the old elite would not survive long.

partisans), as well as territorial units, which in the eyes of the army leadership remained as separate units and were not formally included in the Liberation Army – Hasani, *Histori e pashkruar*, 151.

49 Dervishi, *Historia e shtetit*, 533.

Chapter II: Party and state

1. Yugoslav period

> *Initially, Tito's Yugoslavia found itself at the side of Albania. Its help, although small compared with the needs of our country (as it later turned out), had its hostile aims. It was a conditional program to swallow Albania and shape it into the "seventh republic of Yugoslavia".*[1]

After the end of World War II, the Albanian communists found themselves in a comfortable situation. This was helped by the lack of traditional political parties, as well as the elimination near the end of the war of the majority of potential opponents. The new government inherited a society of millions, which generally treated the ideas of state, parliament and constitution as too abstract and unrelated to the ideas they used in their daily life. In 1944 Albania had an exceptionally large army, formed on the basis of partisan units. The easily-manipulated mass of soldiers with their peasant upbringing created unprecedented possibilities for social advance, simultaneously constituting an obedient and ruthless tool in the pacification of the country. The number of members of the CPA quickly grew during the war. At the end of 1941 it had about 130 members, and in October 1944 that number had already increased to 2250.[2] Only 15% of them were workers, and the dominant group consisted of peasants. In the first post-war years, both the leadership of the communist party, and the armed forces leaders came from the same environment. The unifying factors were the experience of the partisan war, as well as the victory in November 1944.

In August 1945, the I Congress of the National Liberation Front took place in Tirana. In the new reality, the organisation adopted the new name of the Democratic Front, becoming a mass political organisation. Enver Hoxha was selected as the leader of the Front. The Front was intended to become a wide political group, with which the communists intended to win the elections. On September 24, 1945, in Tirana, a meeting of the Anti-Fascist National Liberation Council was held in which a bill concerning elections to the Constitutional Assembly was accepted. Its principles were set out in Act no. 124 from September 28, 1945.[3] In accordance with

---

1 Ramiz Alia, *Jeta ime. Kujtime* (Tirana: Botimet Toena, 2010), 130.

2 Tat'iana Volokitina et al., *Moskva i Vostochnaia Evropa: Stanovlenie politicheskikh rezhimov sovetskogo tipa 1949–1953; Ocherki istorii* (Moscow: ROSSPÉN, 2002), 177.

3 *Gazeta Zyrtare* 54 (1945): 1–2.

the law, all adult citizens of Albania, including women for the first time, were given the right to vote. Exceptions to this included those who had collaborated with the occupants, as well as those who had been sentenced by the military court.

The new government brought with it the idea of ruthless punishment for those guilty of the catastrophic situation in the country. On the basis of the AFCNL's laws from December 15, 1944, 60 former civil servants were tried in the Special Court. Their show trial began on March 1, 1945, in the Kosovo cinema building in Tirana. Among the accused were two former prime ministers (Kostaq Kotta and Ibrahim Biçaku), three former parliamentary leaders, as well as ministers and high-level officers. The primary charges which were made during the trial were treason and collaboration with the occupants. The panel of judges was led by General Koçi Xoxe. On the basis of the sentence announced on April 13, 1945, 17 of the accused were sentenced to death, while the others had to serve long-term prison sentences.

In the days leading up to the parliamentary elections, which were to legalize the communist government, the Tirana trial was a clear signal to potential opponents. The elections were created in such a way that their results were determined before the actual voting. The list of candidates for deputies was presented three weeks before the elections. The electorate was proposed only one list (Democratic Front), which gave the elections the character of a plebiscite.[4] Other political groups did not receive the possibility to register. Any attempt by a different party to register was threatened by the accusation of "collaboration with the occupants" and an appearance in front of the military court.

The non-communist political environment was limited to creating anonymous conspirational discussion clubs. A period of their increased activity were the first four months of 1945. Albanians historians gave them the post-factum names of: "resistance groups," "monarchist groups" or "social-democratic groups." The activists who created them: Sami Qeribashi, Qenan Dibra and Musine Kokalari attempted to bring about the unification of the anti-communist opposition and the creation of a national structure. They also looked for support in western countries, mainly from the United States and Great Britain, which was intended to allow the non-communist political groups to survive. Just before the elections in November 1945 the three largest groups were united into the Democratic Union (Bashkimi Demokratik). Among its organizers were former teachers, writers, and also people working in administrations subordinate to E. Hoxha's government.[5] The majority of them were in favour of overthrowing the dictate of one party for political pluralism. The electoral regulations excluded the Union from participating in legal political life and forced it to cooperate with organisations which planned to overthrow the communist regime by force.

---

4 Dervishi, *Historia e shtetit*, 55–57.

5 Demir Dyrmishi, "Krijimi i organizates opozitare ilegale 'Bashkimi demokratik' dhe veprimtaria e saj ne vitin 1945," *Studime Demokratike* 1–2 (1998): 101–105.

The parliamentary elections took place on December 2, 1945. According to official data, 89.81% of those entitled to vote participated in the elections, of which 93.16% voted for candidates of the Democratic Front.[6] All 84 Front candidates were elected to the Assembly, which in this way became the legal government in the country. The first meeting of the Constitutional Assembly, with the participation of foreign diplomatic missions, began on January 10, 1946. During the first days, at the request of Hysni Kapo, a deputy from Vlore, the Constitutional Assembly unanimously took the decision to suspend the monarchy and proclaimed the People's Republic of Albania. Two months later the Constitutional Assembly passed the Fundamental Statute of the People's Republic of Albania, representing provisional legislation. The document granted the Assembly the highest legislative government, and its presidium was to collectively act as head of state. The government functioned as the highest power.

The victorious Democratic Front was not, however, a united group. The majority of deputies connected with the communist party brought to the parliament a scheme of government typical for partisan groups and a conspiratorial party structure. Above all, the merchants and civil servants from Shkoder, who entered parliament from the Democratic Front list, were dissatisfied. Their informal leader was the merchant Riza Dani, in 1924 one of Fan Noli's co-workers. Representatives of the "deputies group," (as they were later described) spoke in parliament against the monopolization by communists of the most important positions in the country, and the occupation of those positions by uneducated and primitive people, but with partisan backgrounds. The threats directed towards the worried deputies by Enver Hoxha were realized in December 1946. On the wishes of the Minister of Internal Affairs, parliament withdrew the mandate of a group of deputies, with Riza Dani at its head. Their trial was held in September 1947. The deputies were accused of forming a subversive organisation called the Central Committee (Komiteti Qendror), whose aim was to carry out a coup d'etat. On the basis of fabricated evidence, three members of the group, including Riza Dani, were sentenced to death.[7]

The trial of the "deputies group" was one of many after the elections against representatives of the Shkodran "rebels." On January 28, 1946, the military court in Shkoder tried a group of Franciscan priests and pupils of the Franciscan seminary, who were accused of cooperating with war criminals and the formation of the Albanian Union (Bashkimi Shqiptar) organization, with the aim of overthrowing the government. Eight of those accused were sentenced to death, and 27 others were given long prison sentences. The connection between the Catholic clergy and the occupying powers was also exhibited in a trial which took place on February 1–12, 1946, in Shkoder. Among the accused and those sentenced to death were representatives of the pro-German occupying powers from 1943–1944, including the Fran-

6 *Bashkimi*, December 11, 1945, 1–2.

7 Pjetër Pepa, *Dosja e diktaturës* (Tirana: n.p., 1995), 141–150.

ciscan Anton Harapi, and the former prime minister Maliq Bushati. Members of the Democratic Union were arrested and accused of cooperation with the reactive environment and espionage on behalf of the USA and Great Britain in June 1946. The verdict in this case was announced on July 2, 1946, sentencing nine people to the death penalty, and eighteen others to long prison sentences. A group of Albanian engineers, working on the drying of a bog in the region of Maliq were accused of espionage and sabotage. The engineers tried to draw the attention of the central government to the difficult situation of workers, who were underfed and living in terrible conditions, by suggesting that it could lead to a rebellion. This warning was treated very seriously, looking for a connection between the engineers and the Americans from the UNRRA mission, supplying humanitarian aid, who were supposedly trying to bribe and encourage them to sabotage the work.[8] The trial in November 1946 finished with five death sentences, and the Americans were persuaded to leave Albania.

Besides imaginary threats, the communist government also had to face real threats in the form of the armed underground units in the north of the country. The lack of political base for the communists in the north meant that the area was treated by partisans flooding in from the south almost as a conquered area. The local government bodies in this part of the country were created solely by partisans, usually avoiding locals. The conviction of a new occupation was highlighted by the fact that, on public buildings, the Yugoslav *trobojnica* hung beside the Albanian flag. The north of Albania, and especially the Albanian-Yugoslav border became an asylum for units who carried out active fighting with the communist regime. Some of them were a simple continuation of units active during the war (units of Muharrem Bajraktari or the Kryeziu brothers). The new units were full of people who couldn't see a place for themselves in the new reality or had fled from oppression. There was an attempt to unite them in February 1945 by the leader of the Mirdite group, Mark Gjonmarkaj. With the agreement of local leaders, on 15 September 1945 he summoned the northern tribes to a meeting in Bjeshken e Zepës, in the land of the Mirdite.[9] Those gathered decided to form the National Mountain League (Lidhja Kombëtare e Malëve) and Central Committee with its headquarters in Shkoder to direct the organization. On May 6, 1946, the League's coordination office for military affairs was established, as well as a consulting board. The leadership was also responsible for trials and sentencing those cooperating with the communists. The forces loyal to the League were estimated at 500 people, but consisted of small units, most often numbering 5–10 people. The League's leader, Mark Gjonmarkaj, was surrounded with his unit on June 13, 1946, by government forces near Prosek. After

8 William Bland and Ian Price, *A Tangled Web: A History of Anglo-American Relations with Albania (1912–1955)* (London: Albanian Society, 1986), 128–129.

9 The tradition of starting uprisings after decisions taken during meetings dated back to the Ottoman times and gave such activity the character of social consensus.

being heavily wounded in the battle, he committed suicide in order not to fall into enemy hands. After his death, the organisation practically ended all activity.

The culminating moment of armed underground activity in the north of Albania was the Postribe Uprising, which took place in September 1946. Activists of the non-communist resistance movement groups, who remained in the country, as well as a group of Shkodran intelligentsia created the United Committee (Komiteti e Përbashket), which filled the role of coordinator for armed attack preparations. They succeeded in gathering over 400 fighters, who were to attack Shkoder, where military warehouses and prisons were located. Control over the town was to be the start of a wider uprising throughout the northern part of Albania. During the preparations, it was decided to move the attack forward, due to the fear connected with the draft to the army which was aimed at youths from around Shkoder.[10] On September 9, 1946, the uprising forces, gathered in the village of Postribe, attacked Shkoder. The uncoordinated attack, which didn't obtain the expected support of the local people, was stopped in the town's suburbs by army units loyal to the government.[11] The commander of the Shkodran garrison, Musa Daci, effectively blocked the road leading into the town and called for reinforcements from Tirana.[12] 33 of the attackers died during the battle. Twelve captured participants of the uprising were executed in public in Shkoder. The uprising leader, Murat Haxhia, was chased and surrounded by government units in a cave in which he was hiding, and then murdered. For a few more months, units consisting of former partisans conducted a "cleansing operation" in the north shooting those found in possession of a weapon. By the end of 1946, the activity of most anti-communist resistance movement units had ended. Those which survived usually numbered a few or a dozen people and did not pose a serious threat.

Besides eliminating other political groups, the strategic aim of Enver Hoxha's government was to gain recognition on the international arena. The first country which, in May 1945, recognised the new government of Albania was Yugoslavia. A month later, Enver Hoxha, as the head of the government, went on his first foreign mission – to Belgrade. In October, the following countries recognised Albania: Poland, Bulgaria and Czechoslovakia, and soon afterwards the Soviet Union. Among the countries that accepted the change of Albania's government in 1945 were also France and Italy. Many western countries expressed scepticism towards the new government in Albania, while Greece showed open animosity. Between 1944 and 1949, Albania was an important supply base for Greek communists, fighting against the legal government in Athens. The temporary government created by communists found shelter in Albania, and from July 17, 1947, the Greek communists' radio was

10 Butka, *Ringjallje*, 133.

11 Demir Dyrmishi, "Aktivizimi i kundershtareve politike dhe Kryengritja e Postribës," *Studime Historike* 1–2 (1999): 119–121.

12 Butka, *Ringjallje*, 135.

broadcast from its headquarters near Tirana.[13] The Greek government also held the view that the government in Tirana held full responsibility for the participation of Albanian units in the Italian invasion of Greece in 1940, and by supporting the communist rebels they continued their hostile activity against their southern neighbour. The Greek government army often crossed the border into Albania while chasing communist units, causing violent protests in Tirana.

Despite Tirana's attempts, Albanian delegates were not invited in April 1945 to the conference to set up the United Nations Organisation in San Francisco. The dispute over the role of Albania in the Italian invasion of Greece in 1940 meant that its representatives were not invited to the Paris Peace Conference which began in July 1946. Diplomatic support from Moscow meant that a delegation of Albanians was present, but only in an advisory role. During the conference, the Greek representative suggested that Albania, as an ally to the Axis powers, should suffer the consequences of that cooperation. Speaking on behalf of Albania, Enver Hoxha (August 21, 1946) mentioned the number of victims which Albania suffered during the war, as well as the losses inflicted on the Italian and German occupants, estimating them at 53,639 soldiers killed, wounded or captured. Hoxha's stand was supported on behalf of Yugoslavia by Moša Pijade, who described Albania as an ally which deserves the admiration and gratitude of all democratic countries.[14] Because of the peace treaty, signed on February 10, 1947, Italy recognised Albania as an "eternal" sovereign country, agreed to pay for war repairs to the amount of 5 million dollars, and also to relinquish control over the island Sazan.

The request of the Albanian government in January 1945 for official recognition, directed towards the western states, was treated with reserve. In May 1945, an American mission led by Joseph Jacobs arrived in Albania. The Americans linked recognition of the Albanian government to free elections in Albania, respect for previously signed bilateral agreements and the return of property nationalized by the new government to American citizens.[15] Despite the protests of the Albanian government, which did not want to recognise agreements signed by the Kingdom of Albania, the Americans held the view that respecting bilateral agreements by the powers in Tirana was an initial condition to restoring diplomatic relations. The American mission's activity was limited by the suspicion of the communist powers, who regarded all contact with the American mission as subversive. The powers in Tirana regarded the approval by the American Senate of the so-called Pepper resolution (July 29, 1946), recognising the right of Greece to Northern Epirus, as a hostile

---

[13] Charles R. Shrader, *The Withered Vine: Logistics and the Communist Insurgency in Greece, 1945–1949* (Westport, CT: Praeger, 1999), 188.

[14] James O'Donnell, *A Coming of Age: Albania under Enver Hoxha* (Boulder, CO: East European Monographs, 1999), 18.

[15] Bland and Price, *Tangled Web*, 139.

action.[16] In November 1946 the American mission left Albania, thereby ending official contact between the two countries.

Close cooperation with the British, reaching back to the German occupation, was hindered by the Corfu Incident. On October 22, 1946, two British destroyers sailing through the Straits of Corfu were seriously damaged as a result of exploding mines, and 44 sailors lost their lives. E. Hoxha's government held the view that the ships were sailing unlawfully in Albanian territorial water, however, London held the opinion that the width of the water track in this place allowed naval ships to sail, according to the principles of "freedom of the sea." Although it was impossible to decide who had left the mines, the British directed the case to the International Tribunal of Justice in the Hague. In 1949, the Tribunal granted compensation to the British of 843 thousand pounds (1.45 million dollars). Albania did not accept the Tribunal's decision and refused to pay the compensation.[17] In view of Albania's refusal, the British blocked the return of the Albanian gold reserves which were at their disposal.[18] The lack of compromise in the Corfu case broke diplomatic relations between Albania and Great Britain. The opposition of Great Britain and USA blocked, until December 1955, the acceptance of Albania into the membership of the United Nations.

In 1947, the Communist Information Bureau (Cominform) was set up in Szklarska Poręba and included representatives of all communist parties from the Soviet bloc, as well as representatives of communist parties in France and Italy, but there was no place for Albania. During the meeting, it was mentioned that the people's government had won in Albania, but the fact that it was represented by Yugoslavia did not raise any objections.[19] The conference confirmed the acceptance by the Soviet bloc of the Yugoslav protectorate over the "ideologically immature" Albanian communists. The basis for the close relations between the two countries was the understanding signed in 1946: a structure of friendship and mutual help as well as a structure for coordinating economic plans, a customs and currency union.[20] While the USSR created a union with satellite states in order to control them and use their natural resources, Yugoslavia had a similar policy with regard to Albania. Agreements for economic cooperation assumed that mixed Albanian-Yugoslav compa-

16 Edward Capps, *Greece, Albania and Northern Epirus* (Chicago: Argonaut, 1963), 32.

17 Eric Leggett, *The Corfu Incident* (London: Seeley, 1974); Pascal Milo, "Incidenti i Kanalit te Korfuzit 1945–1946," *Studime Historike* 3–4 (2000).

18 Previously the property of the National Bank of Albania, it was confiscated by Germany, and then by the British. Gold weighing 2,399 kg was deposited in the Bank of England, under the supervision of the Restitution of Gold Department of the Tripartite Commission, formed in 1947. This consisted of representatives of Great Britain, France and the United States – Shabtai Rosenne, *The Law and Practice of the International Court, 1920–2005: The Court and the United Nations*, vol. 1 (Leiden: A.W. Sijthoff, 2006), 234–235.

19 Waldemar Dziak, *Albania między Belgradem, Moskwą i Pekinem* (Warsaw: Instytut Studiów Politycznych Polskiej Akademii Nauk, 1991), 24.

20 Ndreçi Plasari and Luan Malltezi, eds., *Marrëdhëniet shqiptaro-jugosllave 1945–1948: Dokumente* (Tirana: Drejtoria e Përgjitshme e Arkivave, 1996), 53.

nies would be established not only for foreign trade and exploitation of natural resources, but also to create rail and electricity networks.[21] The financial backing for these companies was to be the Albanian-Yugoslav bank with a capital of 3 million dinars. The loans issued by Belgrade in 1947–1948 were to equal half of Albania's annual income.[22] During this time, 600 advisers from Yugoslavia travelled to Albania in order to supervise industrial development, while 1,500 Albanians studied in Yugoslav institutions of higher education. The dependence on Yugoslavia was highlighted by the monopoly on supplies of industrial equipment, as well as food and household goods. From the first months of Albania independence, Yugoslavia took it upon itself to support its hungry neighbour. In 1945, 2,900 tons of wheat and 5,700 tons of corn were sent from Yugoslavia, and in 1946 this help was tripled. In his speech to the National Assembly on March 31, 1947, J.B. Tito stated that Yugoslavia can not be indifferent to the fact that "the Albanian nation is hungry and dying."[23]

The monopoly on aid for Albanians, which Yugoslavia reserved for itself, awoke a wide range of controversies and suspicions of paternalism. Lorries carrying aid from the International Red Cross were regularly stopped on the Yugoslav-Albanian border.[24] The supplies of Yugoslav grain which arrived in Albania in July 1945 were generally unfit for human consumption and could be used only to produce alcohol.[25] In August 1946, Belgrade rejected requests from Tirana for increased supplies of printing paper and flags in Albanian national colours. These were needed to decorate Albanian towns during national holidays. Just after the celebration had finished, Belgrade sent a negative response. The Yugoslavs regarded the request for 5,000 flags as excessive and too costly. In some cases, goods sent to Albania had clearly higher prices. The price of Yugoslav ammonite in September 1946 was three times higher than that of the ammonite previously transported from the USSR through Romania.[26]

Belgrade's politics towards Albania divided members of the CPA leadership. Scepticism towards the increasing proximity of Albania and Yugoslavia, and also towards the idea of radical change in Albania itself was felt by Sejfulla Maleshova. Co-opted to the CPA Political Bureau in 1943, Maleshova was the only Marxist in the group, a poet, and also an opponent of the socialist revolution according to Stalin.[27] In 1945 he became the Minister of Culture and the leader of the Economic Plan

---

21 An agreement to create mixed cooperatives was signed on July 1, 1946 – Plasari and Malltezi, *Marrëdhëniet shqiptaro-jugosllave*, 39–43.

22 The largest loan agreement was signed on June 12, 1947. Yugoslavia was to grant Albania 2 billion dinars – Plasari and Malltezi, *Marrëdhëniet shqiptaro-jugosllave*, 102–104.

23 Vladimir Dedijer, *Jugoslovensko-albanskije odnosi (1939–1948)* (Belgrade: Borba, 1949), 173.

24 Bashkim Trenova, "Marrëdhëniet shqiptaro-jugosllave ne fushen ekonomike ne vitet 1944–1946," *Studime Historike* 3 (1990): 54.

25 ASA, Prime Minister's Office, 1945, d. 268, 66.

26 Trenova, "Marrëdhëniet shqiptaro-jugosllave," 56.

27 During his studies in Leningrad, Sejfulla Maleshova translated the "Communist Manifesto" into Albanian – Arshi Pipa, *Albanian Stalinizm: Ideo-Political Aspects* (Boulder, CO: East European Monographs, 1990), 58.

Committee. In both areas, Maleshova was against radical, non-deliberated reform. His caution helped his enemies who were irritated by his "professor's manner" and feeling of superiority towards the majority of the party leadership. At the sitting of the CPA Central Committee Political Bureau in December 1945, Maleshova was accused of right-wing opportunism and anti-Yugoslav actions, and was subsequently removed from the party leadership.[28] Another opponent of Yugoslav domination in Albania, Nako Spiru, also met a tragic fate. One of the few people in Albania with an economic education, he was given the task of economic planning. He was an opponent of the increasing economic dependence on Belgrade. Severely criticised by the party's Political Bureau and deprived of support for his actions, he committed suicide on November 20, 1947.[29]

Spiru's fall was also an effect of the increasing rivalry for power in the party between Enver Hoxha and Koçi Xoxe, neither of whom openly wanted to upset the CPY leadership. Hoxha undoubtedly enjoyed great popularity as a leader of the resistance movement, and was called "Commander" by Albanians.[30] Xoxe was the secretary for party organisation, responsible for personnel matters, and in the government was responsible for internal affairs. His main attributes were also his close relations with Belgrade, especially with the Minister of Internal Affairs – Aleksander Ranković. Despite suggestions from Belgrade, Xoxe did not dare to remove his rival.[31]

The VIII CPA Central Commitee Plenum held between February 26 and March 8, 1948, was a vivid example of increasing Yugoslav influence. A full victory and support from Belgrade was gained by K. Xoxe and his followers. Hoxha was forced to criticise himself and declare that Nako Spiru had poisoned Albanian-Yugoslav relations.[32] In his speech, he also criticised a group of Spiru's former co-workers, expressing the opinion that close cooperation with Yugoslavia was a lifeline for Albania. This self-criticism allowed Hoxha to keep his position as secretary general of the party. The Plenum accepted Xoxe's proposal for full economic and military unification of both countries.

The position of the Kremlin was of key importance for the future of Albanian-Yugoslav relations. In the first few post-war years, the Soviet leadership accepted the particularly close relations between Yugoslavia and Albania, sending economic aid

---

[28] The conclusion of the APL Central Commitee Political Bureau in the matter of the so-called opportunism of Maleshova – *Marrëdhëniet shqiptaro-jugosllave*, 22–24.

[29] Demir Dyrmishi, "Lufta politike në udhëheqjen e PKSh në vitet 1947–1948 dhe mënjanimi i ndërhyrjes Jugosllave," *Studime Historike* 4 (2000): 146.

[30] Dmitrii Chuvakhin, "S diplomaticheskoi missiei w Albanii 1946–1952 gg.," *Novaia i noveishaia istoriia* 1 (1995): 120.

[31] Chuvakhin recalls a conversation with a close co-worker of Hoxha – M. Shehu, who admitted that in his home he had prepared weapons, ammunition and food supplies, in case "Xoxe's agents" came to arrest him – Chuvakhin, "S diplomaticheskoi missiei," 124.

[32] Dyrmishi, "Lufta politike në udhëheqjen," 147–148.

for Albania through Belgrade.[33] The Albanians made their first serious attempt to talk directly with the Kremlin without involving Belgrade in July 1947. Recognising the leading position of Moscow in the world communist movement, the Albanian party leadership turned to Andrei Zhdanov (head of the department of culture and ideology in the Central Committee of the Soviet party) with a request to change the name of the Albanian party.[34] Zhdanov's positive reply created suitable foundations for the visit of the Albanian leadership to Moscow, with E. Hoxha at its head, which took place on 14–26 July 1947. The visit did not go unnoticed by the Yugoslav leadership. This created fear about the possibility of losing control over Tirana. Officially it was presented as a "friendly visit," but the presence of the Minister of Internal Affairs and the Minister of Justice, as well as high-ranking civil servants from the Defence and Foreign Affairs departments, caused suspicion in Belgrade as to the real aim of the visit.[35] The participation of Enver Hoxha in the Moscow talks became a valuable attribute in the constant confrontation with Koçi Xoxe.

From the beginning of 1948, differences between Moscow and Belgrade began to develop. The Soviet leadership had problems accepting the independent politics of Yugoslavia in the Balkans. One of the important issues of the dispute was the question of Albania. The Kremlin was concerned by the question of whether Yugoslavia, itself in need of support for its development, could offer similar aid to Albania.[36] Extreme irritation of the Soviet leaders was caused by the placement of two Yugoslav divisions near Kortcha, with the apparent aim of protecting Albania from Greek aggression. The echo of the increasing conflict reached Tirana with a delay. The lack of knowledge concerning the changing Soviet-Yugoslav relations aided the continuation of the party cleansing, initiated by Koçi Xoxe, with the aim of eliminating followers of Nako Spiru from the CPA. Liri Belishova, N. Spiru's widow, was expelled from the party, as well as members of the Politburo – Tuk Jakova and Bedri Spahiu.

The last list, sent by the Soviet party to the CPY leadership on March 27, 1948, reached all communist parties in Moscow's satellite countries, except for CPA.[37] Knowledge of the worsening Yugoslav-Soviet relations was observed in Albania only on May 13, when a meeting of the CPA Political Bureau took place. The feelings of the party leadership were expressed by Enver Hoxha with the words: "the matter concerns the whole [socialist] camp and our situation is becoming dangerous, but if we don't take bread from Yugoslavia, we will take it from the Soviet Union."[38]

---

33 Enver Hoxha's notes about the meeting with J. Stalin in Moscow, in Plasari and Malltezi *Marrëdhëniet shqiptaro-jugosllave*, 117.

34 The proposition to change the name from CPA to APL (Albanian Party of Labour) was based on the party's social structure, which was dominated by peasants – Volokitina et al., *Moskva i Vostochnaia Evropa*, 467.

35 Ana Lalaj, "Shqipëria dhe Informbyroja," *Studime Historike* 3 (2009): 107.

36 Milovan Djilas, *Conversations with Stalin* (New York: Harcourt, Brace & World, 1962), 102.

37 Extract from a letter sent in March to the leaders of CPY which Albanian leaders found out about only on April 15 – Dervishi, *Historia e shtetit*, 597.

38 Lalaj, "Shqipëria dhe Informbyroja," 130.

On June 28, 1948, Cominform passed a resolution condemning the CPY and excluded the Yugoslav party from its membership. Among the reasons for this decision were the increasing hostility of CPY towards the USSR, the misconception of the party's role in society, the deviation of foreign policy and arrogant behaviour towards other communist parties. A document titled "About the situation in the Yugoslav Communist Party" was published on June 29, 1948, in the Tirana newspaper *Bashkimi*. The message, accompanying the resolution, contained words about the "treacherous, anti-Marxist and ant-Soviet" activity of the CPY, accusing it of attempting to deprive Albania of its independence, and trying to colonize it. On the same day, the Prime Minister, Enver Hoxha ordered the removal of all portraits of Tito from government offices and their replacement with portraits of Stalin and himself. The Albanian diplomatic offices in Moscow, Belgrade, Sofia and Paris received orders to stop all contact with Yugoslav representatives, and if they needed advice to contact Soviet representatives.[39] A day later, the Albanian government ordered Yugoslav diplomats in Tirana to, within 48 hours, treat all Yugoslav specialists and advisers as unnecessary and undesired in Albania. On 1 July 1948, Albania unilaterally annulled all bilateral treaties and agreements, defining them as invalid.[40] Accusing Belgrade of attempting to take control over Albania's economy, the government in Tirana refused to return 500 million dinars, which is how much Yugoslavia estimated as the value of aid given.

2. Soviet period

Albania remains a Stalinist country, the only one in Europe where Stalin's memory continues to haunt the leaders minds. The question arises: if the saga of Stalin as the builder of a greatness of the Soviet Union is liquidated there, what will happen to Hoxha, his "heir" and the architect of Stalinist Albania.[41]

The break with Yugoslavia turned out to be rather beneficial for strengthening the social prestige of the Albanian party leadership. On September 13, 1948, the XI CPA Central Committee Plenum met, during which responsibility for the wave of terror in the first post-war years was placed upon Yugoslavia, and as a result upon its "ally" – Koçi Xoxe. Among the decisions taken during the meeting was a revision

---

39 Lalaj, "Shqipëria dhe Informbyroja," 103–104.

40 On May 27, 1950, all Yugoslav Embassy staff left Tirana, in November the Albanian representative office in Belgrade stopped its activity. For the next three years, the countries had no diplomatic relations. Their restoration in December 1953 followed an Albanian initiative – Lalaj, "Shqipëria dhe Informbyroja," 135.

41 Arshi Pipa, "Stalin and Hoxha: The Master and the Apprentice," in Pipa, *Albanian Stalinism*, 137–138.

of its position in the matter of Nako Spiru, who was regarded as a victim of Yugoslav intrigue and a symbol of resistance against the Yugoslav politics of assimilation.[42]

The September plenum opened the possibility for E. Hoxha of excluding his most dangerous rival and to take full control of the party. The attack on Koçi Xoxe as a close collaborator of Belgrade and the spokesman of Yugoslav influence was simultaneously an attack on the Ministry of Internal Affairs, which Xoxe regarded higher than the party.[43] In the opening speeches, there was mention of murder in prisons and the killing of innocent people. There were attempts to highlight the similarities between Xoxe's methods and those which A. Ranković used in Yugoslavia. Two months later, Xoxe was expelled from the party, and in December 1948 he was arrested and tried together with a group of his closest co-workers (Pandi Kristo, Nesti Kerenxhi and Koçi Blushi). The temperature of the trial was raised by "spontaneous" demonstrations in Tirana, in which participants demanded the highest form of penalty for Xoxe. The judge satisfied "social expectations" on 10 June 1949, with the verdict that the accused were guilty of Trotskyist and Titoist activity. Xoxe was sentenced to death, and his colleagues received long-term prison sentences.

When Xoxe's removal was being prepared, the I CPA Congress took place. In the seventh year of its activity, the party gained "independence," after its break from the maternal CPY, and the Congress was the start of a new era in its history. One of the first decisions taken by those gathered was to condemn the CPY leadership and to announce a postulate cleansing the party of "Titoist" elements, as well as to change the name to the Albanian Party of Labour (APL, Albanian: Partia e Punes e Shqipërise).[44] The position of Secretary General was taken by Enver Hoxha. The Congress was preceded by an internal purge, which expelled 10% of the party membership. This purge was a natural consequence of the dramatic increase in party members in 1947. In just one year, the number of party members almost tripled, reaching the level of 32,583. It is hard to explain this appearance by ideological views alone, but is more likely explained by the generally held opinion of career perspective created by party membership.[45] The party cleansing continued between 1948 and 1951, this time with the removal of the remnants of "titoism." Using this basis, in three years as many as 6 thousand members, in other words about 25% of the membership, were expelled. The vast majority of those expelled were those with little experience in the party – their party membership was issued in 1947–1948.[46]

---

42 Dyrmishi, "Lufta politike në udhëheqjen," 157.

43 Volokitina et al., *Moskva i Vostochnaia Evropa. Stanovlenie politicheskikh rezhimov*, 504.

44 Some former partisans did not agree with the removal of the word "communist" from the party name, but suggestions that such a change was in accordance with the wishes of Stalin meant that the criticism soon died – Chuvakhin, "S diplomaticheskoi missiei," 122.

45 This impressive growth was mainly due to youths who represented about 90% of the party structure. In terms of social background, the dominant group consisted of representatives of peasant families, the proportion of workers equalled 15.3% – Volokitina et al., *Moskva i Vostochnaia Evropa. Stanovlenie politicheskikh rezhimov*, 179.

46 Volokitina et al., *Moskva i Vostochnaia Evropa. Stanovlenie politicheskikh rezhimov*, 183.

From 1948, Tuk Jakova, as the Central Committee secretary for organization, was responsible for party membership politics. The criteria for party positions remained unchanged: a worker-farmer background and participation in the national independence movement. The principle, accepted in November 1944 at the plenum in Berat, of the necessity to control the social structure of the party, so that it did not become a petty-bourgeois social-democratic party, still existed. The awareness of this danger encouraged the attempt to limit access to the party or to make it inaccessible for representatives of intelligent families, rich farmers and representatives of "feudal-tribal" clans from the north. A key role in the ideological preparations for party work was played by five central party courses, which could simultaneously educate 600 listeners. Besides this, there were also courses organized at local level, which 1,200 participants could attend simultaneously. Analysis of their activity, performed by the CPA Political Bureau in 1948 showed that the local courses presented an exceptionally low level and were not suitably controlled by party bodies. The education of participants of such courses was limited to a lecture of *The History of the All-Union Communist Party (Bolsheviks): Short Course* in Albanian, as well as selected fragments of classic Marxist-Leninist works, although for the majority of participants they were completely incomprehensible.

The blame for the inadequate quality of the party education system was placed upon Tuk Jakova by the APL Central Committee in February 1951. In an interview which Enver Hoxha gave in March 1951 with the correspondent of *Pravda* in Albania, I. Bulatov, he blamed T. Jakova for wrongdoings in the party, claiming that his attitude was, for many years, controlled by opportunism and sympathy for enemies of the people. He based this on Jakova's petty-bourgeois background and his social contacts with Catholic clerks in Shkoder. Bulatov travelled around Albania, trying to verify Hoxha's opinion that the party organisation throughout the country was fighting against opportunism and the remnants of capitalist thinking. During his visit in Shkoder, it turned out that the local party committee hardly ever met. The purge was survived by only half the committee members, and those were generally uninterested in party activity in the field. To the surprise of the journalist, in Shkoder there was no clear condemnation of Tuk Jakova's activity, and Hoxha himself did not travel to Shkoder.[47]

The dramatic change in relations with Yugoslavia probably prevented the absorption of Albania into its stronger neighbour, and also opened new and significantly more effective opportunities for economic aid. After the break with Yugoslavia, the role of strategic partner for Albania was taken by the Soviet Union, and as a result its satellite states. Soviet aid for Albania affected almost every sphere of social, economic and even cultural life. It also concerned loans, specialist workers, and the op-

[47] Volokitina et al., *Moskva i Vostochnaia Evropa. Stanovlenie politicheskikh rezhimov*, 187. After his self-criticism, T. Jakova remained in the APL Central Commitee and kept his position as the minister of industry, however, he lost control of the party's membership policy. In 1955 he was removed from the party leadership and interned.

portunity for Albanians to study in educational institutions in the USSR and other Soviet bloc countries. Economic aid for Albania was formalized in 1949 thanks to its entry to Comecon. None of the committee of this organisation had offices in Tirana, but a form of ennoblement for Albania was the organisation of the XI Session of Comecon in Tirana, in May 1959.[48]

Realisation of the aid plan for Albania was taken care of by an exceptionally large number of Soviet advisers for a country of Albania's size. In 1950, their number was estimated at three thousand. The advisers received a salary three times higher than the Albanians employed in similar positions, and also had the right to luxury apartments, cars and larger amounts of food than the locals. The Russians also filled the place of Yugoslav military advisers. Military handbooks, educational programs, and even military uniforms were copied from the Russians. Over 400 Albanian officers were trained in Soviet academies. For a period of twelve years (1948–1960) the Albanian army was supplied in full and trained by the Soviets.[49] The first tanks as well as 12 Jak-9 planes arrived in Albania. The supply of military equipment was intended to lead to the modernization of the Albanian army, which was still at the level of a partisan army in terms of training and equipment. Although no Soviet army units were based in Albania, during the period of Soviet domination, visits of the Black Sea Fleet in Albanian ports were a common occurrence.[50] In September 1957, an Albanian-Soviet agreement to build the Pasha Liman naval base near Vlora was signed. The planned base was designed to strengthen the coastal defence system in Albania, and at the same time to constitute an important bridge-head for the USSR military in the Mediterranean Sea basin.

While intervention plans against "Titoist" Yugoslavia existed, Albania played an important role as a supply base for the planned operation. Thanks to the help of Soviet officers in Peshkopi, an Albanian Intelligence Services training centre was created, where agents were prepared for diversion operations in Yugoslavia. After the break from Yugoslavia, a small war was conducted on the border; by 1953 at least 250 incidents had been noted. A similarly tense situation existed on the border with Greece. Up to 1949 Albania provided active support for the Greek communists fighting against the legal government in Athens. Even after the Civil War in Greece ended, there were almost daily border incidents.[51]

An important factor in Soviet military aid was espionage. This turned out to be priceless in the early 1950s when Albania became one of the quiet fronts of the Cold War. In 1948, reports from British analysts showed that the weakest link in the communist camp, in which it was the easiest to bring about a counter-revolution,

48 Hamm, *Albania*, 39.

49 Skendi, *Albania*, 117–118.

50 Hamm, *Albania*, 27.

51 In the years 1945–1953, 289 Greek Army soldiers were captured by communist units inside the territory of Albania, another 76 soldiers were caught near the border – Beqir Meta, "Raportet midis Greqise dhe Shqipërise në vitet 1950–1953," *Studime Historike* 3 (2002): 107.

was Albania. A group of emigrants, who after suitable training were returned to the country in order to undertake diversion actions, were used to destabilize Albania. In the years 1950–1953, around twenty military actions in Albania were carried out. According to Albanian sources, almost nine hundred people were involved, of which over three hundred had returned to Albania.[52] Among those, at least two hundred people were killed or captured. This Albanian success wouldn't have been possible without information leaks from Soviet intelligence spies, active in the British intelligence services.[53]

In 1953, Turkey, Greece and Yugoslavia signed an agreement of friendship and cooperation, known as the Balkan Pact, which later gained the character of a military union in Bled (August 9, 1954). The statement of the ministers of foreign affairs from the Pact's members declaring that "an independent Albania is a desirable factor of peace and stability in the Balkans," was received in Tirana with anxiety as an attempt to define the future of Albania by two neighbouring states. The feeling of anxiety was clearly reduced in 1955 together with the entry to the Warsaw Pact, as well as the acceptance of Albania, after many years of trying, to the United Nations (December 14, 1955).[54] In the second half of the 1950s, there was a visible increase in Albanian diplomatic activity. The number of countries with whom Albania maintained diplomatic relations grew between 1956 and 1960 from 18 to 32. From 1955 to 1957, Albanian diplomacy made a series of gestures towards Greece. Greek soldiers who had previously been detained in Albania were released, and Tirana agreed to de-mine the Straits of Corfu. However, rapprochement of the two countries was made impossible by the consistent raising by Athens of the question of Northern Epirus.[55] In an interview given to the *New York Times* in August 1957, the Prime Minister of Albania, Mehmet Shehu, provided assurances that Albania was ready to restore diplomatic and trade relations with Washington. Plans to cooperate were hindered by the American Lockheed T-33 spy plane mission, which on December 23, 1957, was forced to land at Rinas airport as a result of an emergency.

The growing dependence on the USSR was not questioned by the leadership of the Albanian Party of Labour while it guaranteed the feelings of safety and constant principles of cooperation. However, after Stalin's death, the USSR underwent some changes which were met with growing anxiety in Tirana. The first worrying signal was the change in the Kremlin's politics towards Yugoslavia. On May 26, 1955, a Soviet government delegation, with N. Khrushchev at its head, flew to Belgrade. At the airport in Belgrade, the Soviet leader made a speech in which he expressed regret about the previous events between the two countries. The Belgrade meeting ended with the signing of a declaration of closer cooperation between the two countries.

---

52 Bland and Price, *Tangled Web*, 280–283.

53 John L. Hart, *The CIA's Russians* (Annapolis, MD: Naval Institute Press, 2003), 5–7.

54 Dervishi, *Historia e shtetit*, 644.

55 Evanthis Hatzivassiliou, *Greece and the Cold War: Frontline State, 1952–1967* (New York: Routledge, 2006), 100.

Albania, who had played a key role in the anti-Yugoslav campaign, began to feel marginalized due to the closer relations between Moscow and Belgrade. Albanian fears deepened during bilateral talks in the Kremlin in the summer of 1955. Mikhail Suslov who was responsible for foreign politics in the CPSU Central Commitee Political Bureau suggested to E. Hoxha that the Albanian party should change its attitude to the Yugoslavia question, and also reassess its view of the K. Xoxe group.[56] In 1955 under Moscow's pressure, a normalization of Albanian-Yugoslav relations took place. This was often of a purely formal character. Portraits of Tito and Ranković, "decorated" with axes covered with the blood of Albanians from Kosovo disappeared from the walls of homes, and songs about "treacherous Tito" were removed from the repertoire of Albanian folk groups.[57] The next change which was a concern for the APL leadership was the questioning of Stalin's internal politics, as well as the purges conducted during his governing. E. Hoxha, as someone who followed the political principles of Stalin, began to feel threatened. Among the Soviet bloc states, the so-called Tito's list – a list of his political enemies whose elimination was the price for understanding with Belgrade, became legendary.[58]

The awakening of the party afraid of repression took place in the spring of 1956. In April 1956, with the participation of 453 delegates a conference of local party committees was held in Tirana.[59] Enver Hoxha did not attend the meeting as he was resting in Vlore. A report of party activity was presented by Fiqrete Shehu, wife of the Prime Minister of Albania – Mehmet Shehu. Deprived of any criticism, the report ended with a declaration to meet all the decisions of the III APL Congress by the party organisation in Tirana. The report caused an uproar in the hall and a range of negative opinions. Participants criticised the country's economic situation, the privileges enjoyed by the party and country leadership, and the groundless purges in the party. Hoxha's reaction was fast and brutal. Twenty seven participants of the conference were arrested, and the main opponents were shot.[60] The unity of the Albanian party was to be shown by the III APL Congress in May–June 1956. The resolution accepted during the proceedings expressed full solidarity with the XX CPSU Congress. In his speech, Enver Hoxha fully agreed with the necessity of restoring the Leninist form of internal party life and the rejection of "the personality cult."

---

56 Enver Hoxha, *Khrushchevtsy. Vospominaniia* (Tirana: Shtëpia Botuese Naim Frashëri, 1980), 148.

57 Grigorii Arsh et al., *Kratkaia istoriia Albanii* (Moscow: Nauka, 1965), 422–423.

58 According to Polish diplomats, the removal of Hoxha was the price to be paid for the recognition of the German Democratic Republic by Yugoslavia and the creation of bilateral relations, however in 1957 the Russians backed away from this idea – see Krzysztof Ruchniewicz and Tadeusz Szumowski, eds., *Polskie dokumenty dyplomatyczne 1957* (Warsaw: Polski Instytut Spraw Międzynarodowych, 2006), 789.

59 Ana Lalaj, "Konferencja e Partise e Tiranes, nje pranvere e deshtuar e se majtes ne Shqiperi (14–19 aprill 1956)," *Studime Historike* 1–2 (2009): 113.

60 Peter Prifti, *Socialist Albania since 1944: Domestic and Foreign Developments* (Cambridge, MA: MIT Press, 1978), 205.

The Albanian government viewed the events of October 1956 in Poland and Hungary with great reserve, observing the threat of revisionist and counter-revolutionary tendencies. There was particular suspicion towards the new Polish leader, Władysław Gomułka, who was regarded as a man who had gained power even though he had been imprisoned for conducting anti-state activity. In his speeches, the Prime Minister of Albania, M. Shehu, called Gomułka a Bukharinist, and the Political Bureau of the PUWP (the Polish United Workers' Party) formed in October 1956 – a creation knocked together illegally.[61] The events in Hungary were a pretext to increased hostility towards Belgrade. After a short break, in November 1956, criticism grew in the Albanian press of Yugoslav politics, although Tito's name didn't appear in the articles. A particularly unpleasant surprise for the leadership of the APL was when the member of the APL Central Committee and the former deputy-minister of defence – General Panajot Plaku fled the country. To the disgust of the leaders in Tirana, Plaku, after arriving in Yugoslavia, announced that Hoxha and his advisers take decisions without taking into consideration the party statute or the law. The Yugoslav press published a range of confidential information about the leadership of the APL, the source of which could only be Plaku.[62]

A break in the previously harmonic Albanian-Soviet cooperation became visible after the visit of Nikita Khrushchev in Tirana in May 1959. This was the first visit of such a high-ranking Soviet politician to Tirana. However, the Soviet leader caused consternation with his protectionist tone and statements, which were difficult for the Albanian party leaders to agree with. They were particularly disturbed by Khrushchev's order to cooperate more closely with Yugoslavia and to change the direction of economic development. The concept of developing heavy industry, so far realized in Albania, turned out to be costly and ineffective for Moscow. During his visit in Tirana, Khrushchev proposed the suspension of forced industrialization and to base Albania's development on the farming-food industry sector. With this idea, Albania would become a great plantation of tropical plants, helped by its natural conditions.[63] His vision of a "great plantation" was unacceptable for the Albanian party leadership, who were fascinated by the transformation of Albania into an industrial-agricultural country.

In view of the growing Soviet-Albanian differences, and the developing Soviet-Chinese dispute, the increasing Chinese interest in Albania became increasingly significant. In September 1956, Enver Hoxha travelled to Beijing as the head of a party-state delegation to participate in the VIIII Chinese Communist Party Congress. The real intention of the visit was easy to work out. In 1955, Chinese participation

[61] Robert Skobelski, "Stosunki polsko-albańskie w latach 1956–1970," *Limes. Studia i materiały z dziejów Europy Środkowo-Wschodniej* 1 (2008): 272.

[62] Smirnova, *Istoriia Albanii*, 317.

[63] A similar idea was reportedly announced in 1953 by A. Mikoian, imploring the Albanian leadership to reject the idea of forced industrialization and to concentrate on agricultural development – Hoxha, *Khrushchevtsy*, 73.

in Albania's foreign trade amounted to just 4.2%, but a year later it had grown to 17%. Support from Beijing became a key element for Tirana in view of the growing pressure from the USSR. Between 1956 and 1959, Albania became an object of the "credit rivalry" between the two super powers. The value of Soviet aid for Albania increased significantly in 1958 as a result of the economic crisis in China (Great Leap Forward campaign).

The open hostility between the APL and CPSU leadership was the opening subject at the Third Romanian Communist Party Congress (20–25 June 1960). The Albanian delegation in Bucharest was led by Hysni Kapo. The meeting was intended to lead to the creation of a joint stand in the matter of the Chinese party and to pronounce it as anti-Marxist and Trotskyist. The continuation of discussions concerning China were opposed by Hysni Kapo, who demanded that the conflict be resolved in bilateral Chinese-Soviet discussions.[64] At the same time, a meeting of the General Council of the World Federation of Trade Unions was held in Beijing, concentrating on representatives of communist countries. The criticism by the Albanian delegate Gogo Nushi of detente politics, and the emphasis placed by Liu Shao-chi on the connections between Albania and China were an obvious declaration against Moscow.

An even more serious conflict between Moscow and Tirana was brought about by the meeting of 81 labour and communist parties, which took place in Moscow (November 1960). The Albanian delegation, led by Enver Hoxha rejected the idea of detente and supported the Chinese position, describing it as the unavoidable war against imperialism. Hoxha's position at the Moscow meeting was met with full approval by the IV APL Congress, which met from 13 to 20 February 1961. There was no direct criticism of the Soviet party during the proceedings, but the delegates of the IV Congress directed many warm words towards the CPCh (Communist Party of China), leading the "fundamental and revolutionary fight," simultaneously criticising the idea of "modern revisionism."[65] An explicitly critical position towards the Albanians was taken by the XXII CPSU Congress (October 1961), where the matter of the APL "disloyalty" was one of the main issues. On October 27, 1961, Khrushchev read out an overview of accusations against the Albanians speaking about the degeneration of the APL leadership and calling the Albanian nation to overthrow Hoxha and Shehu.[66] The majority of the speakers during the Congress were of the opinion that the Albanian party was moving from the Leninist and international position and heading towards nationalism.

After the Moscow meeting, the Soviet leadership decided to use economic sanctions against Albania and annul the loans granted earlier for the realization of Albania's III Five-Year Plan (1961–1965). The suspension of economic aid occurred in a particularly difficult situation which Albania was experiencing in 1960 after

[64] Smirnova, *Istoriia Albanii*, 318.

[65] Smirnova, *Istoriia Albanii*, 327.

[66] Pano, *People's Republic of Albania*, 152.

a series of natural disasters (earthquakes, floods and droughts). After a dramatically poor harvest, in September 1960 the grain reserves in Albanian stores were enough for just 15 days. The Soviet powers agreed to supply Albania with 10 thousand tons of grain (instead of the previously promised 50 thousand tons). The grain, however, didn't reach Albania in September or in October.[67] The only rescue in this situation was the purchase by China in hard currency of Canadian grain and sending it to Albania. Suspension of Soviet economic aid provoked this angry response from E. Hoxha, made on November 6, 1961: "After a delay of 45 days, the USSR promised us 10,000 tons of wheat to be delivered in September or October. These are unbearable pressures. The soviet rats were able to eat whilst the Albanian people were dying of hunger; we were asked to produce gold."[68]

The next point of dispute in the bilateral relations was the matter of the 12 Soviet submarines stationed in the Pasha Liman base.[69] In March 1961, the Soviets demanded the evacuation of all Albanian staff from the base and the handover of full control to the USSR, otherwise the Soviets would close the base. The response from the Albanians, on April 5, 1961, emphasized the temporary character of the mission for Soviet military personnel, connected with training Albanians in the use of Soviet military equipment. This meant that the Soviet officers should leave the base after completing this task.[70] In the same response, Albania claimed the right to all units and equipment found in the base. Based on these political events, on April 29, 1961, Albanian foot soldiers gained control of the Soviet submarines.[71] Finally, the Albanians agreed to allow most of the submarines stationed in the base to leave, keeping only four of them. On May 26, 1961, Soviet ships left Albanian territorial waters, returning through Gibraltar to their homeland. On June 5, 1961, the base's Soviet personnel also left. The four submarines and 22 auxiliary units became part of the Albanian naval fleet. The Kremlin restricted itself in this matter to verbal protests and accusing the Albanians of piracy.

On November 25, 1961, the USSR's deputy minister of foreign affairs, Nikolai Firiubin, submitted to the Albanian representative in Moscow a statement recalling the Soviet representative from Tirana, and demanding the immediate withdrawal of the Albanian representatives from the USSR. When explaining this decision, he accused Albanian diplomats residing in Moscow of attempts to spread materials from the APL Central Committee meetings, which contained "slander against the USSR and other communist countries."[72] On December 3, 1961, N. Firiubin handed over

---

67 Hamm, *Albania*, 18.

68 William Griffith, *Albania and the Sino-Soviet Rift* (Cambridge, MA: MIT Press, 1963), 55.

69 The Soviets spent over 30 million dollars on building and maintaining the base (Pano, *People's Republic of Albania*, 90).

70 Prifti, *Socialist Albania*, 203.

71 Vojtech Mastny and Malcolm Byrne, *A Cardboard Castle?: An inside History of the Warsaw Pact, 1955–1991* (Budapest: Central European Universty Press, 2005), 114.

72 *Pravda o sovetsko-albanskikh otnosheniiakh* (Tirana: Shtëpia Botuese Naim Frashëri, 1961), 14.

another statement concerning the withdrawal of all Soviet diplomatic personnel from Albania, demanding the same from the Albanians. A day later, the Albanian Ministry of Foreign Affairs sent a note to the Soviet representative in Tirana recognising the decision of the USSR as unfair and inconsistent with the principles of international law.[73] The other countries in the Soviet bloc did not break diplomatic relations with Albania, but in December 1961 the ambassadors of Czechoslovakia, East Germany and Hungary left Tirana. The recalled ambassadors were replaced by charge d'affaires, which represents a lowering of the range of mutual contacts.[74]

The break in Albanian cooperation with the Soviet bloc in 1961 meant its exclusion from the collective system of security guaranteed by the Warsaw Pact. Tirana declined to participate in two meetings of the Warsaw Pact countries, which took place in March and August 1961, as well as in a meeting of the Pact's ministers of defence (March 1961). Moscow annulled its military agreement with Albania, cutting it off completely from the supply of weapons and equipment necessary for normal functioning of the Albanian defence system. In the summer of 1961, both in the USSR and in other countries of the Soviet bloc, the training of all Albanian officers, cadets and sub-officers was stopped. The break with the USSR brought about another purge in the APL leadership. The attack was directed at those who had earlier studied at Soviet academies or were responsible for agreements with the CPSU. This group included Liri Belishova, responsible in the Central Committee for propaganda, her husband Maqo Çomo and the veteran of the Albanian communist movement – Koço Tashko. Of particular importance was the removal of Liri Belishova, who, after the death of her first husband, Nako Spiru, and the break from Yugoslavia, was co-opted to the party's Political Bureau, becoming the most influential woman in the party. In July 1960, a group of high officers were also arrested, including the leader of the Albanian fleet, Admiral Teme Sejko.[75] During the trial which took place in May 1961, T. Sejko was charged with preparing a coup d'etat, together with the leaders of the American VI Fleet. The Admiral was found guilty and shot.

73 On December 14, 1961, all Albanian diplomatic personnel left the USSR – Pearson, *Albania*, vol. 3, 615.

74 Arsh et al., *Kratkaia istoriia Albanii*, 428.

75 Gjergj Titani and Proleter Hasani, *Personalitete ushtarake shqiptare ne vite 1912–1997*, vol. 1 (Tirana: Toena, 1997), 215.

3. Chinese period

It is difficult for us to speak about the aid which Albania gave to China, because what the Albanian party and nation did for China and the Chinese nation, it did from a communist perspective and was inspired by feelings of brotherhood and internationalism. But you forced us to speak about it because you, following the example of Khrushchev and Brezhnev, began to count the juans and fens, which you gave Albania.[76]

Proceedings of the IV Congress of the Albanian Party of Labour in 1961 signalled the new challenge which Albania stood before. Both Enver Hoxha and the Prime Minister Mehmet Shehu presented a thesis of war taking place on two fronts – against imperialism and against modern revisionism.[77] The best example of the imperialistic-revisionist conspiracy recognised in Tirana was the treaty signed between the USA and the USSR for the partial ban on nuclear weapon tests (August 1963). The alliance with China changed in principle the political rhetoric of the rulers of Albania. Out of spite to the increasingly regarded *detente* in the world of politics, messages were sent from Tirana about the unavoidable war with imperialism and the necessity to prepare for it. The campaign for peace, organized by the Soviet camp, replaced the universal threat of war. Threatened by the political detente, Albania accepted a position of political isolation on the European continent.

A serious barrier to Chinese-Albanian cooperation was the physical distance between the countries. Ships with Chinese goods and machines sailed through the Pacific, around the Cape of Good Hope and on to Albania. Due to the distance dividing the two countries, Albanian-Chinese trade remained at a low level compared with Albanian-Soviet cooperation before 1961. By taking "economic responsibility" for supporting Albania, China gained a faithful and staunch ally in Europe. Albania announced eight resolutions concerning the acceptance of its new partner to the United Nations. In December 1963, the Albanian representative in the UN, Behar Shtylla criticised the ban on nuclear weapon experiments, and argued that China's problems with joining the United Nations were the systematic obstruction of American imperialists. The American representative Adlai Stevenson described the Albanian speech as a brutal return to the most outspoken demagoguery of the cold war.[78]

When the Chinese performed their first atomic bomb test (October 28, 1964), the Albanian newspaper *Zëri i Popullit* triumphantly described it on its front page as a great success of the Chinese state. On the second anniversary of the explosion, the Albanian leadership sent greetings to Beijing, describing the test as an event of great historical importance, which destroyed the American-Soviet "plot" to main-

[76] *A Letter of the APL CC and Albanian Government to the Chinese Communist Party CC and the Chinese Government* (Tirana: Shtëpia Botuese Naim Frashëri, 1978).

[77] *Kongresi IV i Partisë së Punës së Shqipërisë: (Përmbledhje materialesh) 12–20 shkurt 1961* (Tirana: Shtëpia Botuese Naim Frashëri, 1961), 148.

[78] Pearson, *Albania*, vol. 3, 620.

tain nuclear monopoly in the world.[79] There was a similar reaction to the news of the first Chinese hydrogen bomb explosion (June 18, 1967). In the next congratulatory telegrams sent to Beijing, it was stated that such successes serve in the defence of socialism and create panic in the "American imperialist and Soviet revisionist" camps. A symbol of Albanian-Chinese cooperation was the powerful transmitter, built by the Chinese in the region of Durrës, thanks to which political transmissions from China reached European countries (through Radio Tirana). For over 15 years of the Albanian-Chinese union, Tirana became a regional centre for Europe, representing shelter for revolutionary groups connected with Maoism.

The idea of social-imperialism used in party propaganda, referring to the politics of the USSR, hindered any possible warming in relations with Moscow, despite Soviet declarations which signalled their willingness to enter into negotiations.[80] The new Soviet leadership, after the downfall of N. Khrushchev, tried, with the help of Polish diplomacy, to establish new political cooperation with Tirana. In January 1965, the Polish government sent an invitation to the Albanian leadership to participate in the meeting of the Political Consultative Committee of the Warsaw Pact countries. The Albanian reply, describing this invitation as violation of the rules of the Warsaw Pact and in consequence – as a discriminatory move against the People's Republic of Albania, did not leave any room for compromise.[81] The Albanian press quickly added Khrushchev's successor, Leonid Brezhnev, to the group of "revisionists" and continued its campaign directed against Soviet social-imperialism, using the slogan "Khrushchevism without Khrushchev."[82]

The intervention of the Warsaw Pact countries in Czechoslovakia in 1968 created serious fears in Tirana. Enver Hoxha, who in 1956 praised Soviet intervention in Hungary, this time named similar activity in Czechoslovakia by his former allies as the aggression of Soviet revisionism and its satellites. As a result, on September 13, the Albanian parliament decided to leave the Warsaw Pact. While explaining the reasons for this decision, Hoxha stated that the Pact "from a pact of defence against imperialistic aggression had become a pact of aggression against socialist countries." Albanian officers had not participated in the group's activities since the beginning of the 1960s, and official abandonment of the Pact removed the final pretext to a possible invasion. On September 29, 1968, an Albanian party-state delegation, led by the Minister of Defence, Beqir Balluku, arrived in Beijing. The unusually long visit (until October 10) focused on establishing a new strategy of bilateral military

---

79 Prifti, *Socialist Albania*, 207.

80 GDR diplomats acted as a go-between in discussions with the Kremlin, and had represented Soviet interests in Albania since 1961 – Miranda Vickers and James Pettifer, *Albania: From Anarchy to a Balkan Identity*, 2nd ed. (London: Hurst, 1999), 223.

81 Richard Vaughan, *Twentieth Century Europe: Paths to Unity*, (New York: Taylor & Francis, 1979), 188.

82 Roderick MacFarquhar, *The Origins of the Cultural Revolution*, vol. 3, *The Coming of the Cataclysm, 1961–1966* (Oxford: Oxford University Press, 1997), 365.

cooperation. The presence of the Chinese army Chief of Staff, Huang Yung-sheng, brought about speculation concerning the construction of a Chinese naval base on the coast of Albania, which could protect the country from a possible naval invasion. However, the absence of the Chinese fleet in the Mediterranean Sea basin made such speculation unrealistic.[83]

From the beginning of the 1970s, the Soviet bloc countries tried to weaken the ties between Tirana and Beijing and to restore relations with Albania. This process was hindered by the inflexible stance of the Albanian leaders, who were trying to increase trade relations, but without any political cooperation. Diplomats from the Soviet bloc countries regularly took part in May 1 celebrations in Tirana, as well as in Albanian nationalist holidays. They also consistently boycotted the celebrations if any posters or banners appeared which condemned "Soviet social-imperialism." This was a clear response to Albanian activity which intended to create divisions among the Soviet bloc countries.[84] In 1972, Bulgarian diplomats presented a twelve-point project for normalizing relations in Tirana, but it was rejected. Polish diplomats, after visiting Tirana in May 1972, suggested a strategy of "little steps" towards Tirana and a silencing of criticism directed at the Albanian leadership.[85] For the Poles, the start of the normalisation process was to be the work of a mixed Polish-Albanian committee for trade contacts.

A feeling of threat forced the Albanian leadership to strengthen its relations with its neighbours and partially reduce its aggressive rhetoric. The Albanian inhabitants of Kosovo lost the most as a result of the new relations with Yugoslavia. Tirana observed the waves of social protests which took place in Kosovo in November 1968 in silence. The protesters demanded the recognition of Kosovo as a republic within the Yugoslav Federation, and also drew attention to the issue of the discrimination of Albanians in Kosovo's governments and forces. The policy of openness and unification, despite ideological differences, was the main feature of Belgrade-Tirana relations in the 1970s, helping intensive cultural cooperation between Albanians from Pristina and Tirana.[86] The cooperation with Yugoslavia, which developed intensively from the beginning of the 1970s also had an important economic element. In 1978, the value of trade between the two countries reached 28 million dollars, but

83 Prifti, *Socialist Albania*, 209.

84 Chargé d'affaires of the Polish Embassy in Tirana to the director of the First Department of the Ministry of Foreign Affairs, 11 February 1972, in *Polskie dokumenty dyplomatyczne 1974*, ed. Aleksander Kochański and Mikołaj Morzycki-Markowski (Warsaw: Polski Instytut Spraw Międzynarodowych, 2007), 129.

85 Notes from a stay in Tirana, 2 May 1972, in *Polskie dokumenty dyplomatyczne 1972*, ed. Włodzimierz Borodziej (Warsaw: Polski Instytut Spraw Międzynarodowych, 2005), 232–234.

86 The rapprochement in Albanian-Yugoslav relations was initiated by Belgrade. J.B. Tito in August 1970 appealed to the APL leadership to reject ideological differences on behalf of "common interests in the defence of national sovereignty". In 1971, the diplomatic institutions of both countries were raised to Embassy status (Paulin Kola, *The Search for Greater Albania* (London: Hurst, 2003), 132).

a year later had risen to 60 million and still showed a tendency to grow.[87] A visible change also appeared in relations with Greece. After a few months of negotiations, on May 6, 1971, diplomatic relations were again entered into, although the end of the formal state of war existing since 1940 was not announced.[88]

Albania was the only European country that did not participate in the Conference on Security and Co-operation in Europe (November 1972), despite an invitation from Finland. The Conference was described by Enver Hoxha as a "farce, in which the main actors were the Soviet Union and the United States."[89]

Besides political and economic aspects, the Albanian-Chinese alliance also brought about an attempt to introduce the Chinese form of communism into Albanian conditions. The social reforms, which Albanians experienced in the 1960s, were connected with the reforms of the Chinese cultural revolution, although in Albania they were often described as "revolutionisation" or "a second revolution." As the political expert Arshi Pipa states, the Albanian leader Enver Hoxha described revolutionisation as a bridge from economic revolution to ideological revolution.[90] Isa Blumi's idea of the Albanian cultural revolution refers to the whole of the 1960s, when radical social and economic changes took place. Their aim was the elimination of two threats – a foreign invasion, and the possibility of a reformist movement inside the party, which could result in a change in the political ideology.[91] In this "war for a new Albania," just like the one twenty years earlier, youngsters prepared to fight to rid society of bad habits and the non-beneficial signs for the communist revolution of social conformation and indifference. The new generation of Albanians, who didn't remember the war and had no partisan background were raised with the fear of threats and the awareness that, as part of the conflict, the duty to defend the country against an expected invasion rested with them. The aim was to frighten society, and to force absolute loyalty to the party and state.

Clearly following the Chinese, the APL Central Committee began a campaign against bureaucracy in October 1965. Rallies organized in work places showed support for the new party line, but more and more often expressed obedience to the directors who followed the Soviet school of management. Articles appeared in the press discrediting the bureaucratic framework, showing how many documents particular offices "produce." Using the press, the APL Central Committee appealed to the masses to actively participate in preparation of the next, already the fourth, Five-Year Plan. This represented a symbolic shifting of power over economic plan-

---

87 O'Donnell, *Coming of Age*, 90.

88 Pearson, *Albania*, vol. 3, 628.

89 Enver Hoxha, *Report Announced at the VII Congress of the Albanian Party of Labour* (Tirana: Shtëpia Botuese Naim Frashëri, 1978), 171.

90 Pipa, *Albanian Stalinism*, 86–87.

91 Isa Blumi, "Hoxha's Class War: The Cultural Revolution and State Reformation, 1961–1971," *East European Quarterly* 33 (September 1999): 303.

ning from party bureaucrats directly to the working masses.[92] In the new reform program, the central figure was not the party activist but the worker. In February 1966, an APL Central Committee statement was published in which the need to re-educate clerks through physical work was presented. E. Hoxha's open letter printed in the magazine *Rruga e Partisë* (The Party Road) brought about an open attack on civil service workers as exponents of bureaucracy, which in turn was considered an appearance typical of Khrushchev's revisionism.[93] As Hoxha stated in his letter, elimination of the privileged classes, consisting of the party bureaucracy, business directors, artists and scientists, was a guarantee that Albania would not repeat the Soviet mistakes. A bureaucratic party, dominated by "clerks" was something typical for the Soviet reality, and as Hoxha stated a tool of Soviet counter-revolution, which had strangled the Bolshevik party.[94] In 1966 the party leaders regarded as many as 80% of statistical reports from enterprises, prepared by white-collar workers, as representing examples of unnecessary bureaucracy which should be eliminated.[95]

The postulate of reducing bureaucracy signified an apparent decentralisation of the country. The changes were intended to create a complex of uncertainty among clerks to release them from conformism and comfort. The press reported on the brave decision of eleven clerks, responsible for agriculture in the regional party committee in Durrës, who resigned from their positions voluntarily and began work in cooperatives. The example of the clerks from Durrës was treated as an inspiration to reduce administration in the Ministries.[96] In view of the reduction in the size of the central administration, there was also a reduction in the number of ministers from 19 to 13. Among the liquidated ministries was the Ministry of Justice. The reduction in ministerial positions was closely connected with the process of limiting access to the elite, which was a typical appearance in the 1960s. In 1962, out of 52 APL Central Committee members, as many as 28 were related. After twenty years of rule, the party leadership had become a closed and isolated group, which had an extremely limited range of ties, such as family-social ones with low-level clerks. This differed considerably from the picture in the first few post-war years, when contacts and friendships from the partisan days were maintained. Twenty years later the decision-making order was designated by "a telephone from the Central Committee," which was an order without any negotiation.[97]

---

92 Blumi, "Hoxha's Class War," 312.

93 *Rruga e Partisë* 3 (1966): 2.

94 Hoxha, *Report*, 72.

95 Adi Schnytzer, *Stalinist Economic Strategy in Practice: The Case of Albania* (New York: Oxford University Press, 1982), 49.

96 Officially, there were 15 thousand civil servants who resigned voluntarily, but it is more probable that they were dismissed from their positions during the fight against bureaucracy – Schnytzer, *Stalinist Economic*, 35.

97 "The independence of ministries as institutions was fictional – the minister received orders from the Central Commitee and served only as an agent. There was neither organisation nor systematic operation in this." Naum Prifti, *Teatri ne kohen e krizës* (Tirana: Horizont, 2001), 79.

The Central Committee party letter no. 58 from 30 April 1967 significantly widened the category of white-collar workers who were to be re-educated through physical work. Besides the party's central workers, teachers, officers and intelligent creators were also added. The time for production work equalled 30 days per year, and 15 days for married women.[98] The highest level government workers led by example during the "spectacle" campaign as they presented their engagement in physical work, including the Prime Minister, M. Shehu, who sat behind the wheel of a tractor, pretending to be part of the work in a cooperative.[99] The greatest significance was given, however, to the youth, working in volunteer brigades. The motto "erdhen vullnetaret" (volunteers are coming) represented in the 1960s a form of entreaty justifying the investment which seemed to exceed the development barriers of a small Balkan country. The engagement of volunteers in social work was to be an important part of revolutionisation in social areas and to destroy the social structure and other common laws which a large part of society were still faithful to.[100]

A nine-hour speech from Enver Hoxha at the party's V Congress (November 1966) discussing, among many other topics, the difficult "inheritance of the past," became a signal to widen the area of introduced social-economic reforms. Above all, they concerned farmers, whose land which they could own was reduced to two-thirds of the previous amount. This happened through a "spontaneous and joyful" vote of a bill from production cooperative workers.[101]

The main weapon in the fight against the inappropriate social attitude were wall newspapers. The idea was connected with the Chinese "big-character posters" – *dazibao* (the Albanian version – *flete rrufeja*). Their role was presented on February 6, 1967, during E. Hoxha's speech: "Let everyone, without fear, take a card and write, in large letters, what he thinks about work and about people". The posters became universal at the end of the 1960s. They were placed at workplaces, in schools and hospitals. They presented various problems – economic, political, social, and also cultural. The most important task of the posters were to criticise mistakes and lack of achievements hindering revolutionization, as well as to show who was guilty of negligence. Those who were criticised had a moral duty to respond to the criticism. If they remained quiet, the next papers appeared with more aggressive comments.[102]

At the end of the 1960s, in the spirit of revolutionisation, steps were taken to align workers' wages with those of managers. This meant that there was a systematic increase in the wages of the lowest earners and a decrease in the earnings of those who had previously received the highest salaries (over 1,200 leks). In February 1969, the People's Assembly passed a law which meant that the highest salary could only

---

98 ASA, Central Committee of the APL, 1967, d. 353.

99 Smirnova, *Istoriia Albanii*, 331.

100 There is a wider discussion of these problems in Chapters IV and VII.

101 *Zëri i Popullit*, November 2, 1966, 1–2.

102 Ilia Plaku, "Si i vendosnim flete-rrufete ne vitet 70," *Tirana Observer*, November 19, 2003.

be twice the lowest one.[103] A few months later, the APL Central Committee initiated a motivational campaign for increased proletarian discipline – in order to meet production standards, limit absences from work and increase "voluntary" work activity to help society. The motto of fighting bureaucracy underwent a clear softening. In the 1970s, *flete rrufeja*, which were in worse and worse condition, slowly disappeared from the streets. More and more slander and personal attacks appeared in newspapers, and the authority of mid-level management staff in enterprises (directors) was also undermined, which threatened to weaken discipline at work.

The absurdity of Albanian revolutionisation was not avoided by the army. In October 1965 E. Hoxha sent a letter to "officers, soldiers and people" in which he tried to undermine the authority which officers enjoyed, emphasising the duty of loyalty soldiers had towards the party and its leadership.[104] The new doctrine for the defence of Albania referred to the idea of "a people's war."[105] The realisation of this doctrine assumed that army units would transfer from garrisons to a few thousand "points of resistance," where they would serve every day. In order to liquidate the privileges and unnecessary hierarchy of the army ranks, the rewards of officers were levelled down to the salaries of administrative workers. The idea of a "citizens army" clearly referred to the partisan war, which brought victory to Albanians in the Second World War. Hoxha's view of the future of the Albanian army is best expressed by the words "There is no stronger army than an armed and trained military nation."[106] With the motto of "a pick-axe in one hand, and a rifle in the other" in mind, responsibility for national defence was also given to the youth working in volunteer brigades, and even children, for whom a rifle became an important element of daily fun. The picture of *Kids from my neighbourhood* by Spiro Kristo presented a group of young kids observing with interest an older boy drawing the shape of a rifle on the pavement. In 1967 the *Fatosi* monthly magazine for schoolchildren (to 12 years old) included a number of examples of model pupils, whose greatest dream was to fight with a rifle in hand.[107] The duty to defend the country and the constant improvement of shooting skills was regularly mentioned by the women's weekly *Shqiptarja e Re* (New Albanian Woman).[108]

---

[103] Michael Kaser, "Albania" in *The New Economic Systems of Eastern Europe*, eds. Hans Höhmann, Michael Kaser, and Karl Thalheim (Berkeley: University of California Press, 1975), 266.

[104] Biljana Vankovska and Håkan Wiberg, *Between Past and Future: Civil-Military Relations in the Post-communist Balkans* (London: I.B. Tauris, 2003), 49.

[105] This concept referred to the description used by Lin Piao in September 1965: "The history of the people's war in China and other countries provides conclusive evidence that the growth of the people's revolutionary forces from weak and small beginnings into strong and large forces is a universal law of development of people's war". Alan Lawrance, *China's Foreign Relations since 1949* (London: Routledge, 1975), 181.

[106] Enver Hoxha, *Our Policy is an Open Policy: The Policy of Proletarian Principles* (Tirana: Shtëpia Botuese 8 Nëntori, 1974), 29.

[107] "A do te merrni edhe mua ne aksion," *Fatosi* 1 (1967): 8.

[108] R. Lahi, "Çdo dite, çdo ore te stervitemi," *Shqiptarja e Re* 10 (1985): 11.

Despite its formal entry to the Warsaw Pact in September 1968, Albania increased its annual defence budget by 38%. In the following years, the budget systematically increased, but at an insignificant level.[109] The limited defence possibilities against potential aggression was the inspiration behind the fortification of the country. The idea of building a million bunkers throughout the country came from Mehmet Shehu, who believed that it would be the most effective form of defence in such specific geographical conditions.[110] The first bunkers were built in 1958, but the majority of them were constructed at the end of the 1970s and beginning of the 1980s. Three times more concrete was used to build this system than for the whole of the Maginot Line. The construction of over 700 thousand concrete bunkers practically stopped all investment in the construction area. The cost of building one bunker exceeded 350 thousand leks and was similar to the cost of a two-room flat in a block.[111] The presence of bunkers near homes was a reminder of the constant threat, and was also supposed to bring about a national mental state of being a fortress. Complementary to this defence system were millions of concrete poles topped with iron spearheads to impale hostile paratroopers.[112]

The change in the Albanian defence doctrine was a pretext to the largest purge in the Albanian army. The party leadership received more and more disturbing signals of frequent examples of insubordination and disregard of regulations. In addition, during the soldiers' training process, political training was neglected, and especially that of Enver Hoxha's works. The officers' salaries were also extremely low which encouraged some of them to leave the army.

The report of the Minister of Defence, Beqir Balluku, presented in 1975, criticised the results of creating a "citizens army," suggesting that it was a destructive process of the armed forces and a fall in their professionalism was noticeable. The report, named by E. Hoxha "the black thesis," led to accusations against B. Balluku of irregularities in the reform of the armed forces.[113].

Balluku's dismissal and imprisonment began a process of eliminating generals, accused of spreading defeatism and holding similar views to the arrested minister. General Petrit Dume lost his position as Army Chief of Staff, as did his deputy, General Rahman Perllaku. The Army Political Directorate Chief, General Hito Cako and his deputy, General Halim Ramohito, were also removed. On November 5, 1975, the High Court in Tirana sentenced B. Balluku, P. Dume and H. Cako to the death penalty, and the others to long-term prison sentences. While the generals were being sentenced, there was another purge among the group of economists running

109 Prifti, *Socialist Albania*, 220.

110 Bardho Hyseni, *Beteja dhe duele. Esse dhe kujtime* (Athina: Alcaeus, 2000), 43.

111 Michael Kaser, "Economic System" in *Albanien*, ed. Klaus-Detlev Grothusen (Göttingen: Vandenhoeck & Ruprecht, 1993), 293.

112 Johannes Stahl, *Rent from the Land: A Political Ecology of Postsocialist Rural Transformation* (London: Anthem Press, 2010), 17.

113 Prifti, *Socialist Albania*, 215.

the Albanian economy. Abdul Kellezi and Koco Theodhosi were deprived of their government positions, after being accused of introducing the Yugoslav method of management into the Albanian economy, thereby weakening the idea of centralization. Their activity was described in court as "sabotage."

The peak of social-political change in the period of revolutionization were two documents – the exceptionally restrictive penal code from 1975, and the new basic law, accepted on November 28, 1976, by the People's Assembly. The document defined the official name of the country as the People's Socialist Republic of Albania. Among the organizations whose activity was banned by the constitution were those of fascist, anti-democratic, anti-socialist and... religious nature. The constitution also defined fixed principles in relation to other countries – a ban on accepting foreign loans and the stationing of foreign troops on Albanian territory.

From the end of the 1960s, greater and greater cracks appeared in Chinese-Albanian relations. Tirana's angry reaction was provoked by the Chinese premier Chou En-lai, who in September 1969 met with his Soviet counterpart Aleksei Kosygin in Beijing to discuss the dispute over the border.[114] The results of the Albanian delegation's visit to Beijing) with Abdyl Kellezi at its head (16 October 1970) might have showed that small misunderstandings did not influence Chinese-Albanian cooperation. During the visit, four bilateral agreements were signed. They concerned loans for Albania and the handover of machines and equipment necessary for the next Five-Year Plan (1971–1975).[115] Another worrying signal for the APL leadership was the meeting of Chou En-lai with special American envoy, Henry Kissinger (July 1971), and the warming of relations between the two countries. At the APL Congress in November 1971, doubts as to whether Beijing had decided to cooperate with the imperialist world were openly expressed.

The usefulness of Albania for Beijing decreased after China's acceptance into the UN, which took place on October 25, 1971.[116] At the VI APL Congress (November 1–7, 1971) not even one Chinese party representative appeared. This did not signify the suspension of Chinese credit for Albania, and the Albanian-Chinese system of economic and trade cooperation, signed on June 3, 1975, in Beijing by Deputy Prime Minister Adil Çarçani, gave the impression that China had not resigned from the Albanian card. The Albanian leaders commemorated the death of Mao Zedong in September 1976 with a 3-day period of mourning. A letter sent to the CPCh leadership contained condolences and a conviction that both parties, Chinese and

[114] Albanians found out about the meeting after it had taken place, which increased their irritation – Harry Harding, *A Fragile Relationship: The United States and China since 1972* (Washington, D.C.: Brookings Institution, 1992), 395.

[115] Pearson, *Albania*, vol. 3, 627.

[116] A resolution in this matter was announced by the Albanian minister of foreign affairs Nesti Nase. Pearson, *Albania*, vol. 3, 628.

Albanian, would cooperate more closely and continue to fight against their common enemies.[117]

The changes which took place in China after Mao Zedong's death were unacceptable for Tirana. The new leader of the CPCh, Hua Guofeng, disappointed the Albanians in August 1977, when he announced at the XI CPCh Congress the Three Worlds Theory as an official doctrine of the Chinese foreign policy. This theory, aimed against the hegemony of the two super-powers, the USSR and the USA, assumed that those two countries created the first world, which fights both socialist and capitalist countries (the second world), and also third world countries (China, Romania, Asian countries, Africa and Latin America).[118] The Three Worlds Theory was attacked on 7 July 1977 in the APL Central Committee organ – *Zëri i Popullit*, where it was described as totally opposite to Marxist-Leninist ideas. Acquisition of power by Deng Xiaoping in 1978 was the beginning of a political strategy leading to a free market economy, which was also impossible for Tirana to accept.[119]

Josip Broz Tito stayed in Beijing between August 30 and September 7, 1977. The visit of the Yugoslav leader to China was a surprise for Tirana and gave birth to a wide range of suspicions and fears as to the real reason for the meeting, which had not been consulted with the APL leadership earlier. The Plenum of the Albanian party Central Committee, which was held in November 1977, severely criticised the developing Chinese-Yugoslav relationship. Party organisations throughout the country received the transcript of E. Hoxha's speech in which he criticised Beijing for "demonstrative widening of national and party relations with Yugoslavia."[120]

The year 1978 saw an increase in the ideological dispute with Beijing, as well as the gradually sharper comments which both sides began to make connected with breaches of the bilateral agreements made in 1975.[121] On July 7, 1978, the Chinese Ministry of Foreign Affairs gave the Albanian ambassador in Beijing a diplomatic note informing of the suspension of aid supplies and the recall of economic and military advisers from Albania with immediate effect.[122] Albanians were accused of sabotaging economic cooperation. Beijing appeared to be particularly irritated with the attitude of the Albanian Minister of Industry, who refused to consult his decisions with Chinese advisers. The Chinese placed the blame on the Albanians for the unsuccessful joint projects in the field of petro-chemicals, as well as in the defence infrastructure. The letter also contained estimations of the level of aid for Albania,

117 O'Donnell, *Coming of Age*, 75.

118 This idea was first used by the deputy prime minister of China, Deng Xiaoping, during his speech on April 10, 1974, at the UN General Assembly – Ku-cheng Li, *A Glossary of Political Terms of the People's Republic of China* (Hong Kong: Chinese University Press, 1995), 363.

119 Robert J. Alexander, *Maoism in the Developed World* (Westport, CT: Praeger, 2001), 4.

120 Smirnova, *Istoriia Albanii*, 343.

121 Xhelal Gjecovi, ed., *Historia e Popullit Shqiptar ne kater vellime*, vol. 4 (Tirana: Toena, 2008), 305.

122 During this period, 513 Chinese advisers worked in Albania. Following their recall, 57 Albanian students stopped their studies at Chinese universities. Edwin E. Jacques, *The Albanians: An Ethnic History from Prehistoric Times to the Present* (Jefferson, NC: McFarland, 1995), 546.

which in the years 1964–1975 alone, was estimated at over 10 billion juan (approx. 5.27 billion dollars).

The Chinese note was the main theme of the meeting of the APL Political Bureau, which took place on July 11. According to the Albanian leaders, the crisis in the bilateral relations was not due to economic reasons, but the growing ideological conflict between the APL and the CPCh. Chinese actions towards Albania were described as "brutal and arbitrary," and not in accordance with international standards. The Albanians also questioned the value of Chinese aid, estimating it at 2.6 billion juans (1.4 billion dollars), of which part had been repaid. The Chinese had omitted the mineral resources supplied to China within the framework of the clearing agreement. The 56-page-long Albanian response to the note of July 7 expressed hope that the worsening bilateral relations were of a temporary nature, and that the "Albanian government and nation would fight to maintain the friendship between the two countries."[123] This time the break did not take such a severe form as in 1961, and both countries decided to maintain diplomatic relations. Despite the questioning of the level of Chinese aid by the Albanians, there is no doubt that no other country has to this day, (including Italian aid in the inter-war years), been the patron of Albania for such a long period of time.

4. Period of isolation

> *We know how to deepen the contradictions between the enemies of socialism, and we deepen them as much as we can, but first of all respect our principles. We always call a spade a spade..*[124]

After breaking cooperation with China, the most important challenge for Albanian foreign policy was the necessity to compensate for the loss of its most important market, as well as its strategic creditor. This was so difficult that, in the constitution of 1976, the country banned the borrowing of foreign money. An additional problem was the barter system used in the trade with China. In the report of the Ministry of Foreign Trade from 1978, there was a dramatic sounding statement: "in our bank there is almost no foreign currency and in this situation it is necessary to gain new loans to maintain imports."[125] In view of the catastrophic lack of foreign

[123] *Zëri i Popullit*, July 30, 1978, 1. Albania started trading with China after a five-year break, in 1983, but political cooperation was only resumed after the visit of the Albanian minister of foreign affairs, Reis Malile, in January 1991 (Ian Jeffries, *Socialist Economies and the Transition to the Market* [London: Routledge, 2003], 227–288).

[124] Enver Hoxha, *Reflections on China, II, 1973-1977. Extracts from the Political Diary*" [Tirana, The „8 Nentori" Publishing House, 1979], 109.

[125] Per Sandström and Örjan Sjöberg, "Albanian Economic Performance: Stagnation in the 1980's," *Soviet Studies* 5 (1991): 931–932.

currency and the limited imports, the Albania leadership considered the possibility of increased trade with Western Europe, without becoming economically dependent.[126] The European perspective in foreign policy, clearly neglected during the cooperation with China gained a strategic significance. The change of direction in Albanian foreign policy was connected with the belief that it was possible to increase the range of trade, without political changes and the maintenance of isolation from the international community. Some countries in Western Europe were regarded as "safe trading partners," with whom cooperation didn't cause any negative ideological consequences. Besides Italy and France, the Albanian leadership also included the Scandinavian countries, the Benelux countries, Austria and Switzerland.[127]

The APL leadership considered the greatest threat to be the tendency of detente in international politics. This was a result of the belief that Albania was of great significance in European politics, and also out of the fear that collaboration between the super powers could overthrow the regime in Albania. The axiom of full sovereignty for the Albanian state consistently presented by the APL leadership was connected with the belief that there was a Marxist fight with the countries of Western Europe, the USA, as well as the countries of Eastern Europe.[128] The doctrine of isolation was fully supported by the VIII APL Congress, in November 1981. All signs of revisionism and imperialism were criticised, even in the communist countries, as they had also, according to Tirana, thrown out the principles of Marxism-Leninism.

The ageing Enver Hoxha become increasingly suspicious of his environment and those who could succeed him. During his long reign, he had skilfully eliminated people who could pose a threat in any way. Out of the 22 people who, in 1941, had formed the first Political Bureau of the party, as many as fifteen had been removed from the party accused of conducting hostile activity. In 1981, the victim of Hoxha's suspicion was his closest ally, regarded as his right-hand man in the party hierarchy, Mehmet Shehu. The first official statement concerning his death stated that he had committed suicide as a result of a nervous breakdown.[129] What the last hours of Shehu's life really looked like was never revealed, but the dictator publicly "revealed" him to be a long-term spy for the American, British, Yugoslav and Soviet intelligence services.

The obsessive conviction of the permanent threat of foreign invasion became a reality on September 25-26, 1982. There was an attempted invasion by an armed group, led by Xhevdet Mustafa, on the southern coast of Albania. According to the official version, the group, whose number was not given, reached the coast of Al-

126 Sadikaj, "Politika e jashtme," 149.

127 In the 1970s, Albania entered into diplomatic relations with 22 countries. They did not enter into relations with countries considered to be hostile towards Albania: West Germany, Spain and Great Britain – Stephen Bowers, "Stalinism in Albania: Domestic Affairs under Enver Hoxha," *East European Quarterly* 1989 (January): 449–451.

128 Prifti, *Socialist Albania*, 246.

129 Jacques, *Albanians*, 510.

bania by boat and was discovered in the morning by locals, who then informed the government. After a few hours of fighting with an Albanian army unit, Mustafa's group was "totally liquidated."[130] Those most likely to be behind the attack were the exiled Albanian politicians, although Hoxha accused the Yugoslav intelligence service, the UDBA, of organizing the attack.[131]

The terrible state of foreign currency reserves forced Albanian diplomats in 1979 to desperately attempt to regain gold reserves, taken during World War II by the German army in Albania, and deposited in English banks after the war. The aim of the Albanian diplomats was to solve the matter through bilateral negotiations with Great Britain, without the participation of other countries. Officially, the two countries did not maintain diplomatic relations, but informal contact regarding the gold took place in 1979 in Belgrade. The British Ambassador in Yugoslavia, Edwin Bolland, passed the Albanian proposition to his government, and the government in turn to the Trilateral Commission (consisting of representatives of the USA, Great Britain and France), which was to decide on the fate of the gold deposit. The Commission met after a long break in July 1984 and prepared a seven-point protocol with the conditions to be met by Tirana in order to open the possibility of gold return. The most important of these was the requirement for Albania to pay compensation to the victims of the incident in the Corfu Straits (1,900 thousand dollars), as well as compensation for American citizens whose property was nationalized by the Albanian communist government (estimated at 2 million dollars). The Albanians did not question the claims of Great Britain and the USA, but demanded the return of the whole deposit (1,570 kg of gold), together with interest resulting from its deposit in English banks, as well as a document signed by the British confirming that, after payment of the compensation, London would treat the Corfu issue as closed and would not make any further claims. As for the American claims, the Albanians demanded the full property records which the Americans had based their claims on. The Albanian proposition was rejected by the Americans.[132]

In 1984, Enver Hoxha met a group of foreign journalists in Tirana and discussed the current situation in Albania. These discussions constituted a kind of summary of the government of E. Hoxha, which in respect of the upcoming events became a political testament. Hoxha proudly emphasized that in Albania there had been no uprising of "red bourgeoisie," who had enjoyed special privileges, not accessible for the average party member.[133] In Hoxha's opinion, the rejection of the idea of "proletariat dictatorship" was to unavoidably lead to the deprivation of power for workers and its acquisition by "new revisionist bourgeoisie," with the best example being the Soviet states. While the majority of the Marxist-Leninist party in the world tried to modify its image, the APL leadership regarded all modifications as unjust and

[130] Pearson, *Albania*, vol. 3, 642.

[131] Enver Hoxha, *The Titoites: Historical Notes* (Tirana: Shtëpia Botuese 8 Nëntori, 1982), 630.

[132] Sadikaj, "Politika e jashtme...," 149.

[133] Bowers, "Stalinism in Albania," 444.

improper. Despite Hoxha's declaration, the Albanian state did not deal with the following challenges and difficulties. In January 1985, for a week Albania experienced large snowfalls which blocked most of the roads in the northern part of the country, between Shkoder and Bajram Curri. Telephone connections were also broken. All the lorries, bulldozers and helicopters, as well as all doctors and soldiers in the country were mobilized. 50 people fell victim to the winter, including directors and workers of cooperatives.[134]

Enver Hoxha, who had suffered from diabetes for many years, died on April 11, 1985. No foreign representatives were invited to his funeral. At the first meeting of the Political Bureau after his death, Muho Asllani proposed that the capital should take his name. This proposition caused mixed feelings, and Ramiz Alia, in response to Asllani's proposal, claimed that the name of Hoxha was identified with the whole of Albania and not just Tirana.[135] Hoxha's main monument was a giant pyramid, constructed according to the design of his daughter, in the centre of Tirana. The university in Tirana, the port in Durrës and one of the factories were also given the name of the leader. On the eightieth anniversary of Hoxha's birth, October 14, 1988, the Enver Hoxha Museum was opened in Tirana. In the same month, three monuments were revealed: in Tirana, Kortcha and Gjirokastra. Hoxha's legacy includes 71 volumes, generally with the character of political journals, as well as works of a theoretical character. They include the volume *Imperialism and Revolution*, a polemics with Lenin's work *State and Revolution*. His response to *Eurocommunism and the State* by Santiago Carrillo was the work *Eurocommunism is Anti-communism*.

After Hoxha's death, Ramiz Alia was chosen as his replacement. One of the main ideologists in the party, he enjoyed Hoxha's trust even as far back as the war, when he was named as a political commissioner of the VII Shock Brigade, even though he was only 19 years old. Between 1955 and 1958, he was the Minister of Culture and Art, and from 1970 a member of the party's Political Bureau. Alia played a key role in the cultural revolution, developing and defining subjects indicated by Hoxha. He was one of the few members of the party leadership who came from the north of the country, which led to his alienation among the older party activists. As a loyal executor of Hoxha's decisions, he was also a representative of a generation, which gave him credibility on the public forum during the difficult years of revolutionisation.

Under the direction of the new leader, the IX APL Congress took place in November 1986. During the Congress he emphasized the necessity to continue the politics of Enver Hoxha and the unchanged basic principles: "rely on our own strength" and "no foreign loans." Despite the visible stagnation, during the proceedings two small signals of the coming change appeared. The first was the acceptance of implementing material incentives for workers, which was designed to increase their

134 Osman Allkja, ... *fije nga Ditari i Kryeministrisë* (Tirana: O. Allkja, 2000), 27–29; "Te gjithe në kembe," *Pionieri*, January 29, 1985, 2.

135 Dervishi, *Historia e shtetit*, 767–768.

efficiency. The second signal was found in the final Congress Report, which contained the statement that Albania is a European country, and its inhabitants should be aware of what is happening on the European continent.

In the mid 1980s, a visible shift in Albanian foreign policy took place. Yugoslavia, until this time the key partner for Albania in the Balkans lost its position to Greece, whose government declared in 1987 the end of the state of war between the two countries (lasting since 1940) and recognised the dependence of Northern Epirus to Albania. The deteriorating Albanian-Yugoslav relations was a direct result of the events in Kosovo in the spring of 1981. The demonstration of Albanian students in Prishtina became a pretext for the Yugoslav government to carry out a purge, both in the Union of Communists in Yugoslavia, as well as in administration and education. The Albanian press angrily reported on the implementation in April 1981 by the Yugoslav government of a ban on the carrying of any Albanian language publications, music recordings and films into the country.[136] The internal problems in Albania meant that in the 1980s it was not really able to influence the events unfolding in Kosovo. The growth in separatist tendencies among Albanians in Kosovo became a serious dilemma for the government in Tirana, with economic cooperation with Yugoslavia and security issues forcing it to be cautious in its support for Albanian rebels in Kosovo.[137] Both countries were connected by joint interests, one of the most important being the construction of a railway line through Montenegro which would connect Albania with Europe. Its construction began in 1948, but for political reasons it was not completed until 1986, due to Albanian negligence, even though it was the only rail connection with the outside world. A controversial problem, which caused particular irritation for Tirana was Yugoslavia's raising of the issue of the Slavic minority in Albania. The Albanians confirmed the existence of a small number of Macedonians inside the country, but refused to accept the right for a Serbian minority to exist. The Yugoslav press estimated that the Slavic minority in Albania equalled 100 thousand. Tirana viewed the attempt to combine the issue of cultural cooperation with the necessity of guaranteeing rights to the Slavic minority with clear irritation, regarding such politics from Belgrade as "multiplying unnecessary obstacles." The riots of the Kosovar Albanians in 1988–1989 and the annulment of Kosovo's autonomy by Belgrade were bitter pills to swallow. The Albanian press increasingly wrote about oppression of Albanians by the Serbian government, and the question of Kosovo regularly appeared at the forum of the General Assembly of the UN. In response, Belgrade accused Albania of inspiring ethnic conflict in Kosovo, also adding the question of negating the rights of the Slavic minority living in Albania.

Against the background of increasing conflict with Yugoslavia, there was a slow but steady normalisation process in Greek-Albanian relations. From 1981 the Greek

---

[136] *Zëri i Popullit*, July 25, 1985, 4.

[137] Vickers and Pettifer, *Albania*, 145.

political scene was dominated by socialists from the PASOK party. Some of them had previously sought shelter in Albania, when Greece was ruled by the "black colonels" junta (1967–1974). A gesture of good will towards Athens was the amnesty in 1984, which concerned a few Greeks captured inside Albania and serving time for espionage. At the request of Athens, the remains of the orthodox saint (St. Kosmas), which were located in the Albanian Fieri, were transported to Greece.[138] However, negotiations concerning the creation of a Greek Language School, with the intention of using an educational program based on course-books published in Greece, hit a dead point.

The architect of the improving Greek-Albanian relations was considered to be the Minister of Foreign Affairs, Karolos Papoulias, whose family originated from Pogon near Gjirokastra, one of the most active Greek minority centres in Albania. In December 1984, Papoulias visited Tirana and signed five bilateral agreements concerning economic, technological and scientific cooperation, as well as cultural exchange. As part of one of the agreements, Greek engineers helped to develop the communications infrastructure in the south of the country.[139]

After a forty-year break, the border crossing in Kakavia was reopened in 1985, as was the Corfu-Saranda ferry connection.[140] The border crossing in Kakavia opened the possibility of contact between residents of the borderland villages. In June 1986, in the borderland region of Dropulli, a ceremony to celebrate the new irrigation system took place. The Secretary of the APL Central Committee, Foto Çami participated and stated that there was no "real conflict" between Albania and Greece, and that "problems from the past" could be resolved through mutual understanding.[141] The final breakthrough in relations with Athens occurred in 1987. The three-day visit to Tirana of the Greek Minister of Foreign Affairs, Karolos Papoulias (November 1987) was a precursor to a meeting between the prime ministers of the two countries: Andreas Papandreu and Adil Çarçani, which happened in 1988.

The increasing significance of Greece in Albanian foreign policy also stemmed from the crisis in Albanian-Italy relations. At the beginning of the 1980s, Italy was the most important "road to the West" for Albania. This was visible from the in-

---

138 Mystehak Xhemali, "Enigma e një murgu endacak dhe legjenda e tij si Shenjt," *Albania*, May 4, 2007, 4.

139 Pearson, *Albania*, vol. 3, 643.

140 In the building which had been used since 1976 by Greek trade representatives in Tirana, a new diplomatic institution was created. The Albanian Embassy was set up in an exclusive area of Athens – Kolonaki, where it neighboured with the American Embassy – David Turnock, *The Economy of East Central Europe 1815–1989: Stages of Transformation in a Peripheral Region* (London: Routledge, 2006), 568.

141 *Zëri i Popullit*, June 2, 1986, 3. The realisation of F. Çami's postulates had the character of "diplomatic football." The Luftetari sports club from Gjirokastra invited the Greek club Pindos, based just across the border in Konitza. Together with the football players, local civil servants from Konitza, as well as a few hundred supporters, travelled for the friendly match to Gjirokastra – *Zëri i Popullit*, June 9, 1986, 2.

creasing trade between the countries as well as their cultural cooperation.[142] The small differences as to the nature of the cooperation resulted from the fact that the Albanians tried to develop trade, whereas the Italians were more interested in widening political and cultural cooperation. The crisis in the bilateral relations began on December 10, 1985. On that day, the seven-member Popaj family managed to enter the grounds of the Italian Embassy in Tirana and requested political asylum.[143] The Italians helped the Albanian family, ignoring the demands of the Albanian Foreign Ministry to hand the escapees into the hands of the police. The issue was difficult to resolve as the Albanians could not enter the grounds of the Embassy, and the Italians could not take the family out of the country without the agreement of the Albanian government. The Albanian press portrayed the family as spies working for Yugoslavia, and the attitude of the Italians as one of hostility towards the Albania.[144] During talks in Tirana and Rome, the Albanians repeatedly demanded the handover of the "escapees," while the Italians unsuccessfully demanded a guarantee that the Popaj family would not be sentenced to the death penalty, in accordance with the Albanian penal code.[145]

Cooperation with France did not suffer from negative emotions connected with the past. The French tradition among the Albanian political elite reached back to the inter-war years, and even E. Hoxha himself fondly looked back on his student years in Montpellier. The work of French Albania experts was particularly valued in Tirana, especially as the scientists avoided the negative evaluations of E. Hoxha's regime. In the second half of the 1980s, France became not only a valued partner for Albania in scientific cooperation, but also as a supplier of machines, which enabled the largest investments of the decade to be finalised.[146] Austria and Switzerland were also valued partners for the Albanians from the end of the 1970s. The Albanian leadership valued the virtues of Swiss banking, as well as its role in providing shelter for thousands of Albanians from Kosovo, who in the 1980s migrated to Switzerland for political or economic reasons. The empathy towards Austria resulted from its

---

[142] Hamit Kaba, "Demshperblimet Italiane te Luftes se Dyte Botërore per Shqipërine (1945–1960)," *Studime Historike* 1–2 (2003).

[143] Sadikaj, "Politika e jashtme," 155.

[144] One of the direct consequences of the cooling Albanian-Italian relations was the refusal of Albtourist to accept 700 Italian tourists, despite a previously signed agreement – Sadikaj, "Politika e jashtme," 156.

[145] The stubbornness of the Albanian rulers lasted until May 1989, when Albania was visited by the UN General Secretary, Javier Perez de Cuellar. The Popaj family finally travelled to Rome in May 1990, during the period of transformation – Dorina Topollaj, "Te denuarit qe u futen ne ambasada," *Tirana Observer*, June 29, 2006, 6.

[146] The import of French turbines made it possible to finish one of the largest investments – the hydroelectric plant on the River Drin, which had been suspended since the end of the 1970s. The French-Albanian firm ADA was probably the first joint-venture company which operated at the end of the 1980s in Albania – Vickers and Pettifer, *Albania*, 222.

neutral political policy, as well as from the key role of Austro-Hungary in shaping an independent Albanian state.

More complicated, because of the Albanian claims for compensation, was the question of normalisation of relations with the Federal Republic of Germany. Due to the dramatic economic situation which the Albanian state found itself in, the issue of war compensation for the military occupation in 1943–1944 gained particular significance. Bonn did not react to the claims for compensation until 1979, when talks between the ambassadors of Albania and West Germany took place for the first time in Belgrade.[147] During secret talks in Bonn, Albania was represented by a high-level civil servant from the Foreign Ministry. A normalisation of relations in exchange for the payment of compensation was provisionally agreed upon. In August 1984 the Premier of Bavaria, Franz Joseph Strauss, flew to Tirana. Strauss proposed a concept for settlement of compensation by offering cheap loans, however, this was rejected by the leader of the Albanian delegation, Manush Myftiu. He argued that, in accordance with the constitution of 1976, Albania could not take loans from other countries. The turning point in relations took place in October 1987, when diplomatic relations with West Germany were restored. The German Vice-Chancellor and Minister of Foreign Affairs, Hans Dietrich Genscher, visited Tirana on October 23, 1987. The Genscher-Alia meeting in the Brigade Palace in Tirana was regarded as a great success for Albanian diplomacy. The basis of future mutual relations was an agreement concerning economic and scientific-technical cooperation, for a period of 10 years. Genscher's declaration of cooperation in the fields of culture and tourism was accepted with satisfaction. The nature of Albanian-German cooperation was finalized in 1988. A German delegation led by the Federal Minister of the Economy, Erich Riedl, visited Tirana. During the talks, it was repeatedly emphasised that German firms were interested in entering the Albanian market, as well as in Albanian goods.[148] These declarations forced the Albanians into creating a set of principles under which firms from Western Europe could enter the Albanian market. By supplying products to Albania, the ban on accepting foreign loans could be avoided. Among the first firms that appeared on the Albanian market were German firms from the exploitation and food industry sectors (GFE and AMEKON).

Albania's close cooperation with West Germany was met with an angry reaction from the leaders of East Germany. When the West German diplomatic office in Tirana received the status of an Embassy in 1987, Berlin gave Albanian representatives a note demanding a similar change in respect of its diplomatic office. Berlin considered the accusations directed in 1960 against Albania (resulting in the withdrawal of the ambassador from Tirana) as no longer valid. Discussions conducted with the Albanian representative in Berlin ended in 1988 with the signing of an agreement which

147 Shpëtim Çaushi, *Diplomacia shqiptare ne normalizimin e marredhenieve me Gjermanine* (Tirana: Ombra GVG, 2002), 156–158.

148 Sadikaj, "Politika e jashtme," 152.

nullified the decision of the East German government in 1961, thereby creating the possibility of increasing the level of mutual contacts to full diplomatic status.[149]

The return of Albanian diplomats to international forums and the breaking of its position of isolation was possible thanks to the help of Greece. In October 1987, Albania agreed to send its representative to the Conference of Ministers of Foreign Affairs of the Balkan States. At the Conference in Belgrade (February 24–26, 1988), the Albanian minister, Reis Malile, delivered a speech supporting the idea of creating an atomic and chemical weapon free zone in the Balkans. He also spoke about protecting the rights of minority groups, emphasising the need for this issue to be closely connected with political stabilization of the region. R. Malile's participation in the Belgrade meeting created huge interest among the media, which had previously treated Albania as a closed reservation. The journalists, who were surprised by the activity of Albanian diplomats, were told by Malile – "it's not us who are changing, others are."[150] Participation in the conference was an indication of the lasting tendency to return the country to the "Balkan club." The next such conference, in October 1990, was held in Tirana itself.

The break from isolation by the Albanian diplomats did not immediately bring about significant changes in Albania's domestic politics. The first small suggestions in 1988 from the intellectual environment to begin a program of economic reform, with privatization of part of the national companies, were rejected by the APL leadership as "of secondary importance." More attention was given to scientific methods of fighting Gorbachev's deviation than to attempting any political or economic reform.[151] On 24 June 1988, the newspaper *Zëri i Popullit* published an article with the title "*Perestroika*, a program and strategy to strengthen Soviet social-imperialism," in which the basic aim of *perestroika* was explained to be privatisation of the economy, and glasnost was just a trick serving the ennoblement of bourgeois ideals.[152] The statue of Stalin, which still stood in its honorary place in Tirana, represented an obvious challenge to the journalists and writers of the *perestroika* period who were discrediting Stalin's achievements. In his speech at the VIII Central Committee Plenum (September 26, 1989) Ramiz Alia ensured that "there will never be agreement to open the road toward private property and capitalist exploitation," in Albania there would be no weakening of the proletariat dictatorship and there was no place for the idea of pluralism propagated by the bourgeoisie.[153] In 1989, the Albanian press filled many pages with the appearance of social crises being experienced by the countries of Eastern Europe, who were entering the road leading to democracy and a market economy.

---

149 On June 20–22, 1989, the Minister of Foreign Affairs of East Germany, Oscar Fischer, visited Tirana. This was the first visit since 1961 of such a high-ranking politician from the Soviet Block states.

150 Smirnova, *Istoriia Albanii*, 353.

151 Elez Biberaj, *Shqipëria ne tranzicion: Rruga e veshtire drejt Demokracise* (Tirana: ORA Botime, 2001), 62.

152 Pipa, *Albanian Stalinism*, 174.

153 *Zëri i Popullit*, September 27, 1989, 1.

Chapter III: Economy

Having experienced a Stalinist development strategy for more than 30 years, Albanian economic structure differs from that of these African states [Angola and Mozambique] *in that only a little less than half the population live in towns.*[1]

In communist Albania, discussions concerning the progress and changes in civilization which took place after 1944 most frequently began with a presentation of the actual situation of Albanian development before 1939. Such a presentation led to the simplified conclusion that, from a level of one of the least developed European states, with an archaic economy and an illiterate society, Albania succeeded during the years of communism in becoming a modern country, in which heavy industry played a key role.

There is no doubt that pre-war Albania belonged to the least developed economic areas in Europe. The basis of survival for most people was archaic agriculture and shepherding. Even against the background of the other Balkan states, the perspective of modernizing Albania seemed to be especially limited. In the mid-30s, as many as 86% of the population worked on the land. In comparison, the figure in Yugoslavia was 80.8%, in Bulgaria 74.6%, and in Greece only 61%.[2] The scale of illiteracy in Albania in the 1930s exceeded 80%, while in the other Balkan states it was less than 50%.[3] The basic obstacle to developing agriculture in Albania was the landscape of the country. As much as 70% of the county's surface is over 300 m a.s.l., which is twice the level of the European average. The shape of the land restricted the possibility of mechanizing agriculture to a minimum. The arable land in Albania constituted just 12% of the country's surface. There was a similar figure in Greece (14.8%), but in Bulgaria and Yugoslavia over 30% of the country was made up of arable land.

At the turn of the 19th Century, half of the arable land in Albania belonged to less than 4% of the population. This group consisted mainly of representatives of the Ottoman Empire civil servants – Begs, Ags and Bajraktars. A few family groups (Vlora, Vrioni and Toptani) owned about 50–60 thousand ha each. Petty farmers

1 Adi Schnytzer, "The Socialist People's Republic of Albania," in: Peter J. Wiles, ed., *The New Communist Third World: An Essay in Political Economy* (New York: St. Martin's Press, 1982), 297.

2 John Lampe and Marvin Jackson, *Balkan Economic History, 1550–1950: From Imperial Borderlands to Developing Nations* (Bloomington: Indiana University Press, 1982), 334–336.

3 Karl Kaser, *Patriarchy after Patriarchy: Gender Relations in Turkey and in the Balkans 1500–2000* (Berlin: Lit, 2008), 92.

represented about 84–86% of the rural population, whereas about 14–16% did not own any land.[4] The latter survived by renting land in exchange for 30–50% of their annual income (in addition, they also paid tax to the state). The tenant farmers were totally dependent on the landowners and represented the poorest layer of society. The burdensome tax system, associated earlier with the Ottoman "foreign power," was particularly perceptible in the inter-war years. Besides the taxes on agricultural production and breeding, each family had to pay a tax on education (for schools) estimated at 2% of their income, and every building owner paid an annual tax which equalled 3% of the building's value. Another form of service to the state, which was inherited from the Ottoman times, was the unpaid work on the construction of public roads for 10 days per year. The increasing tax burden forced some Albanian farmers into economic emigration – initially to Bulgaria, Romania and Italy, and at the end of the 19th Century also to the USA and Australia. The Albanian village before 1944 was regarded in Europe as an extremely under-developed area, and the symbol of Albanian agriculture, deprived of machines, fertilizers and irrigation systems was the universally used wooden plough.[5]

The most frequent element of criticism directed towards the economic politics of the pre-war government of Albania was the question of economic dependence on other countries. The firms which gained concessions in Albania most often operated in the exploitation sector and represented American, British, Italian and German capital. After 1925, Italy began to dominate the Albanian market, thanks to political pressure and increasing investment. Between 1925 and 1939, Italian loans designated to the construction of the Albanian infrastructure amounted to 130 million franks, and their division was controlled by over 250 Italian specialists, working in Albania. Italy's economic domination was defined by their monopoly in oil and copper ore exploitation, electric energy production, and concessions connected with agriculture and forestry.[6]

Despite the financial crisis which the Albanian state permanently found itself in, during the inter-war years a visible leap in civilization took place. The most visible result of cooperation with the Italians was the construction of a network of hardened roads and bridges, which provided connections between the capital and most regions which had previously been isolated from the main administrative centres. At the end of the 1930s, the first electricity generating plant was built in Kortcha. In a few towns, electric power stations using Diesel engines was created. The capital

[4] Wojciech Roszkowski, *Land Reforms in East Central Europe after World War One* (Warsaw: Institute of Political Studies, Polish Academy of Sciences, 1995), 51.

[5] Derek Hall, *Albania and the Albanians* (London: Pinter Reference, 1994), 116–117.

[6] In 1936 in southern Albania, 300 Italian settlers arrived and set up plantations in land which had previously not been cultivated – Örjan Sjöberg, *Rural Change and Development in Albania* (Boulder, CO: Westview Press, 1991), 31.

was also modernized, and the modern Zog and Mussolini boulevards were built. In 1927, the town was partially electrified, and lights appeared on the main streets.[7]

The development of civilization in Albania also took place during the Italian occupation. The old and primitive water mills were gradually replaced by modern constructions with motors. In Elbasan and Vlore, modern oil presses were built, as well as a range of small factories producing cleaning products. There was a development in the wood industry and a growth in the interest of wood as a raw material for handicrafts. Although most of the wood from Albania was exported as a raw material, more and more began to remain inside the country where it was used as a raw material by furniture factories and producers of household goods. Transports of Italian food arrived in places particularly affected by poor crops. Until 1941, the attitude of Albanians towards the Italian occupants was not unequivocal. After the war with Greece ended in 1941, the occupation began to be more difficult to accept. Corruption and bureaucracy in the country were no greater than during the time of Zog, but it was much more irritating because the greatest gains were made by foreigners.[8] The war with Greece reduced the level of Italian food aid, and as a result there was a dramatic increase in the price of food articles. The relatively short German occupation deepened the food supply crisis in the south and led to a significant increase in its market price. With the help of Austrian geologists in 1944, there was a systematic increase in mineral resource exploitation, which came together with the characteristic wasteful economic exploitation. German companies took control of chromium ore and copper exploitation, as well as oil exploitation.

The last months of the war, and especially the operations carried out against the partisans in the south, came with considerable human and material losses. The report of the International Center for Relief to Civilian Populations (with its headquarters in Geneva), published in 1945, described Albania as one of the most damaged countries in Europe.[9] In 1944, most of the infrastructure built in the years 1939–1944 was unfit for use. The most important exploitation centres (Selenica, Rubik, Kuçova, Patos) had been so devastated that it was impossible to use the sources of oil and chromium ore. As for residential buildings, the scale of the losses was quite uneven. In towns in the central and northern parts of the country, the damage was almost invisible, as most damage was carried out in the south.[10] When the war ended, Albania had no financial possibilities even to partially rebuild the country, whereas its gold reserves had been taken out of the country by King Zog or the occupants.

In the first post-war years, the country's budgetary needs were met by the confiscation of private property, as well as the introduction of a war tax. This covered income gained from trade during the years 1939–1944. A list of enterprises and

7 Bernd J. Fischer, *King Zog and the Struggle for Stability in Albania* (Boulder, CO: East European Monographs, 1984), 162.

8 Fischer, *Albania at War*, 90.

9 Jacques, *Albanians*, 426.

10 Fischer, *Albania at War*, 269.

merchants, together with the level of "extraordinary tax," was published on March 15, 1945 in the newspaper *Bashkimi*. The taxes were so high that for most firms it signified the need to sell assets or to enter bankruptcy.[11] In December 1944, the property of those suspected of collaboration and those who had entered political exile was confiscated, and a month later German and Italian property was confiscated. On January 14, 1945, a law was passed which allowed the confiscation of private property by the state. Generally this concerned private companies, employing paid workers (besides craft producers). The companies were taken over by state civil servants, designating a new administration among people who usually had no management qualifications, but who had shown loyalty towards the new government. In order to manage the property confiscated by the state, the Ministry of the Economy, in accordance with the Soviet example, was established.

In July 1945, the Anti-Fascist National Liberation Council leadership passed the first act concerning employment protection.[12] In the new social-political reality, ensuring the suitable number of workplaces and eliminating unemployment was one of the key tasks of the state. The act of July 1945 defined the acceptable length of working time, the right to holidays and equal pay for the same work (regardless of gender).[13] The Labour Code which was passed by parliament as Act 527 from August 25, 1947, was complemented by an act on social insurance from August 26, 1947, the first in Albania's history.[14]

The I CPA Congress, which was held in 1948, accepted the basic directive in the Two-Year Plan of economic development, which it intended to carry out in 1949–1950. The basic plan was to develop heavy industry, for which 46% of the total investment funds were designated.[15] The targets of the Two-Year Plan were not fully met, but the growth in industrial production was impressive. Among the key investments of the Two-Year Plan were the Joseph Stalin textile factory in Tirana, the sugar processing plant in Maliq, and the hydro-electricity plant in Selite. The realization of such an ambitious industrialization plan would not have been possible without the help of the USSR and the Soviet bloc countries. Accepting the role of Albania's patron, the USSR provided 40% of Albania's income. The acceptance of the Soviet model for economic development came across a serious obstacle in the form of the lack of qualified workers, as well as administrative workers necessary to undertake central planning.

---

11 In 1945/1946, income from the War Tax represented 53% of the Albanian State's income – Iljaz Fishta and Veniamin Toci, *Ekonomia e Shqiperise ne vitet e para te ndertimit socialist (Nentor 1944–Nentor 1948)* (Tirana: Akademia e Shkencave e RPS të Shqipërisë, Instituti i Historisë, 1984), 142–144, 153.

12 "Mbi kohen e sherbimit, mbrojtjen dhe shperblimin e punës," *Gazeta Zyrtare* 12 (1945): 1.

13 Feti Gjilani, "Rruga historike e lindjes dhe e zhvillimit te legislacjonit te punës ne RPSh," *Studime Historike* 4 (1971): 130.

14 *Gazeta Zytare* 87 (1947): 2.

15 Smirnova, *Istoriia Albanii*, 300.

During the first Five-Year Plan (1951–1955), as much as 43% of the investment funds were designated to the development of industry, while agriculture (employing 70% of the population) received only 14% of the funds. According to official data, at the end of the first five-year period, the value of industrial production was twice the level of agricultural production. This was a vivid contrast to data from 1938, when industrial production generated only 18% of the national income.[16]

In February 1949, Albania entered Comecon. This brought with it a formalization of aid for the country from other member states. Besides the low-interest loans (in practice, non-returnable), machines, raw materials and a wide group of specialists arrived in Albania. The value of loans provided to Albania, which increased year after year, reached its peak during the second Five-Year Plan (1956–1960). One of the plan's goals was to achieve 14% growth in industrial production annually. At the end of the 1950s, this reached 17% annually and belonged to the highest in the world.[17] In 1959, Albania received aid from the USSR worth 83.8 million dollars. Over 35 million dollars was given by other countries belonging to Comecon, and 13.8 million dollars by China. At the end of the 1950s, 95% of Albanian oil and 76% of tobacco entered the Russian market. The break in economic cooperation with Comecon brought about significant changes in investment policies. Not only the USSR, but also a few other countries from Eastern Europe annulled promised loans to Albania.[18]

Albania's industrial development in the 1960s concerned individual yet enormous investments for a country of its size, leaving the development of infrastructure and light industry on the back burner. In 1961 an Albanian-Chinese agreement was signed in Tirana in which Peking agreed to lend Albania 125 million dollars to complete investments planned in the 1950s. Despite support from China, as many as 250 projects planned within the framework of the third Five-Year Plan (1961–1965) had to be suspended, and 40% of them had still not been successfully completed by 1965.[19] The distance separating Albania and China, as well as the limited range of Chinese business interests in Europe, meant that the Albanian leaders were given significantly greater freedom in their economic decisions. In the mid 1960s, a new concept for economic development based on the absolute priority of developing heavy industry was implemented. This became possible thanks to Chinese loans, as well as supplies of Chinese household goods, which were not produced at all, or only in small amounts, in Albania. The break of economic cooperation with China in 1978 signified the breakdown of ambitious investment plans. Among 35 objects which were planned to be finished in the 1970s with Chinese aid, only fifteen had been completed by 1978.[20] None of the three fundamental investments realized with

16 O'Donnell, *Coming of Age*, 167.

17 O'Donnell, *Coming of Age*, 168.

18 Schnytzer, *Stalinist Economic Strategy*, 73.

19 Smirnova, *Istoriia Albanii*, 328.

20 Smirnova, *Istoriia Albanii*, 343.

Peking's help (the hydro-electricity plant in Fierze, the oil refinery in Ballsh and the metallurgical complex in Elbasan) were finished according to schedule.

From 1972 there was a noticeable tendency to diversify imports. Trade with Western Europe grew from 12% (1972) to 18.2% in 1974. During the same time, China's participation in Albanian foreign trade dropped from 50.6% to 42.3%.[21] The loss of its strategic partner in 1978 forced the Albanian leadership into greater openness towards cooperation with European countries. The drop in demand for Albanian chromium ore and food products restricted the scale of imports to a minimum and marked the 1980s with the problem of a lack of goods. In the 1980s, foreign trade gradually fell. The turning point in this trend took place in 1988. This particularly concerned trade with Western Europe. In 1989, the value of imports from the West equalled 165 million dollars, but a year later it was already 245 million dollars.[22] Albania purchased machines, replacement parts, and weapons. The main exports from Albania were oil, ferro-chrome, nickel ore and agricultural products.

One of the axioms of Albanian economic policy up to the end of the 1980s was the principle of central control of the economy, This was generally performed by party activists who had no basic knowledge of economics. A few reasons for the standstill in the economy were revealed during the proceedings of the IX APL Congress (November 1986). After Hoxha's death, it was easier to express the previously unpopular opinion that the economic problems were not the result of external blockades, but resulted from internal reasons. Despite the growing crisis, the IX Congress was still dominated by the belief that it was necessary to keep the three fundamental principles: rely on your own strength, no foreign loans and balanced foreign trade (no import without export).[23] In this period, GDP for one inhabitant of Albania did not exceed 930 dollars, which was one of the lowest in Europe.[24] Small attempts to change economic policy were initiated in 1987. The Council of Ministers passed an act to introduce financial rewards for workers employed in the national economy in order to increase their work efficiency.

1. Agriculture

Just like in other communist countries, one of the first social-economic reforms in Albania concerned agriculture, realized after the act of August 29, 1945. According to official data from the beginning of 1945, as many as 87% of peasant families

---

21 O'Donnell, *Coming of Age*, 73.

22 David Seddon and Ruth Davey, "The Politics of Economic Reform in Albania" in *Political and Economic Liberalization: Dynamic and Linkages in Comparative Perspective*, ed. Gerd Nonneman (New York: Lynne Rienner Publishers, 1996), 131.

23 Smirnova, *Istoriia Albanii*, 351.

24 Nicholas Pano, "The Process of Democratization in Albania" in *Politics, Power, and the Struggle for Democracy in South-East Europe*, eds. Karen Dawisha and Bruce Parrott (Cambridge: Cambridge University Press, 1997), 297.

either possessed no land at all, or had an area no greater than 3 ha at their disposal.[25] The reforms introduced the principle of "the land belongs to the person who cultivates it." The range of the reform was widened on May 27, 1946, by the next act concerning the expropriation of vineyards and orchards.[26]

The act from August 1945 allowed the confiscation of all large land properties, consisting of 1/3 of all arable land in the country. Land belonging to religious communities was also targeted. The previous owners were left with 20 to 40 ha of land, depending on the level of farming-techniques. The former owners could demand compensation for the lost land only in very few cases. The land collected during the reforms was divided among the peasant families who owned no or very little land with the provision that it could not be sold or leased. Among those who received land, the majority were former tenant farmers and families who helped the partisans during the war. About 70 thousand families took advantage of the beneficial reforms, together receiving 156,159 ha of land, as well as bulls and swine, confiscated from the former landowners.[27] In practice, only some of the landless farmers succeeded in receiving land, as the amount confiscated from the landowners turned out to be insufficient. The reform ended in November 1948.

The reform of agriculture represented an introduction to the second phase of changes in property ownership, which in fact constituted the realization of the Soviet idea of village collectivism. In February 1946 at the V CPA Central Committee Plenum, the motto of socialist agricultural reconstruction was heard, which meant the gradual merging of individual farms. The first cooperative (Kooperative Bujqesore) was established in autumn 1946 in Krutje near Lushnje.[28] 26 families settled there. In the same year the next six cooperatives were set up, including the first ones in the south of the country (Risilse near Vlore and Cifligut near Saranda). The first seven cooperatives, established in 1946, consisted of just 217 families, who had received 943 ha of arable land. The average area at the sole disposal of families working in the cooperative was around 0.1 ha. Members of agricultural cooperatives had the right to breed poultry and rabbits, possess beehives and a limited number of farm animals. The meat could be used for personal consumption or sold to the cooperative or at the local market place. There were a range of issues connected with free-market sales, so the majority of farmers sold what they could breed to the cooperative, at significantly lower prices than those at the market.

---

25 In 1930, with the help of Italian advisers, an agricultural reform program was created with the aim of solving the problem of landless families. The reforms were not carried out due to the lack of staff necessary to prepare the plan, as well as objections from landowners. Skendi, *Albania*, 157.

26 Władysław Góra, ed., *Reformy agrarne w socjalistycznych państwach Europy (1944–1948)* (Wrocław: Zakład Narodowy im. Ossolińskich, 1987), 37–50.

27 Nina D. Smirnova, *Obrazovanie Narodnoi Respubliki Albanii 1939–1946* (Moscow: Izdatel'stvo Akademii nauk SSSR, 1960), 166.

28 Kristo Frashëri, *The History of Albania: Brief Survey* (Tirana: Shtëpia Botuese Naim Frashëri, 1964), 334.

The lack of an agricultural cooperative tradition hindered the understanding of society of the principle of collectivism and created an attitude of unwillingness, and even hostility against the cooperatives. This was also helped by the growing economic pressure on individual farms. In 1949, peasants were burdened with the duty to supply a defined amount of agricultural produce to the state. This amount was defined by the authorities based on the size of the farm and the class of land. Those who didn't meet the defined amount were fined and sometimes the land was confiscated and divided out. In 1947–1948, a wave of protests by peasant farmers swept through Albania, taking extreme forms in the regions of Shijak and Tepelena. The peasants, driven to desperation, executed sentences on officials who had been sent to supervise the confiscation of grain.[29]

Despite economic pressures, the collectivization process at the beginning of the fifties was still voluntary, and as a result was rather slow. Even in 1954, collective agriculture covered only 12.8% of arable land. Directives which violently hastened collectivism appeared at the party plenum in December 1955. Between January 1 and March 15, 1956, 151 new cooperatives were established, in other words, the same number as between 1946 and 1954.[30] The vast majority of these were small cooperatives with up to 30 families, with small areas which usually did not exceed 100 ha. Cooperatives with an area of over 200 ha were rare. By 1960, the areas without cooperatives were generally mountainous areas and areas unfit for crops.[31] The acceleration of collectivism also became possible due to the direction of people experienced in organizing kolkhozes to the most isolated corners of the country. In the 1960s, such activity perfectly suited the program of revolutionization and modernization of the most under-developed rural areas.[32]

The violent acceleration of collectivism deepened the crisis in agriculture, and especially in breeding. Problems with food supplies caused a systematic reduction in the number of cattle per head.[33] Albania was clearly behind other Soviet bloc countries in terms of animal-based agricultural production. The indicator of meat and milk production per inhabitant was half of that in Bulgaria, while the number of eggs was six times lower.[34]

---

29 Arshi Pipa, *Albanian Stalinism: Ideo-Political Aspects* (Boulder, CO: East European Monographs, 1990), 24.

30 Iljaz Fishta, "Kolektivizimi ne mase and prodhuesve te vegjel te fshatit (1956–1960)," *Studime Historike* 3 (1990), 35.

31 ASA, Prime Minister's Office, (f. 890), 1956, d. 726.

32 Social research conducted in the village of Bogë (north-west Albania) showed that, despite the introduced changes in property ownership, the lifestyle and habits of local society did not change much. This testified to the bonds with arranged marriages, exogamy, and traditional dress – Steve Cook and Marash Rakaj, "Social Changes in the Albanian Alps during Communism," *Middle States Geographer* 28 (1995), 85–89.

33 Smirnova, *Istoriia Albanii*, 338.

34 Michał Skarżyński, *Rozwój gospodarczy Ludowej Republiki Albanii 1944–1970* (Warsaw: Polski Instytut Spraw Międzynarodowych, 1971), 31.

Table 1. **Changes in the structure of arable land ownership in the years 1950–1990 [%]**

Type of property	1950	1960	1970	1980	1990
Private property	91.3	13.6	0	0	0
Family-owned land			3.5	2.7	4.3
Cooperatives	5.4	72.2	75.8	75.8	71.6
State property	3.3	14.2	20.7	21.5	24.1
Total	100.0	100.0	100.0	100.0	100.0
Surface area (thousand ha)	391	457	599	702	704

Source: Hall, *Albania and the Albanians*, 121.

Further changes in property ownership and the rationalization of production were supposed to defeat the crisis. From the mid 1960s, cooperative land was reduced by at least half, with the allowed level of live inventory per head also halved. The idea of rationalizing production meant, in practice, that more Chinese tractors and agricultural machines were used, and the smallest cooperatives were integrated into larger units. Their number fell from 1915 in 1959 to 423 in 1978, while the average number of families in one cooperative grew from 114 to 235. In 1971, the creation of higher type cooperatives (HTC) began. These differed from other cooperatives in level of mechanization, as well as the more rational system of remuneration. The level of pay in HTCs depended not only on the level of production plan realization, but also on weather conditions and the real possibility of performing work. By 1981, 41% of cooperatives had already been transformed into HTCs, and owned 23% of the arable land in the country.[35]

The isolation of Albania on the international arena and the threat of war encouraged the government to take action in order to ensure food self-sufficiency during such times. Between 1946 and 1990, the area of arable land in Albania was increased by 52,200 ha. This was due mainly to the drying of coastal areas, as well as an increase in the use of mountainous areas. The enthusiasm connected with the concept of extensive agriculture was dampened in the mid 1970s, when the area of arable land began to decrease, and more attention was given to proper melioration and fertilization of land. This was possible due to the establishment of chemical plants and the production of the first Albanian artificial fertilizers.

The catastrophic drop in Albanian agricultural production in the 1980s led to a supply crisis, similar to the one that communist Albania experienced in the first few post-war years. One of the factors that led to this situation was a drought, which

35 Andrew H. Dawson, *Planning in Eastern Europe* (New York: St. Martin's Press, 1987), 45.

affected both agriculture and the energy sector.[36] The situation was intensified by the lack of investment in agriculture and the gradual elimination of private property in cooperatives. Queues of people in front of shops in towns, waiting from the early morning for the chance to buy basic food articles, became part of daily life in the last decade of communism.

The attempts to introduce small economic reforms at the end of the eighties reached the agricultural cooperatives with a visible delay. A system of remuneration, with levels defined according to economic results for given cooperatives, was introduced in 1989. In the experiment's first phase, only ten cooperatives in the whole country participated.[37]

2. Industry

When discussing the development of industry in Albania, it is possible to speak only about the time after World War II. The rural poverty meant that it represented a limited market for domestic producers. Without counting a few mines operating during the inter-war years, the majority of Albanian consumer needs before 1939 were met by small craft workshops, as well as imports from neighbouring countries. At the beginning of the 1940s, the list of enterprises operating in Albania was dominated by food producers, printers, brickworks and exploitation units. Only a few of them employed over 10 people. During the Italian occupation, modern machines as well as serious investment in the infrastructure in the south of the country appeared. This came with an increase in the demand for building materials. The small brickworks which had operated since the 1930s in Tirana, Elbasan and Kortcha, as well as the cement producers in Shkoder and Vlore were taken over in 1940 by Italian capital and significantly modernized. After the war with Greece ended in 1941, the demand for building materials dropped and the short "industrial boom" ended. When the war ended, the work of industrial units was hampered by a lack of raw materials and fuel, the damaged energy network, and the destroyed machinery. Among the first industrial units which reopened were mines, mills and printing houses. The production of cement started in Shkoder in May 1945.[38]

The first two Five-Year Plans in the 1950s were realized with help from the members of Comecon. A key role was played by the activation of the industrial-exploitation sector, as well as the heavy industry connected with it. Albania's showpiece as a member of Comecon was the development of the exploitation industry, and

[36] Per Sandström and Örjan Sjöberg, "Albanian Economic Performance: Stagnation in the 1980s," *Soviet Studies* 5 (1991), 932.

[37] Smirnova, *Istoriia Albanii*, 354–355.

[38] Dilaver Sadikaj, "Rindertimi i industries ne vitet 1945–46," *Studime Historike* 3 (1975), 43.

chromium ore in particular.[39] During the realization of the second Five-Year Plan (1956–1960), Albania became one of the leading producers of chromium, occupying first place in the world for the production of chromium *per capita*. As a member of Comecon, Albania exported a large amount of oil (254 thousand tons in 1955), which mainly reached Black Sea ports and Gdansk, at the same time importing petro-chemical products from Romania. The first refinery started operations in 1967 in Cerrik, and soon afterwards the next one opened in Kucova.[40] The showpiece of industrial Albania were the mills (textile in Tirana and wood in Elbasan), as well as the huge electricity generating plants, with a special role played by the Karl Marx hydro-electricity plant on the River Mati, producing 120 million Kwh annually.[41] During the II Five-Year Plan, the value of industrial production exceeded the value of agricultural production in Albania for the first time.

The largest financial investment by China, whose significance in terms of potential future wars is difficult to overestimate, was the construction of the largest industrial complex in Albania – the metal works in Elbasan, with the aim of fully satisfying the country's requirements in steel production.[42] The symbol of Chinese-Albanian cooperation was the chemical industry which was built from scratch. Thanks to Chinese aid, it was possible to purchase a production line in Italy for nitrogen fertilizer and to start production in Fier. Within the framework of the policy to sensibly use natural resources, new investments were more reasonably planned so that the production plants were located near the source of raw materials. However, the motto of "harmonic and proportional location of industry" encouraged at least some industrial branches to look for locations in accordance with social interests, and not economic ones.

One reason for Albanians to be proud was its energy self-sufficiency. The completion of two large hydro-electricity generating plants: Bistrica near Saranda and Vaut të Dejës on the River Drin, as well as the development of the hydro-energy complex on the River Mat, enabled the completion of the plan to provide electricity to the whole country. October 25, 1970, celebrated as the Day of Light, became a symbolic date in the Albanian drive towards a modern country.[43] In an atmosphere reminiscent of the Chinese Great Leap Forward, the press reported that Albania was the only country in the world in which the whole country was supplied with electricity. After the break with China, Albania successfully maintained its energy security. Supplies of electricity from the hydro-electricity plants allowed the country's needs to be met, and was also exported to Greece, Yugoslavia, and even Austria.

[39] Skarżyński, *Rozwój gospodarczy*, 23.

[40] Skarżyński, *Rozwój gospodarczy*, 21.

[41] Prifti, *Socialist Albania*, 57.

[42] Jacques, *Albanians*, 53.

[43] Wolfgang Bartke, *The Economic Aid of the PR China to Developing and Socialist Countries* (New York: K.G. Saur, 1989), 150.

The growing indicators of industrial production in Albania to a low level concerned light industry, and the food industry, which was growing particularly dynamically in other Balkan countries. The participation of these branches of industry in total production systematically fell. In the 1950s, the food industry generated 55% of total industrial production, but in 1970 the figure had fallen to 32%.[44] This was influenced by both the low productivity of agriculture and the small amount of funds for investment. The flagship of the Albanian food industry remained the capital's Ali Kelmendi Food Factory. Established in 1960 as a small manufacturer of spirits, in the 1970s it developed production of fruit-vegetable products, and in the next decade it also began to produce sweets and soft drinks.[45] Besides the capital's factory, the food industry was dominated by small companies producing fish products in port towns, vegetable and fruit product factories, as well as a few sugar mills and alcohol distilleries. The traditional exports from Albania were marmalade and jam, as well as alcoholic drinks (brandy and wine).

In 1967, the process of liquidating the last "remnant of capitalism," as craftsmanship was regarded, began. Craft workshops were replaced by craft cooperatives, whose organizational structure resembled the agricultural cooperatives. The result of this change was the increasingly difficult lack of household articles, despite increasing imports from China. In 1975, concessions for small craft workshops were restored. The majority of these were connected with the production of clothes and shoes. The rebirth of private enterprises, even in such a limited form came with some negative side-effects – the theft of material from state factories, and the lower efficiency of those workers who also "moonlighted" in workshops.[46]

The whole of the 1980s passed under the cloud of a lasting crisis. Daily problems for Tirana's inhabitants were cuts in water and electricity supplies. The decrease in the global price of chromium placed Albania in a particularly difficult situation – both because of the low productivity of Albanian mines and the low quality of its raw materials. In the 1980s, the mines had ageing technology, low quality products, and the production efficiency decreased. In the 1980s, problems concerning the availability of spare parts and some raw materials deepened. Due to the increasing number of pauses at the end of the decade, a demoralizing principle was introduced into production enterprises that some employees would stay at home as a "reserve," receiving 80% of the remuneration of those working. A good example of the technological chaos which ruled in the 1980s was the textile factory in Kortcha. The factory still used Mauser Special machines, from the 1930s, with the other machines being of Chinese, Italian or East German production. Only the Czechoslovakian loom for

44 Skarżyński, *Rozwój gospodarczy*, 20.

45 Murat Klosi, *Ndertimet në pushtetin popullor* (Tirana: Shtëpia Botuese Naim Frashëri, 1968), 143.

46 Schnytzer, *Stalinist Economic Strategy*, 57.

weaving socks and German machines for weaving lace were relatively new. The factory used Albanian cotton and artificial fabric imported from Greece.[47]

At the end of the 1980s, the ecological threat which industrial development brought with it was considered for the first time. In 1988, there was a ministerial order that new industrial units should be built a minimum of 4–5 km away from residential areas. The largest metal works in Elbasan produced steel, ferro-chrome, nickel, cobalt, and building materials. The neighbouring Bradashesh valley was covered by woods with abnormally high levels of sulphur, phenol and cyanide. During its period of peak production, every year 180 tonnes of ammonia, almost 10 t of heavy metal salt and a ton of phenol entered the River Shkumbini. The same river supplied irrigation water for the areas around Durrës and Elbasan.

3. Communication and transport

One of the most important barriers to modernization was always communication. In such a mountainous country as Albania, all investments in communication turned out to be exceptionally expensive. In 1912, there was only 138.5 km of hardened road in Albania. The longest road was 42 km long and connected Shkoder and Lezha. Between 1921 and 1937, with Italian help the road network was increased to 2,202 km, including the creation of connections between Tirana–Elbasan and Shkoder–Puke in very difficult conditions. In the inter-war period, internal communication was served by horse wagons and a small number of buses. In 1938, around 2 thousand cars drove on Albanian roads. Communication with the outside world was provided by ships sailing to Bari and Corfu, as well as planes flying to Italy, Greece, Bulgaria and Romania. Planes from Italian transport companies served Tirana and small airports in Shkoder, Vlora and Kortcha.

The roads connecting the main towns in the country were reopened for use in the first months of 1945.[48] The communist leaders estimated that they inherited just 2,800 km of hardened road. In the next forty years, the road system was increased to 6,700 km.[49] Transport never belonged to the economic priorities of the communist government. On average, 8% of total investment was dedicated to road construction. Only 40% of the constructed roads were made of asphalt. The terrible road surface significantly influenced the abnormally high level of vehicle defects. Rural inhabitants still used vehicles with metal wheels, which destroyed the road surface.[50]

[47] Adi Schnytzer and Ramat Gan, "Industry" in *Albanien*, ed. Klaus-Detlev Grothusen (Göttingen: Vandenhoeck & Ruprecht, 1993), 333.

[48] Fishta and Toci, *Ekonomia e Shqiperise*, 90.

[49] Raymond Hutchings, "The Infrastructure of the Albanian Economy" in *Albanien im Umbruch: eine Bestandsaufnahme*, ed. Franz L. Altmann and Robert Elsie (Munich: Südost-Institut, 1990), 148.

[50] Hutchings, "The Infrastructure," 149.

Another danger, especially in rural areas was the tradition of *kalldermi* – leaving large stones on the road to help pedestrians to walk there.[51] During the period of revolutionisation, the attention of the party leadership concentrated on the inappropriate use of means of transport at the disposal of enterprises. It was a common occurrence to use lorries for "unplanned" transport of relatives and friends, and even for the transport of workers to picnics.[52]

In the mid 1980s, wheeled transport covered 2/3 of the transport needs of both goods and people. The streets of towns were dominated by bicycles, buses and a few company cars. Public transport mainly consisted of Skoda buses, some of which dated back to the end of the 1940s. The worsening technical condition of the buses and a lack of spare parts meant that a decision was made in the 1980s to import used buses and lorries from France, Switzerland, West Germany, Italy and Holland. The majority of them were used for public transport in large towns. Domestic travel restrictions did not help the development of long-distance travel connections. The first international connection between Kortcha and Istanbul opened in January 1990.[53] From 1960 to the end of the 1980s there was a ban on the use of private cars.

Table 2. Albanian transport network lengths in the years 1950–1990 [km]

Type of roads	1950	1960	1970	1980	1985	1989	1990
Roads asphalted	181	446	1,213	2,254	2,457	2,800	2,850
Roads asphalted %	5.8	12.8	22.9	36	35.5	38.6	38.3
Roads not asphalted	2,919	3,024	4,091	4,002	4,472	4,450	4,600
Roads total	3,100	3,470	5,304	6,256	6,929	7,250	7,450
Railways	121	121	203	337	608	684	720

Source: Hall, *Albania and the Albanians*, 126.

Before World War II, Albania had no rail connections, with the exception of small sections of narrow-gauge routes for the transportation of minerals from mines to ports. In 1947, a 42-kilometre-long section, connecting Durrës and Peqin, was opened.[54] A year later the line was extended to Tirana. The first trains in Albania came from Czechoslovakia and Poland. In the 1980s, the government managed to purchase five German steam engines which had been withdrawn from service in West Germany. Intensive development of the railway system took place in the

51 In 1967 school children were encouraged to remove *kalldermi* from roads as part of community service – *Zëri i Rinise*, February 8, 1967, 5.

52 Schnytzer, *Stalinist Economic Strategy*, 49.

53 *Zëri i Popullit*, January 18, 1990, 4.

54 *35 Vjet Shqipëri socialiste: te Dhena statistikore për zhvillimin e ekonomise dhe të cultures* (Tirana: Shtëpia Botuese Mihal Duri, 1979), 120.

1960s. The youth press provided a range of examples of the non-human engagement of youths, for whom the motto "perpara per ndertimin e hekurudhes" (forward to build the railway) became a slogan for life.[55] Thanks to the voluntary work of youth brigades, it was possible to connect the south of the country with the northern railway line running along the sea coast. In 1988, Albanian trains made 36 daily connections, carrying 29 thousand passengers.[56] Up to the mid-1980s, Albanian trains had no connections with the outside world. Finally, in 1986, after a few years of bilateral negotiations, the connection between Shkoder and Titograd (today Podgorica in Montenegro) was opened.[57] The connection was used solely by freight trains, which transported Albanian ferro-nickel to Czechoslovakia. The drawback of this form of transport was the high fees for Yugoslav transportation.[58]

In maritime transport, a leading role was played by the port in Durrës, which served 80% of the units sailing into the coast of Albania. The ports in Shengjin and Saranda, whose infrastructure was extremely modest and could handle only a few ships, played a significantly smaller role. The port in Vlora was used mainly for military purposes, together with the submarine base built by the USSR. The first ferry connections between Albania and the outside world were opened in 1983. A ferry from Trieste sailed into Durrës three times a month.

The only airport used by civilians was located in Rinas, 20 km south of Tirana. Until the end of the 1980s, the airport served six international connections per week. Initially, these were Eastern European planes (JAT, MALEV and TAROM), but in the eighties there was a connection with Jannina served by OLYMPIC and a connection with Zurich (SWISSAIR). The crisis in Albanian-Yugoslav relations led to the suspension of flights served by JAT in 1989. In the same year, Air France planes with connections to Paris appeared in Rinas.

The Albanian leadership placed little economic significance on the development of tourism. In 1956, Albtourist was established following the example of the Soviet Intourist. At the end of the 1950s, organized groups from communist countries (mainly Russian and Czechs) arrived on the coast of Albania. A hotel complex was created for foreign guests in Durrës and the Czechs built some tourist buildings in Dhermi, by the Ionian Sea. The break in Soviet-Albanian relations in 1961 restricted tourism to a minimum. A program to build hotels in order to stimulate tourism in Albania was begun in the 1970s. In 1979, the hotel "Tirana" was built in the capital with 324 beds and became the flagship of the Albanian tourist industry. The Hotel Iliria in Kortcha and Butrinti in Saranda were a little smaller. By 1982, 11 hotels had been built, with 1,500 beds.[59] The restrictions and demands placed on foreign tour-

---

55 "Përpara për ndertimin e hekurudhes," *Zëri i Rinise*, January 21, 1967, 4.

56 Hutchings, "The Infrastructure," 145.

57 Jacques, *Albanians*, 587.

58 Hutchings, "The Infrastructure," 143.

59 Derek Hall, *Tourism and Economic Development in Eastern Europe and the Soviet Union* (London: Belhaven Press, 1991), 262.

ists did not help the interest in visiting Albania to grow, but instead led to Albania being treated as a tourist "curiosity."[60] Every foreign tourist had to apply for permission at least two months prior to the planned trip. Only organized groups, with a minimum of 15 people, under the strict supervision of the Albtourist "guide" were tolerated. The arrivals were not allowed to take any literature of a political or religious character into Albania, or take any Albanian newspapers out of the country. The program, together with the "obligatory" Albanian folk music concerts had to be accepted by Albtourist. Only a selected group of people could have any contact with foreigners, with the typical Albanian subjected to repression in the event of contact with the tourists. According to Albanian estimates, in 1989 over 14 thousand tourists visited Albania, with the vast majority being citizens of Yugoslavia and Greece.[61] From the 1950s, there was also a visible decline in the holiday bases for Albanians utilizing the right to paid holiday leave. In 1960, there were 14 recreational centres in which workers could spend their holidays, paying 1/3 of the real cost. In 1967 that number had fallen to eight, and the number of people using the holiday centres did not exceed 11,000.[62]

---

60 Irena Ateljević and Derek Hall, "The Embodiment of the Macho Gaze in South-Eastern Europe: Performing Femininity and Masculinity in Albania and Croatia" in *Tourism and Gender: Embodiment, Sensuality and Experience*, eds. Annette Pritchard et al. (Wallingford: CABI, 2006), 144.

61 *Zëri i Popullit* 12 (1990): 2.

62 Skarżyński, *Rozwój gospodarczy*, 50.

Chapter IV: Socio-demographic changes

This is the basic defect in Albanian existence – the inability (caused by a lack of cultural tools) to care for mutual property as an attribute of mankind and the inability to organize themselves into a community. [...] That's how it was during communism, because specific features, resulting from the socialization of mankind, nursed by religion, and then humanistic and enlightened culture, did not develop, but became totally alien because of the dictatorship.[1]

When the communist party came into power, just like at the beginning of the 20th Century, the vast majority of Albanian society were inhabitants of villages. The northern part of the country, traditionally dominated by shepherding still had tribal structures. The social order in this area was determined by common law, and the basic form of social organisation remained clans. In the south, agriculture dominated south of the River Shkumbin. In this area, society recognized common law to a lower extent than in the north, and foreign influence meant that there was a corrosion in the institutions of clan and patriarchal family. The pre-war demographic structure in Albania was characterized by high birth and death rates.[2] The average population density in 1938 equalled 38 people per square km and was clearly lower than in other countries, such as Greece and Yugoslavia. The populations of the northern and north-eastern mountain areas were extremely low. The largest populations centred around the capital, in the region of Shkoder, and in the fertile land near Kortcha. The population growth rate of 34.4/1000 was one of the highest in Europe. Against the background of European countries, the mortality rate was also exceptionally high at 17.6/1000, which could be explained not only by poverty, but also the practice of *bloody revenge* which was of the principles of common law.[3] The low level of migration from villages to towns clearly grew during World War II. The development of industry and services during the Italian occupation (1939–1943) increased the attraction of towns and the possibility of finding employment.

As a result of the property reform, as well as repression in the first post-war years, the small group of producers and merchants, as well as the influential layer of landowners, practically disappeared from social life. In accordance with the Soviet

[1] Fatos Lubonja, „Państwo socjalne i filozofia 'wyrywaj i znikaj'" in Fatos Lubonja, *Albania – wolność zagrożona: Wybór publicystyki z lat 1991–2002*, trans. Dorota Horodyska (Sejny: Pogranicze, 2005), 344–345.

[2] Arjan Gjonça, *Communism, Health and Lifestyle: The Paradox of Mortality Transition in Albania 1950–1990* (Westport, CT: Greenwood Press, 2001), 9.

[3] Derek Hall, *Albania and the Albanians* (London: Pinter Reference, 1994), 61–63.

model, the new society had space for just two social groups; workers *(klasa punetore)* and peasants (*fshataresia*). Together with the intelligentsia, also known as the popular intelligentsia (*inteligjencia popullore*), these two classes created the working people (*populli punonjes*), also defined as the working masses (*masat punonjese*).[4] The idea of intelligentsia in communist Albania was also applied to clerks, engineers and artists. The two dominant classes in society: workers and peasants, were not antagonized groups in party propaganda but were shown as being under sentence to co-act.[5]

The creation of a state administration was one of the most difficult tasks for the new rulers. Most of the pre-war administrative elite had fled the country, and a wave of repression reduced the number of people who were ready to fill administrative functions to a minimum. According to the census of September 1945, 1,122,044 people lived in Albania, of which 78.7% lived in the countryside. Among those, there were no more than six hundred representatives of the "intelligentsia," in other words, people with secondary school education or higher. They were all included in the program of "mobilization of citizens," which meant forced work in defined administrative positions in locations indicated by the central government. The law concerning the mobilization of citizens, from 15 December 1944, sanctioned the principle that all people who do not follow the principles of mobilization would be treated as "war saboteurs."[6] The lack of workers, essential in the building process of the new country helped former partisans in their quest to fill the key positions, and in the longer-term perspective created a mechanism for "social advance." The idea of what is important in terms of social change in communist countries in the Albanian reality referred, above all, to the realization of the first two Five-Year Plans. The great investments of the 1950s drew youngsters away from the countryside, and the lack of administrative workers helped the chances of promotion both in enterprises and social and political organisations. One of the simplest routes of advance was connected with party membership. The number of party members never exceeded 5% of the population. A party member gained a wide range of new duties, and together with promotion, had to spend increasingly more time at conferences and meetings. In the mid-1960s, party members who were workers (36%) outnumbered clerks (34%) for the first time. As in other communist countries, a group of prominent party members was selected, described as the *nomenklatura*. They were created by the highest ranking party officials and their families. They were able to use a range of privileges – they were chauffeur-driven in state cars and could buy goods in special shops. The symbol of their social position was the separated part of the capital which was closed for others (defined by residents as the *bllok*), in which the standard of life was much higher than that of the other Albanians.

---

4 Örjan Sjöberg, "Social Structure" in: *Albanien*, ed. Klaus D. Grothusen (Göttingen: Vandenhoeck & Ruprecht, 1993), 493.

5 Sjöberg, "Social Structure," 496.

6 Ismet Elezi, *Zhvillimi historik legislacjonit penal në Shqipëri* (Tirana: Albin, 1997), 79.

The basis for the new social structure of the communist country were the workers. At the beginning of the 1960s, most employed people were workers in cooperatives (53% in 1960), but with time the dominant position was taken by workers, who accounted for 58% of those employed in the middle of the eighties. In 1938 there were 15,000 workers employed in Albania, but by 1973 their number had risen to 357,000, and in 1976 to 373,000. In the same time, the percentage of cooperative workers fell to 42%, although their number increased during this period. From the 1960s, social mobility underwent a visible deceleration. It became rare for somebody to advance from the worker environment to the group of white-collar workers, and even more difficult for cooperative workers. In this last group it was more likely for women who broke through the "class barrier" through marriage.[7]

The idea of female emancipation was already discussed in Albania in the 1930s. Under the patronage of Senije, the sister of King Zog I, the "Gruaja Shqiptare" (Albanian Woman) association had been active since 1929, spreading a model of the woman-citizen, previously unknown in Albanian public life.[8] In reality, this association's activities created very little interest. The declaration of the National Liberation Council in November 1944 had much more important consequences, as it granted equal rights to women concerning participation in the country's political and social life.[9] In the National Liberation Army, women represented a large, over 6 thousand strong, group. Some of them died in the war, but some, like Bule Naipi and Persefone Kokedhima, lived to be treated at the same level as the male-heroes enjoyed.

The experience of the partisan wars was a serious challenge for the traditional family model and the traditional role of the woman. The partisan mentality tended to avoid formal unions which were treated as a bourgeois remnant. The former partisans who settled in large towns brought with them a new model of behaviour. Family life was less important than social duty. This lifestyle went against the typical Albanian subordinate role of women, and also limited the time spent raising children to a minimum. The new challenges, countless meetings, and the need to self-educate shifted plans connected with private life to the back burner. According to the act of 1948, it was possible to get married at the age of 18, regardless of gender, but at the age of 16 it was possible to marry with the permission of the People's Court. In such cases, minors did not need the permission of their parents, and were legally treated as "emancipated." Marriage in accordance with the family code was based on equal rights for both husband and wife, with equal rights to choose their profession and place of residence. The idea of a family head, key in common law and pre-communist civil law was deprived of significance. The act of 1948, as well as the family code from 1965, sanctioned equal rights to divorce for both husband and wife. In 1947,

7 Sjöberg, "Social Structure," 500.

8 Fatmira Musa, "Gruaja në revistën 'Shqiptarija' (1929–1931)," *Studime Historike* 1–4 (1993), 79.

9 Prifti, *Socialist Albania*, 97.

there were 100 recorded divorces based on claims issued by the wife, but in 1968 the number had risen to 342.[10] Enver Hoxha considered the right of women to divorce as one of the greatest victories of socialist Albania.[11]

The basic forum of public activity for women was the Union of Albanian Women (Bashkimi i Grave të Shqipërise, BGSh).[12] According to its program, the organisation supported the initiatives taken by the party, but also tried to maintain contact with women from other socialist countries and all "progressive women" in the world. From the 1960s, in accordance with the defined program of revolutionization, one of the most important tasks of women's organisations was to fight the remnants of common law, including arranged marriages. The inspiration for such activity was the widely-reported case of Mereme Sulati from the village of Shenavlash near Durrës. In 1960, Mereme's father "promised" his 13-year-old daughter to his neighbour in exchange for 80 thousand leks. The wedding, which took place in October 1966, became a pretext to imprison the "degenerate father," and activists from youth organizations decided to conduct a campaign of propaganda "in the defence of women's dignity."[13]

During the process of revolutionisation, E. Hoxha's speech (February 6, 1967) on the issue of full emancipation for women presented it as one of the key tasks facing the party and state. In the same year in Tirana, a brochure called *About Women*, containing quotes from the works of Marx, Engels, Lenin, Stalin and Mao concerning the emancipation of women, was edited. The proceedings of the II APL Central Committee Plenum in June 1967 were dominated by the problematic position of women in Albanian society. Ramiz Alia, at the II Central Committee Plenum, paid attention to the fact that only 8,280 women belonged to the party (representing just 12.4% of its membership), and the vast majority of employed women performed simple tasks which didn't require any qualifications.

In 1967 the press carried stories of a number of actions in the women's environment, of the women activists fighting for a change in their traditional perception. One example was the initiative of Limone Çudari from the village of Thenepel, who started a course for female tractor drivers in cooperatives, in order to change the ste-

---

10 Bajram Mejdiaj, "Mbi te drejten e gruas per te kerkuar zgjidhen e marteses," *Studime Historike* 1 (1970): 82. The number of divorces systematically rose – from 850 in 1960 to 2,024 in 1980, and 2,675 in 1990. This took place despite the humiliating divorce procedure, which included the presentation of the problem before the People's Assembly and public answering of questions asked by judges.

11 Enver Hoxha, *Mbi problemin e gruas: pjesë nga fjalime, raporte e biseda* (Tirana: Shtëpia Botuese Naim Frashëri, 1967), 197.

12 The organisation was formed in 1946 based on the Union of Anti-Fascist Women of Albania which had been active since September. Its first leader was the wife of Enver Hoxha – Nexhmije – Sharon Wolchik and Alfred Meyer, *Women, State, and Party in Eastern Europe* (Durham, NC: Duke University Press, 1985), 144.

13 L. Mrati, P. Ceri, and V. Belovoda, "U denua nje akt kriminel qe cenon dinjitetin e te rejave," *Zëri i Rinise*, February 15, 1967, 2.

reotype of the perceived "suitable" and "unsuitable" work for women.[14] The symbol of change in Tirana was the creation of a women's brigade in professions which had previously been reserved for men. In the 21 December building enterprise, a women's building brigade was established, and a women's repair brigade was formed at a tractor manufacturers.[15] At the end of 1967, the number of women working in Tirana's industrial factories exceeded 54%. The lowest ratios of emancipation were recorded in building enterprises, and in science and culture. Among the lecturers of the University of Tirana, women represented only 12%[16].

Table 3. Percentage of women in the work-force in the years 1960–1990

Field of activity	1960	1970	1980	1990
Industry	27.8	44.2	43.6	44.5
Construction	5.6	9.4	9.0	9.5
Agriculture	43.8	52.8	52.2	52.2
Transport & Communication	6.7	14.9	15.8	15.9
Trade	39.6	39.6	53.3	54.5
Education and Culture	41.4	48.7	50.5	53.0
Health	72.3	77.5	78.7	80.5
Total	35.9	45.3	45.9	45.1

Source: Jane Falkingham and Arjan Gjonça, "Fertility transition in Communist Albania 1950–1990," *Population Studies* 55 (2001): 317.

Revolutionization did not create better chances of professional promotion for women. In 1973, women occupied only 5.6% of management positions in industry and 3% of management positions in cooperatives. This situation only began to visibly change in the 1980s, when the percentage of women among the students in higher education exceeded 45%. An example of a scientific career which was no longer reserved solely for man was provided by Andromaqi Gjergji. The archaeologist from Kortcha became the first Albanian woman to gain a PhD in 1980.[17]

Although the number of women in the party had grown to 27% by 1976, at the higher levels of the party hierarchy it was more difficult to meet a female-activist. The ceiling of acceptance for women among the leadership was the APL Political

---

14 Dilaver Sadikaj, "Rritja e rolit te gruas ne prodhimin shoqeror faktor vendimtar and emancipimit te saj te plote (Nendor 1966–Dhjetor 1968)," *Studime Historike* 4 (1976), 23.

15 Alfreda Tase, "Aspekte te luftes per emancipimin e plote te gruas ne rrethin e Tiranes ne vitet 1961–1970," *Studime Historike* 3 (1984), 22.

16 Tase, "Aspekte te luftes," 23.

17 Susan E. Pritchett Post, *Woman in Modern Albania* (London: McFarland., 1998), 77.

Bureau. Here, revolutionization had not brought about great change, and the only woman who had succeeded in reaching the group of candidates in 1976 for the Political Bureau was Lenka Çuko. A high position in the party-state hierarchy was also occupied by Nexhmije Hoxha, who had taken the position of leader of the Democratic Front after her husband's death in 1985.[18] There was an equally low level of female representation in the central structure of justice. Among the deputies in the People's Assembly's VIII term, who were selected on October 6, 1974, there were 83 women (33.6%), which was the highest level of feminism in the Albanian parliament to date.

Table 4. Albania: proportion of female deputies in the People's Assembly in the years 1945–1987

Deputies			
Date of elections	**Total**	**No. of women**	**% of women**
December 2, 1945	82	6	7.3
May 28, 1950	121	17	14
May 30, 1954	134	15	11.2
June 1, 1958	188	17	9
June 3, 1962	214	25	11.7
June 10, 1966	240	39	16.3
September 20, 1970	264	72	27.3
October 6, 1974	250	83	33.6
November 12, 1978	250	81	32.6
November 14, 1982	250	76	30.4
February 1, 1987	250	73	29.2

Source: *Ligjvënësit Shqiptare 1920–2005* (Tirana: Kuvendi i Shqipërisë, 2005).

Before the war, the population density of Albania placed it near the end of the regional ranking, however, at the end of the 1980s it was higher than in the other Balkan states.[19] Society underwent a demographic explosion which peaked in the second half of the 1970s. In this time, the speed of natural population growth was five times higher than the European average. In 1978 there were 13,000 women with

[18] Fahri Balliu (author of Nexhmije Hoxha's biography), describes her role in political purges and wider, in personal policy of Party as crucial, especially in the last decade of Enver Hoxha's life. Fahri Balliu, *The Ghoulish Lady Nexhmije Hoxha* (Tirana: Shtëpia Botuese 55, 2005), 245–250.

[19] Derek Hall, "Albania" in *Environmental Problems of East Central Europe*, eds. Francis W. Carter, David Turnock (New York: Routledge, 2002), 255.

more than seven children. A significant number of them had reached that level before their thirtieth birthday. A symbolic display of approval for motherhood was the introduction in 1955 (based on the Soviet example) of the Mother Heroines (Nenë Heroinë) medal, for every Albanian woman who had given birth and raised at least ten children.

The state introduced a law making abortion illegal, and simultaneously offered a wide range of social benefits for families with many children.[20] A family received help for each child from the state. In 1981, the period of paid maternity leave was extended to 6 months, with the guarantee that the mother could return to work after that time. Like in other socialist states, both in workplaces and in housing estates, networks of canteens and eating houses, as well as laundrettes, were created – institutions which were designed to help women to combine their professional lives with their role as mothers. In 1938 only 2,400 children attended kindergarten, but in 1950 the number had risen to 10,000, and ten years later 15,867 children attended 434 kindergartens.[21]

The continual announcement of pro-family policies and the encouragement to have many children visibly softened at the end of the 1980s. At the X Congress of the Union of Albanian Women in June 1988, during the proceedings there was not a single appeal for an increase in children, despite a clear decline in the level of child birth. The increasing problems with food supplies, the worsening living conditions and the lack of essential goods forced the government into a more pragmatic approach to the issue of birth rate. The reduction in family size was especially visible in towns. In towns in 1980, the number of families with at least 10 members represented less than 1% of urban families (in 1960 it was 2.2%). In rural areas, large families equalled 6.3% (in 1960 the figure was 9.1%).

Due to the relatively low salaries, it was an economic necessity for both partners to work. It is true that from the 1970s men were encouraged to share domestic duties with their wives, but the response to this proposition appeared to be minimal. Research among a group of 450 women living in Tirana, conducted in 1986, showed that the vast majority of them were so burdened by domestic duties and child care that they had no time for any cultural activity, or to raise their professional qualifications.[22] Only 20% of men admitted to performing any kind of housework in the research.

Albania belonged to the countries in Europe with the lowest level of urbanization. At the close of the discussed period, 1989, only 35% of Albanians lived in towns. The most intensive urbanization process took place during the first Five-Year

[20] The ban on abortion, with the possibility of financial punishment or imprisonment of up to 12 months was introduced by the Penal Code in 1952. George F. Cole, Stanisław Frankowski, *Abortion and Protection of the Human Fetus: Legal Problems in a Cross-cultural Perspective* (Boston: Martinus Nijhoff Publishers, 1987), 258.

[21] Demir Dyrmishi, "Arsimi dhe shkenca ne vitet 1949–1960," *Studime Historike* 1–2 (2001): 112.

[22] Hall, *Albania and the Albanians*, 87.

Plan (1951–1955). In the 1960s, the main trend of migration was to move from small towns to Tirana.[23] Twenty years later, Albanian society experienced the unique, in Europe, appearance of de-urbanization. Due to the high birth rate in towns, the accommodation crisis deepened. The construction of new dwellings lost out to industrial investments, and the bunker project only added to the accommodation crisis. In this situation, urban inhabitants (often youths entering into adult life) decided to "escape to the village," where there were fewer problems with obtaining food and accommodation.[24]

Table 5. Urbanization in the years 1945–1968

Population	1945	1955	1960	1968
Total	1,122,044	1,391,449	1,626,315	2,018,800
Urban population	238,812	383,169	502,455	671,700
Urban population %	21.3	27.5	30.9	33.3

Source: Pandi Geço, "Rritja e popullsise qytetare ne RPSh dhe shperndarja e re gjeografike," *Studime Historike* 2 (1970), 86.

The problems connected with accommodation accompanied Albanians constantly from the end of World War II. As a result of military action, over 62 thousand homes were destroyed or seriously damaged, amounting to almost ¼ of the prewar total.[25] Between 1945 and 1970, they succeeded in building 185 thousand new flats. In reality, this meant that, on average, 7,400 families could move into new flats every year, whereas the population increase was at the level of 40–50 thousand per year. The construction of new flats had to cover not only the losses sustained during wartime, but also the damage caused by numerous earthquakes, (especially in the regions of Kortcha and Shkoder). Despite the realization of the concept of forced industrialization, no plan connected to the construction of apartments for the influx of new workers flooding into towns was made. One solution was the introduction in the 1960s of voluntary work in building brigades – the factory's workers worked in their free time to build blocks of flats designated for the employees. In the same period, there was a drastic decline in the number of privately-built houses in towns

[23] Pandi Geço, "Aspekte të rritjes se popullsise se qytetit të Tiranës pas çlirimit," *Studime Historike* 1 (1971): 49.

[24] The construction of residential buildings in rural areas was helped by loans from the state. The appearance of young married couples settling there in their own homes was intended to accelerate the process of destroying "large families," typical of the northern part of the country. Steve Cook, Marash Rakaj, "Social Changes in the Albanian Alps during Communism," *Middle States Geographer* 28 (1995): 87.

[25] Gogo Nushi, "Mbi planin ekonomik të shtetit" in *Kongresi I-rë i Partise Komuniste të Shqipërise: (8–22 nëntor 1948)* (Tirana: Botimi i Partisë Punës se Shqipërisë, 1950), 449–450.

– mainly due to the lack of building materials. The situation was different in rural areas where the greatest number of buildings built privately were constructed in the years 1966–1970. In the 1980s, residential buildings represented just 4% of the gross output of the construction sector. At that time, over 80% of the population lived in buildings built before 1944.[26] The difficulty of obtaining a flat, which was a particularly difficult problem for young marriages, meant that new flats in towns were, in the 1980s, often inhabited before they were completed, often without fixtures and fittings. This was partially due to the lack of quality control in new flats.

Table 6. Albania: dwelling completions by five year periods in the years 1945–1990

Period	Dwellings built	State total number	State %	Self build	
				urban	rural
1945–1950	12,114	1,114	9.2	–	11,000
1951–1955	26,110	7,596	29.1	1,619	16,895
1956–1960	47,413	11,734	24.7	3,514	32,165
1961–1965	44,693	15,808	35.4	2,091	26,794
1966–1970	73,213	29,045	39.7	2,382	41,786
1971–1975	61,908	32,038	51.8	1,476	28,394
1976–1980	56,390	26,326	46.7	1,240	28,824
1981–1985	75,362	41,187	54.7	1,388	32,787
1986–1990	75,522	37,799	52.1	1,082	32,641

Source: Hall, *Albania and the Albanians*, 97.

A great success of the Albanian state was the full electrification of the country, which was successfully realized in October 1970. According to official propaganda, Albania was one of the first countries in the world which was completely electrified. The supply of electricity to all villages also allowed universal access to the radio, a key tool for the intensification of ideological messages to the most isolated regions of the country. After this success, in 1971 the plan to provide telephone connections to the whole country began, as did the construction of hardened roads, enabling-wheeled transport to reach every town. Both of these ambitious plans were not successfully carried out. The lack of investment funds also hindered the proper supply of drinking water. In the mid-1980s, over half of all Albanian villages suffered from

[26] Mario Blejer, *Albania, from Isolation toward Reform* (Washington, DC: International Monetary Fund, 1992), 21; Hall, *Albania and the Albanians*, 95.

a lack of water. This was a result of either the distance to a water source, or more frequently because of dried-up rivers and streams supplying villages. In 1986 a plan was made to supply drinking water to every village in Albania. The plan assumed the construction of reservoirs, whose size was to be suited to the number of people in a given area, but this idea had not been realized by the end of the 1980s. In Tirana, Durrës and Vlore, increasingly frequent cuts in water supplies resulted from the worsening condition of the communal infrastructure. In the 1980s, cold water appeared in taps in the capital most frequently between 3.00 and 5.00 in the morning.[27]

The average life expectancy of an Albanian woman, which in 1950 did not exceed 54 years, had grown in 1980 to 70 years.[28] This represented an undoubted success, especially as the average life expectancy in the inter-war Albania was lower than 40. Thanks to great investments in irrigation and the drying of bogs, malaria was eliminated. In the inter-war period this had been one of the symbols of Albanian poverty and under-development. Even in 1949, there were 238,266 recorded cases of malaria, which meant that 20% of the population suffered from this illness.[29] Twenty years later, the illness practically did not exist in Albania. There was also a successful reduction in cases of tuberculosis and syphilis, which were commonplace before 1944. In the 1950s, tuberculosis was responsible for 15% of all deaths.[30]

In communist Albania, free medical care was available to all workers and their families. Health centres were open next to every factory, every agricultural cooperative, and also in towns regardless of their size. By 1959, 55 hospitals and 108 other health service centres (clinics, sanatoriums and childbirth clinics) had opened. In the mid 1980s, all births in towns and over 98% in villages took place in hospitals or childbirth clinics, under the supervision of doctors or midwives.[31] In 1938, for every doctor working in Albania there were 10,000 inhabitants, in 1960 this had fallen to 3,360, and in the 1980s to less than a thousand. This growth was impressive especially when the birth rate is taken into account.[32]

The increased availability of medical care did not go hand-in-hand with quality. Doctors did not have access to modern equipment or medicines. The lack of investment in hospitals and terrible hygienic conditions posed a real threat to the health and life of patients. In the hospitals in Tirana, there was a universal practice of repeatedly using needles, syringes and equipment for blood transfusions. A black mark on the Albanian health service was the high level of infant fatality. In the inter-war years, Albania estimated it at 80.9/1000 healthy births. Despite clear progress in

---

27 Hall, *Albania and the Albanians*, 98.

28 O'Donnell, *Coming of Age*, 121.

29 Skendi, *Albania*, 260.

30 Arjon Gjonca, *Communism*, 16.

31 In comparison, in 1938 there were 10 hospitals and 1 birth centre in all Albania – Kadri Kërçiku, *Zhvillimi i shëndetësisë në Shkodër: Gjatë shekujve. XVIII–XX* (Tirana: Shtëpia Botuese Mihal Duri, 1962), 294.

32 O'Donnell, *Coming of Age*, 120.

health care, it was only at the end of the 1960s that the pre-war figure was reached. At the end of the 1970s, the mortality rate was successfully lowered to the level of 50/1000 births.[33] Another serious challenge for the medical service was bureaucratic procedures. Dr Kastriot Melyshi, quoted by J. O'Donnell, analysed the case of transporting the seriously ill from small towns to specialist centres. In this case, the bureaucratic procedures demanded by such a transfer reduced the patient's chance of survival. For a patient to reach Shkoder from his village, it required a minimum of two weeks; and another month passed if the patient was to be treated in Tirana.[34]

The standard of living for Albanians in the 1980s seemed to be low for European standards, but it is also difficult to speak about poverty, especially in the towns. Each resident had access to electricity, each family had a radio, and the number of televisions and fridges systematically increased. Albanians did not have cars, but the bicycle was a universal form of transport. Despite the deficit of household goods in shops, prices in state shops were controlled by the state and practically did not change. The whole system of education – from kindergarten to university was financed by the state, the families of pupils and students had to cover only the cost of course-books. The social security system included a packet of benefits "from birth to death" and was one of the most progressive in Europe. The state gave financial support to invalids and pensioners, and paid for funerals.

33 O'Donnell, *Coming of Age*, 119.

34 O'Donnell, *Coming of Age*, 123–124.

Chapter V: The apparatus of repression

> *Agitation and propaganda of a fascist, anti-democratic, religious, war-inciting, anti-socialist nature as well as the preparation, distribution or storage with the aim of distribution, of literature with content aiming to weaken or overthrow the state's proletarian dictatorship will be punished by: imprisonment for three to ten years. These actions, if conducted during wartime or leading to especially serious results, shall be punished by imprisonment for no less than 10 years or the death penalty.*[1]

The idea of introducing a modern legal structure similar to those in Western Europe into the Albanian reality appeared in the 1920s. The new penal code came into life in June 1927, replacing the previously used Ottoman code from 1879. The introduction of the new code was preceded by the act of 1925 which sharpened the punishment for political crimes, as well as for "activities of propaganda" directed against the state or against the "head of state." The Code of 1927 was based on Italian law and was extended in 1932 with the Military Penal Code. Before censorship was increased in 1937, the press published examples of excesses in particular ministries. The Ministry of Justice was heavily criticised, as it was accused of unjustified suspension of investigations into murders. The effectiveness of justice was burdened by the spectre of *Kanun* (Albanian customary law), which meant that judges were personally responsible for sentences, although they issued them on behalf of the state. A good method to reduce crime was the increased effectiveness of the police, which was respected even in the north of the country. In 1932, an act concerning arms production and handling was passed which did not ban the possession of weapons, but did ban their appearance in public. Evidence that the law was not ignored is the fact that the number of victims of "bloody revenge" (*gjakmarrja*) fell in the second half of the 1930s.[2] The fall in crime was also a result of more effective police action. The number of gendarmes at the beginning of the 1930s was 3 thousand, serving at 400 stations located throughout the country. This organisation performed typical police duties, but also acted as escorts during the collection of taxes in villages.

The period of Italian occupation drastically lowered the level of security in Albania. Outside the larger towns, where the *carabinieri* units took care of public security, in other parts of the country there was a significant increase in crime.[3] Before the

---

1 "Art. 55 of the Penal Code of the People's Republic of Albania," *Drejtesia Popullore* 3 (1977): 61.

2 Jason Tomes, *King Zog: Self-Made Monarch of Albania* (Stroud: Sutton Publishing, 2003), 153.

3 Fischer, *Albania at war*, 102.

invasion in 1939, the Italian press presented Albania as a country in which the practice of bloody revenge was leading to self-destruction, which could only be prevented by the Italian invasion. In reality, the *vendetta* which was suppressed by the Royal Gendarmerie in the 1930s again became a serious social problem in 1940 and 1941.

From 1943, in the communist led National Liberation Movement (LNÇ), there were structures responsible for security in the regions controlled by partisans, and the first justice structures. The LNÇ military court was established by the order of the National Liberation Army Chief of Staff on August 17, 1943.[4] Its continuation was the Special Court established by the decision of the National Liberation Council in December 1944. It consisted of ten people. Proceedings of the Court were chaired by Koçi Xoxe, and the main prosecutor was Bedri Spahiu.

The acquisition of power by the communists in 1944 brought a basic change in penal law. With the aim of eliminating potential political opponents, the Albanian communists used penal law, which was characterized by imprecision and led to the "justification" of excessive force in the name of the state. The Penal Code from 1927 was maintained, but only as a kind of general legal guideline. On January 25, 1947, the People's Assembly Presidium passed Decree 392, which defined the code from 1927 as legal rules (*regulla juridike*), which can not remain opposed to the "new democratic spirit" and legal acts passed by the people's government.[5] These included two acts from December 1944 concerning "Military and people's government sabotage" and the second about "war crimes." The idea of "war criminal" (*kriminel lufte*) was defined in more detail by the act on the organisation and functioning of military courts (passed on January 14, 1945), which introduced a wide range of possible "collaboration with the occupants" both through supporting in wartime the activity of the occupant's administration or their military groups, as well as through inspiring others to such activities. The idea of war criminals was also applied to people who acted against "Albanian independence," as well as against the undefined "highest interests of the Fatherland."

On January 14, 1945, the leadership of the Anti-Fascist National Liberation Council decided to widen the range of activities of military courts and to adapt them to the mass punishment of political opponents. The military court was established for each of the existing bodies, as well as the Highest Military Court (Gjyqi i Nalte Ushtarak). On March 1, 1945, it dealt with the case of 48 people accused of collaboration with the occupants. 17 of the accused were sentenced to the death penalty, and 8 received life imprisonment.[6] The show trials, which frequently took place in theatres and concert halls, were attended by large numbers of people. The statements of the accused were interrupted by whistles and jeering from the halls, and the audience was inclined to pass sentence without deliberation. The majority of

---

4 Koço Nova, "Aspekte nga veprimtaria gjyqesore revolucionare gjate luftes N.Cl.," *Studime Historike* 4 (1971): 109.

5 Ismet Elezi, *Zhvillimi historik legislacjonit penal në Shqipëri* (Tirana: Albin, 1997), 79.

6 Fehmi Sufaj, *Historia e burgjeve te Shqipërisë gjate shekullit XX* (Tirana: Albin, 2000), 110.

the accused were "prepared" for the process by long investigations, and the panels of judges were dominated by officers with no legal training. The participants of public manifestations organized in this period demanded the highest form of punishment for the accused.

On May 19, 1945, an act was passed concerning the temporary organisation of justice, which was to work through the People's Assembly, regional courts at a prefecture level and the High Court. The judges were assigned by the local national independence councils, with the exception of the High Court judges. The new justice bodies were used to eliminate the alternative, non-communist political environment. After independence, a few non-formal organisations were established, consisting of Balli Kombetar and Legaliteti activists. Many underground groups were formed in the first four months of 1945. Luan Omari, quoting a source from the Foreign Ministry, claims that in 1945 there were 84 armed units acting illegally, containing 1,500 people. By 1951, their number had drastically decreased, and in 1953 the last ones were eliminated.[7]

The next acts, introduced in 1945, penalized all actions against the reforms and social changes conducted in the country.[8] The new basic law, accepted on March 14, 1946, only referred to penal law in the country in Art. 19. There was a clause that no person can be charged for actions not defined in the law as crimes.[9] This clause was used on numerous occasions as an example of the principle of law and order in the country, although the lack of precision in the penal act meant that, in practice, this clause was of little significance.

On December 24, 1946, the People's Assembly accepted the law on "the basic execution of the penal code." This document consisted of 9 chapters and 55 articles representing a type of provisional penal code. In Art. 5 of the act, it was written that nobody could avoid responsibility for their actions by claiming ignorance of the law. The act also widened the meaning of hostile action against the new political reality and the organs of the state, including the withholding of information in this category of crime.[10] In May 1948, the People's Assembly accepted the first penal code in communist Albania. The Code's authors sacrificed a great deal of space to crimes against the state and public order, as well as against social organisations active in the country. The Code proclaimed penal responsibility for all those over 14 years of age. The catalogue of punishment defined by the code included the death penalty (with the option of changing to life imprisonment), hard labour and imprisonment from 6 months to 20 years. The Code lasted for four years. On May 22, 1952, in a speech to parliament, the Minister of Justice, Bilbil Klosi, presented the new Code, based on "the basic principles of Soviet justice" and reflecting the continuing class strug-

---

[7] Luan Omari, "Mbi funksionet e brendshme te shtetit tone socialist," *Studime Historike* 4 (1971), 56.

[8] Elezi, "Zhvillimi historik," 81.

[9] Elezi, "Zhvillimi historik," 82.

[10] Elezi, "Zhvillimi historik," 85.

gles.[11] In according with Klosi's words, the new document copied solutions known from the Soviet code from the years 1922–1926 and introduced a range of economic crimes, including those connected with work discipline. In the case of some serious crimes, the Code from 1952 allowed the possibility of penalizing people who were over 12 years old. For the repression to be effective, it was also decided to punish the accused's next of kin. For crimes against the state or improper behaviour, the whole family could be isolated from society in one of the villages designated for internees.[12] The Code, with small changes, lasted twenty five years.

The revolutionization of the 1960s led to the degeneration of justice. The Ministry of Justice was closed, and the place of classic courts was taken by military courts and people's tribunals. The decentralization of justice was based on the assumption that mass social participation in judging others was the best practical lesson of revolutionization. The spirit of revolutionization was reflected by the new Penal Code which entered into life in October 1977. This expanded the ideas of crime against the state and treason.[13] This predicted the highest level of punishment for 33 types of crime, and one of the most important achievements of Albanian penal law was regarded as the option of early release from prison. Treason, as was understood by attempts to illegally leave the country, was threatened by punishment of 15–17 years of imprisonment. In practice, this was often extended using any possible pretext. There was also the infamous Article 55, predicting high prison sentences for "hostile agitation and propaganda," which meant that the majority of political prisoners were sentenced according to this article. The Article contained the provision that, during wartime, or if the court considered the crime as one of high social damage, the length of imprisonment could not be shorter than ten years, or could be as high as the death penalty. The changes in the legal system, introduced in 1977, restricted the rights of those accused to a minimum, and they were rarely defended by competent people during trials. The accused's lawyer usually sacrificed little attention to his clients, and generally concentrated on solutions of an ideological character.

Changes in the Penal Code, introduced by a decree of September 15, 1988, introduced the beginning of the democratization of penal code. There was a significant reduction in the use of the death penalty for crimes against the state. The highest punishment was to be used only for the most serious crimes, such as diversion or terrorist activity.[14]

---

11 Pearson, *Albania*, vol. 3, 445.

12 Elezi, "Zhvillimi historik," 88–92.

13 "Kodi Penal i Republikes Popullorë te Shqipërisë," *Drejtesia Popullore* 3 (1977): 45–106.

14 Elezi, "Zhvillimi historik," 100–101.

1. Sigurimi

During the period of Soviet domination, there was an increase in the Albanian secret police (full name of Sigurimi i Shtetit – State Security). On March 20, 1943, the first structures responsible for internal security were established in the Albanian resistance movement with the name of War Information Services (Sherbimi Informativ i Luftes). In October 1944, when the government was established in Berat, it was renamed in accordance with the Yugoslav pattern to the Department of People's Defence (DPD, Drejtoria e Mbrojtjes se Popullit). It was run by Haxhi Lleshi, and was subordinate to the Ministry of War. 5,000 people were sent to work in the Department, selected from former partisans.[15] In 1945, the creation of local structures of DPD began. In particular, People's Defence Sections were established. In March 1946, there was a reorganization of DPD, which formally became part of the Ministry of Internal Affairs, and was directed by one of the deputy ministers. During this time, DPD was again restructured and renamed as the State Security (Sigurimi i Shtetit), with Nesti Kerenxhi at its head. The Services were under direct Yugoslav supervision.[16] After the break with Yugoslavia, in 1948 the APL Political Bureau took direct control over the political police. During the 1950s, the structure of Sigurimi was considerably developed. Three separate pillars were created (directorates): counter-intelligence, intelligence and security for state leadership. The Intelligence Directorate was located on the fourth floor of the Ministry of Foreign Affairs, and its officers were officially diplomatic service workers. Among the Sigurimi co-workers were many representatives of "politically suspicious" families, whose relatives belonged to the pre-war social-political elite and had fled the country or been interned. Co-workers of the Sigurimi included: residents (organizing networks of agents), agents (secret co-workers) and owners of properties which were used by the Sigurimi (Albanian: *strehues*).[17] An APL member could not be a co-worker of the Sigurimi, without the agreement of the party leadership.

The main aim of Sigurimi activity was to prevent any attempt to overthrow the communist regime or deceit with the intention of changing the governing elite, as well as fighting all forms of political opposition which could threaten the stability of the regime. One of the Sigurimi's first "shows of strength" were actions taken after a bomb attack on the Soviet Embassy on February 19, 1951. In fact, the explosion of dynamite did not damage the building and did not have any human casualties, but for the next few days the Sigurimi looked for people allegedly involved in the conspiracy, concentrating on the intelligentsia. Although the names of those involved were known by the police before the attack, and the dynamite was supplied by an

---

15 The majority of DMP officers only had a primary education, and 22% were illiterate – Kastriot Dervishi, *Historia e shtetit shqiptar 1912–2005* (Tirana: Shtëpia Botuese 55, 2006), 614.

16 Dervishi, *Historia*, 615; Uran Butka, *Ringjallje* (Tetove: Botues Phoenix, 1996), 316.

17 Kastriot Dervishi, "Si funksiononte Sigurimi i Shtetit," *Albania*, September 22, 2001, 2.

officer, the case became an example of excellent action of the Albanian security organs. 23 people from the intelligentsia were linked to the organisation of the explosion. They were all sentenced to the death penalty, despite not having anything to do with the attack.[18]

Within the Sigurimi framework, there were specialized structures dealing with censorship, as well as the organisation of prisons and work camps. The Sigurimi's regional structures acted in each district (rreth), and in each workplace. Diplomatic units, as well as Albanian trade and cultural representatives operating outside the country's borders, were also under Sigurimi supervision. The Sigurimi workers were active in all state institutions, as well as in production enterprises. In the 1980s, five motorized military units, which would act during any attempted overthrow of the communist party leadership, were also part of the Sigurimi. At that time, the number of Sigurimi workers exceeded 10,000 people. The Border Guards, numbering 7,000 soldiers in the 1980s, were also linked to the Sigurimi.[19] This formation was organised so that it was subject to the Ministry of Internal Affairs. The Guards had to protect the borders of Albania from all external threats, make smuggling impossible, and also to prevent people from fleeing the country.

Against the background of the Sigurimi, a secondary role in Albanian repression was played by the People's Police. This was established on October 6, 1945, and initially provided support and protection for particular national independence councils. In December 1946 the People's Police was reshaped into a body for executing state administration, which was subordinate to the Ministry of the Interior. Besides the police, there were also separate police formations "for general duties" established to control road traffic, as well as the "fire police."[20] In the first post-war years, the police forces included many police officers from the times of King Zog I, who taught the younger officers the basics of their profession. The People's Police was organized in five divisions. These included the economic police, which protected factories, building sites, and state buildings. The communications police protected bridges, roads, telephone and telegraph networks, whereas the prison police served in prisons and work camps. A separate police structure controlled road traffic and conducted investigations into criminal matters. The former main commander of the police between 1967 and 1987 emphasised that the police did not deal with political matters, and that the detection of crime of a criminal nature exceeded 80%.[21]

---

18 Butka, *Ringjallje*, 147–153.

19 Lavinia Stan, *Transitional Justice in Eastern Europe and the Former Soviet Union* (London: Routledge, 2008), 179.

20 Ariste Jano, *Forcimi dhe demokratizimi i pushtetit popullor në Shqipëri (nentor 1944–nentor 1948)* (Tirana: Akademia e Shkencave e RPS të Shqipërisë, Instituti i Historisë, 1986), 54.

21 Kasëm Kaçi, "20 vitet e mia si Drejtor i Pergjitshem i Policise," *Tirana Observer* 6 (2007): 4.

2. Prisons and labour camps

The changes in 1944 led to a significant change in leadership of Albanian prisons. The vast majority of workers, from directors to guards, were dismissed, and most of the directors during the occupation were imprisoned. New people appeared in their place, however, the majority had no experience in this type of work and no qualifications. In 1945, intensive courses for prison workers were introduced, with the aim of making up for the basic lack of education. A few people working as directors were sent to the USSR in order to undergo further training there. The report from 1954 concerning the personnel in the main prison in Tirana showed that most guards had only finished the 7th year of school education in schools specially created by the Minister of the Interior.[22] The guards' level of education did not change until the 1970s, when it became a standard for directors in Albanian prisons to be created by graduates of military or police schools.

A serious problem that affected the difficulty of serving punishments was the turnover of personnel, resulting most frequently from breaches of discipline. In 1954, in the average Albanian prison, there was one guard for 10 prisoners, which significantly differed from the standard in developed countries, where there was one guard for 2–6 prisoners.[23] In each prison, besides the Commander and Political Commissioner, there were two officers responsible for record-keeping, as well as one doctor and a nurse. Next to the main prison in Tirana, there was a prison hospital, which also treated sick prisoners from other prisons.

In the first post-war years, there were 18 prisons in Albania. Eight of them were designated exclusively for political prisoners, seven for social criminals, and the remaining three were for both types of prisoner. Prison administration services in 1945 estimated their capacity at 3,000. Before new prisons had been built, the old ones, some from the Ottoman times, had to hold over 7,000 accused[24]. The overflowing prisons became a serious social problem. During the Italian occupation, the highest level of prison inmates was in 1942, when the combined number of those imprisoned or interned amounted to 2,500 people. In 1947, there were 4,749 people in Albanian prisons, of which 3,659 were political prisoners, and 1,090 had been sentenced for criminal activities.[25] In January 1950, the number of inmates had risen to 9,168, of which 7,168 stayed in prisons and about 2,000 were detained in camps. In 1953, four prisons with the worst conditions (Berat, Durrës, Elbasan, and Gjirokastra) were closed. The report of the Main Prison Service in 1954 stated

[22] Sufaj, *Historia*, 112.

[23] Sufaj, *Historia*, 114.

[24] The main prison in Tirana, with a maximum capacity of 478 inmates, contained 902 political prisoners and 873 criminals in 1951. Sufaj, *Historia*, 118.

[25] Sufaj, *Historia*, 106.

that the situation in prisons was improving systematically. Evidence of this was the elimination of escapes and better care for the inmates.[26]

The prison in Burrel was particularly important in the penitentiary system. Political prisoners with the longest sentences, as well as victims of the party purges, were placed there.[27] The conditions for serving time in Burrel were described in detail by Agim Musta:

> My cell, number 9, was 6 x 4 m, and had two small windows with bars. 40 prisoners lived in 24 square metres. By the door, there were two large buckets, used for excrement and urine. Prisoners were only allowed to go to the toilet 3 times per day, for just 5 minutes, in a group. During the night, it was forbidden. Regardless of the season, wake-up call was at 5 in the morning. The corridors rang with the whistles of guards. Prisoners had to tidy their bedsheets and wait for the guards to get to the morning roll-call. Often the doors were opened with such force that the bucket with urine was knocked over. The smell of ammonia took your breath away. The inmates next to the door had the worst situation. After the morning roll-call we went to wash and use the toilet. There was only 5 minutes for this. Those who suffered from constipation or prostrate problems were the most unfortunate. There were often arguments among the inmates about their place in the toilet. If you were more than 5 minutes late, you had to go to isolation. After these activities, we returned to our cells and waited for our one hour of fresh air. This was the most important part of the day. We met prisoners from other cells, we spoke, and learnt about news from meetings with families. According to the regulations, it should have been one hour, but it was never so long as the guards, on the orders of the supervisors, shortened it to 30, or even to 15 minutes. After getting some fresh air, we returned to the cells, where we read newspapers or books, played chess or dominoes. Some time was spent on repairing old clothes, learning foreign languages and thinking. At 1pm, we received soup for lunch, it was a green liquid, in which pieces of potato, grains or rice or beans floated. The bread was taken in a carton by the cell leader and distributed evenly. There was 500 g for 24 hours. The bread was made of very poor quality whole grains. At 6 pm, tea was handed out, this was a warm coloured water, but the portion of sugar which we had the right to receive was stolen by the guards together with the inmate-cooks. Before the evening curfew, there was a roll-call conducted by an officer or sub-officer. Every inmate, upon hearing his name stood to attention, however, they were often read incorrectly. Half of the officers and sub-officers were illiterate and often deformed the names so badly that it created a comical situation.[28]

For those found guilty of political crimes, a network of labour camps was created in order to solve the problem of prison overcrowding. The largest ones had between 800 and 1000 inmates at any one time. The rooms which the inmates lived in were not adapted to this aim, which affected the state of health of those living there. In the Porto Palermo camp, the inmates slept in an old fort without any light.[29] The condition in the camps were an insult to human dignity, and the daily portion of food for

---

26 In the same year, according to the Director's data, 77 inmates died in the prison – Sufaj, *Historia*, 116.

27 Sufaj, *Historia*, 133.

28 Agim Musta, *Dosjet e gjalla* (Tirana: Shtëpia Botuese Bilal Xhaferri, 1995), 36.

29 Sufaj, *Historia*, 121.

Table 7. Number of prisoners serving time for political crimes (1957–1962)

Prison (localization)	1957	November 1962 (before the amnesty)
Bulqize	–	4
Tirana*	868	1,191
Burrel	240	306
Shkoder	127	124
Kortcha	105	12
Terbuf	557	–
Vlore	262	172
Zadrime	93	–
Total	2,252	1,809

* In Tirana, those convicted of political crimes served time in three prisons (designated as prisons 303, 309 and 313).

Source: F. Sufaj, *Historia e burgjeve te Shqipersie gjate shekullit XX* (Tirana: Albin, 2000), 127.

one prisoner was less than 300 g – mainly wheat and rice. In 1947, there were four labour camps, with the biggest one in Maliq, where over a thousand prisoners worked on the drying of a bog. The growing demand for a cheap workforce during the first Five-Year Plan encouraged the development of camps. They were most frequently set up in places where the largest investments were in progress (building of factories, railway lines and canals) or with great projects for re-cultivation of arable land.[30] After the construction process had ended, the camp was closed, and the prisoners were transferred to another camp. In January 1966, the Re-education Section, as the camp for women was described, was established in Kuçova. A few hundred women, who had earlier served time in Tirana, were sent to this camp. They lived in wooden barracks and worked on the land. In 1975, this camp was moved to the village of Kosove near Lushnje. The new camp could hold 500 women. Among those serving time for political crimes were foreigners who had married Albanians.[31]

In 1961 there were 14 camps for political prisoners and, during the next decade, their number grew to 18. The camps near mines were permanent ones. Among

30 Anton Logoreci, *The Albanians: Europe's Forgotten Survivors* (London: V. Gollancz, 1977), 197–198.

31 After the break in Albanian-Soviet cooperation in 1961, about 300 foreigners (including around 150 Russians) who were married to Albanians were the victims of repression. The Albanian powers pressed them into leaving the country or into accepting Albanian citizenship. Those who did not want to follow these orders were forced to live in the provinces or were sent to work camps. Robert Skobelski, "Stosunki polsko-albańskie w latach 1956–1970," *Limes. Studia i materiały z dziejów Europy Środkowo-Wschodniej* 1 (2008): 282; Sufaj, *Historia*, 121.

those, labour camp number 303, located near a piryte mine in Spac in the north of the country, was particularly infamous. The prisoners worked in the mine for 8 hours per day, six or seven days per week. During the long winters, the temperature in the camp fell below –15°C, and the area of the camp was covered in snow for a few months per year. They lived in small cells with concrete floors. The daily food rations were just 900 g of bread, 250 g of potatoes, 10–25 g of sugar and 150 g of jam. The prisoners unable to work received considerably less.[32] The camp's notoriety resulted not only from the difficult work conditions, but also from the sadism of the guards who guarded the prisoners. The protests of the prisoners against the unjustified drastic punishment they received were ignored, which led to a rebellion on May 21, 1973. A group of prisoners acquired weapons, took control of the camp and hung a flag of Albania without the communist stars. In their postulate they demanded the improvement of conditions. Alarmed by the events in Spac, the Political Bureau took the decision at its extraordinary meeting of "liquidation of the uprising at all costs." On May 23, Sigurimi units took control of the camp, but four of the organizers were lost near the camp. The rebellion in Spac was the largest of a few similar events in Albanian labour camps.[33]

From the first post-war years, the communist government used other forms of repression besides prisons and camps, described with the name of "political internment." In 1947 such punishment had already been given to 1272 people in the country. Those interned were placed in so-called closed villages, with free movement forbidden and under close supervision of Sigurimi officers. For residents of the "free" part of the village, contact with "marked" people was too risky and put their families into danger. The settlers generally avoided contact with the residents of the "free world." Their stay in the settlement could last up to twenty years.

Among those repressed were both members of families sentenced to imprisonment or time in camps and those who were burdened by a "bad biography" (*biografi e keqe*), in other words, who came from families of civil servants and officers from the inter-war years, landowners or other "enemies of the nation." In each group there was a group of people experiencing social ostracism. They were enemies of the people (*armiq te popullit*), and most of them were descendants of rich farmers, who were disinherited by the communist state. Children from such families could only complete primary school and were not allowed to attend further education, and all forms of contact with them created suspicion from the government.[34] Clarisa de Waal presented the example of two brothers, who despite their advanced age couldn't set up a family. One of the brothers who had previously belonged to Balli Kombetar marked his brother with a "bad biography." For people from such families, it meant there was no chance to make a career and find good work.[35]

---

32 *Voices for freedom* (London: Amnesty International Publications, 1986), 188.

33 Musta, *Dosjet e gjalla*, 184–185.

34 Stahl, *Rent from the Land*, 17.

35 Clarissa de Waal, *Albania Today: A Portrait of Post-communist Turbulence* (London: I.B. Tauris, 2005), 63. On the problem of "collective shame" in Albania, see Nicola Nixon, "'You can't Eat Shame

The application of group responsibility became a really effective way of eliminating potential threats. From the 1960s, it was difficult to find in Albanian society any organized, conscious form of resistance. Awareness of the threat to next of kin stopped all attempts to contest the existing political and social order. Regardless of the developed structure of the Sigurimi, society itself joined in actively in the search for actual and potential enemies of the state. Many people did so out of fear, conformism, and others out of jealousy or the desire to make a career. In the country, in which one inappropriately spoken word or the lack of engagement was considered as a crime, gossip or information complemented by fabricated evidence was enough to convict a man to tens of years in prison.

Between 1945 and 1956 over 80,000 people were arrested for political reasons, of which 16 thousand either died in prison or were shot (the population in Albania was less than 2 million). In the whole history of communist Albania, 5,487 people were executed (including 450 women).[36] Among the amnesties announced during the communist rule, particular significance was given to the one announced on the 50th anniversary of Albanian independence. In November 1962, 1,211 people convicted of social crimes and 144 convicted of political crimes were released.[37]

---

with Bread': Gender and Collective Shame in Albanian Society," *Southeast European and Black Sea Studies* 1–2 (March–June 2009).

36 Agim Musta, *Burgjet e shtetit burg* (Tirana: Toena, 2000), 5.

37 Sufaj, *Historia*, 127.

Chapter VI: Culture and education

Writers and artists, led by the party's teachings, let them see the life of the nation, create art for people, nice, clear and understandable for everyone, art for all people. The life of the nation, its sharp words, psychology and humour of the people, let them take their place in literature and artistic works, especially in plays. The art of revolution is created by artists of the revolution, whose hearts beat together with the heart of the nation.[1]

Before the outbreak of World War II, Albania belonged to the countries with the highest level of illiteracy in Europe. Although the duty to attend school for all children between 7 and 12 years old was introduced in 1913, even in the 1930s just one in five children attended school. The level of illiteracy was defined at 80% of society, while in mountainous areas it reached even 95%. Despite the relatively large number of primary schools, only a few secondary schools operated; the school in Kortcha run by French people, the teaching school in Elbasan, the American Harry Fultz technical school and the agricultural school financed by Italians. In 1939, Albania was the only European country which did not have its own university. The state budget financed a small number of scholarships so that Albanians could study abroad. In 1938, 16 people studied with state scholarships, and over 400 people studied with funding from their families. The graduates who returned to the country had great problems finding work, without suitable protection. Their frustration meant that they became a natural basis for political radicalism. Representatives of this group could be found among activists of the first syndicalist groups, as well as the forming communist groups. The Italian occupants developed the scholarship system for Albanians between 1939 and 1943, with the intention of creating support for Italian politics in the country.

The development of the education system was one of the priorities in the policy of the communist government, who also aimed to take full control of education. In 1945, they succeeded in opening 928 schools and mobilize 1,743 teachers.[2] The act concerning educational reform in 1946 introduced mandatory and free learning for all children, financed by the state. The whole system of education was financed by the state and was unprofessional. Besides the seven-year primary school, technical

---

1 Enver Hoxha, *Report Announced at the VII APL Congress of the Albanian Party of Labour* (Tirana: Shtëpia Botuese Naim Frashëri, 1978), 138.

2 The vast majority of teachers were graduates of secondary and primary schools. In the Tirana area, the number of teachers in 1947 with a higher or semi-higher level of education represented only 8% of teaching staff. Jano, *Forcimi dhe demokratizimi*, 62.

secondary schools were opened, as was the two-year Teaching Institute, which educated teachers. In September 1949, a new law concerning special care for all illiterate people between the ages of 12 and 40 was passed. Evening courses were organized for them in which they learnt how to read and write.[3] In 1955, the liquidation of illiteracy among all citizens under 40 years of age was considered as completed.

In the 1952/1953 school year, the seven-year school became mandatory for all Albanian children. Besides those schools, they also managed to open 13 secondary schools, which were attended by over 3,000 pupils.[4] In 1947, the first artistic school opened in Tirana, with the intention of educating musicians and dancers. The network of new schools developed at an impressive speed, even in those regions of the country where schools had never existed before.

Among the semi-higher schools, the two-year teaching school, educating teachers in Elbasan, had the longest tradition. For graduates of secondary school, in October 1950 two institutions were opened: agricultural and mechanical, and learning in the teaching school was extended to four years. By 1956 the number of such institutions had risen to seven.[5] The right to education at the semi-higher and higher level was dependent on political criteria. In each region, there was a commission which analysed the backgrounds of candidates, giving a suitable opinion, while the Ministry of Education also issued an opinion in the case of each candidate. During the 1951/1952 school year, there were 480 applications, of which 339 (70%) were approved. 89 candidates were delegated by work crews.[6]

In 1947, the Institute of Science was established, with its headquarters in Tirana. The Institute coordinated scientific research conducted in Albania. Before 1955, Albanian scientists did not have titles or degrees. In 1955, the Council of Ministers introduced the title of assistant professor, which was given to 20 teachers, and a special commission operating at the Ministry of Education was created to evaluate and qualify teachers.[7] In the second half of the 1950s the titles of "doctor of science" and "scientific candidate" were borrowed from the USSR and introduced. Due to the lack of its own higher education institute, the Albanian government sent candidates to study in the USSR and other Soviet bloc countries. In the years 1949–1953, 671 Albanians completed their higher education in this way. The breakthrough in Albanian scientific events was the establishment in September 1957 of the University of Tirana (Universiteti shtetëror i Tiranës). Its staff was created by graduates of Soviet institutions, as well as a group of Russian teachers, including Prof. V. Makarow from

---

3 The first such courses were organized in November 1944. Muharrem Dezhgiu, *Veprimtaria e Shtetit te Ri te Demokracise Popullore (maj–nentor 1944)* (Tirana: Akademia e Shkencave e RPS të Shqipërisë, Instituti i Historisë, 1982), 94.

4 Demir Dyrmishi, "Arsimi dhe shkenca ne vitet 1949–1960," *Studime Historike* 1–2 (2001), 113–114.

5 Vladimir Misja, "Aspekte te zhvillimit te arsimit te larte në RPS te Shqipërise," *Studime Historike* 3 (1986), 19.

6 Dyrmishi, "Arsimi," 114.

7 Dyrmishi, "Arsimi," 122.

Tomsk, who was one of the designers behind the institution.[8] With its 200-person teaching staff, the institution was attended by 3,600 students in the first year. In the first ten years of its functioning, 6,700 students graduated from the capital's institution. Even after the break from the USSR in 1961, the basic foreign language learnt by students of the University of Tirana was Russian.[9]

On June 20, 1972, the Albanian government announced the establishment of the Academy of Science of the People's Republic of Albania (Akademia e Shkencave e Republikës Popullore te Shqipërise). The task of the Academy was to develop research based on scientific criteria and Marxist-Leninist methodologies. The Academy's team was to include 117 members and five member-correspondents. Six months after its official establishment, 25 people from the world of science were selected to join it. The list of academics included the historians Aleks Buda and Androkli Kostallari, the writer Dhimiter Shuteriqi and Bedri Dedja – the Deputy Minister of Education and Culture. The Academy's first chairman was Aleks Buda.[10] Two journals were created in which the achievements of Albanian archaeology were presented (*Monumentet* and *Shqipëria arkeologjike*). The latter also published research from Yugoslavia, France, Belgium, England, and even Iceland.

The financial difficulties in Albania during the inter-war period meant that it was possible in only a few cases to talk about the state's cultural policy. Most funds were designated for education, and to a lesser extent supported libraries and museums. Cultural activity appeared mainly in the associations and clubs active at a local level. The informal capital of Albanian culture was Shkoder, where the best writers and poets of the time lived, and the greatest number of music groups were formed.

From 1944, the state and its bodies aspired to be the only organizer and sponsor of cultural activity. Never before in Albania's history had culture been given the opportunity to develop as during the communist period. The size of the potential audience of culture significantly increased. The state patronage over culture resulted from the valued role it could play in the indoctrination of society. Culture was to be also a tool to defeat the under-development of Albanian villages and to extract the country from the Ottoman traditions. The classic indicator of cultural development in Albania are the publishing statistics in the country. Albanians emphasised proudly that in just 12 years (1945–1957) more Albanian books were published than in the previous four hundred years, since the first text was published in Albanian. Constantly available in the publishing market were classic works from the 19th and the beginning of the 20th centuries, such as Andon Zako Cajupi, Fan Noli and Migjeni. These writers were regarded as pioneers of progressive and revolutionary literature, which replaced romance, pacifism and individualism, and were therefore in line with the style of socialist realism.

---

8 Pearson, *Albania*, vol. 3, 528.

9 Luan Omari, Stefanaq Pollo, and Bardhyl Golemi, eds., *Universiteti Shtetëror i Tiranës 1957–1967* (Tirana: N.I.Sh. Shtypshkronjave Mihal Duri, 1967), 104–112.

10 "Ligje për krijimin e Akademia e Shkencave e RPS," *Studime Historike* 1 (1973): 3–6.

The political changes in Albania at the end of the war forced many excellent writers to leave the country. Among them were Ernest Koliqi, Branko Merxhani and the left-wing writer Tajar Zavalani.[11] Among the pre-war writers, victims of repression included the poet and arch-bishop Vincenc Prennushi, and Kristo Floqi, a drama writer from Kortcha, who in 1944 decided to remain in the country. The drama writer Ethem Haxhiademi in 1945 was the leader of the Literature Union and began to work as a teacher in the teaching school in Elbasan. He was arrested in 1947 and sentenced to the death penalty, which was changed into life imprisonment.[12] The Shkodran literature environment was the first to be affected by repression. Traditionally in this environment, the connection with Italian culture helped the state to burden the artists with charges of collaboration. Among those sentenced to the death penalty were writers and poets: Ndre Zadeja, Lazer Shantoja and Anton Harapi. The writers Petro Marko and Mitrush Kuteli died in prison, and up to twenty others were imprisoned.[13]

In October 1945, the Union of Writers in Albania was established, with the poet Sejfulla Maleshova as its head. Criticised by the party leadership for moderation and unwillingness towards radicalism, from 1946 Maleshova was increasingly often the object of attacks. In October 1949, the III Congress of the Literature Union took place, which assessed Maleshova's activity. The majority of the speakers accused him of "opportunism," and tolerating anti-national writers, as Gjergji Fishta and Ernest Koliqi were regarded. Maleshova was dismissed from his position as Union leader, and a year later was expelled from the organisation.[14] The most important effect of the Congress in 1949 was the acceptance of the socialist realism pattern as the only one for Albanian literature. The method of socialist realism was mechanically transferred from the Soviet Union. The dependence on the Soviet model was most clearly expressed in the proceedings by Nonda Bulka: "Our inspiration is Soviet literature. [...] Today Soviet writers should show us the right direction. We need guidelines from Soviet literature, like a lighthouse for our works."[15] The key task of Albanian literature in the future was to create works about workers, and to do it in such a way that they could be understood by the workers.

In the framework designated by the III Congress, there was no place for experimental works, or works for a more refined audience. From 1954 to the end of communist rule, the Union of Writers and Artists published the monthly magazine *Nen-*

11 Robert Elsie, *Zarys historii literatury albańskiej. Współczesna literatura albańska* (Toruń: Wydawnictwo Uniwersytetu Mikołaja Kopernika, 2005), 125.

12 He died in 1965 in the prison in Burrel. Tomor Plangaric, "Me rastin e 101-vjetorit të lindjes së shkrimtarit Ethem Haxhiademi," *Gazeta 55*, April 23, 2002, 4.

13 Elsie, *Zarys historii literatury*, 126.

14 "Ditari i Skender Luarasit: Si u likujduam. Debatet qe fshehu diktatura," *Standard*, November 23, 2010, 2.

15 "Konferenca e vitit 1949. Si do te shkruhej letersia e realizmit socialist," *Standard*, November 27, 2010, 4.

dori (November), which served as a guideline for the mandatory ideological line in Albanian literature. In socialist realism convention, in the 1950s a large group of writers-graphic artists appeared. Their works had no artistic value but were fully accordant with ideological recommendations and, thanks to that, were circulated in society.[16] Russian writers dominated the list of those most frequently translated into Albanian. Besides Maksim Gorkii, Mikhail Sholokhov and Konstantin Paustovskii, Albanian readers could meet the classics of Russian literature – Pushkin, Tolstoy, Chekhov and Gogol. Among other translations, French and German classics from the 19th Century, as well as the more modern works of Pablo Neruda and Rabindranath Tagore, dominated.

From the list of the most well-known literature from the 1950s, it is worth mentioning the tales of Sterjo Spasse – *They were not alone* (Ata nuk ishin vetem) and *The dead river* (Lumi i vdekur) by Jakov Xoxa. Both these works tackled the problem of peasant poverty in pre-war Albania. The participation of Albanians in the civil war in Spain was treated by Petro Marko in his tale *Hasta la vista*. The portrait of a new hero in socialist Albania was described by Dhimiter Xhuvani in the story *Standing up again* (Perseri ne kembe). Among Albanian poets, those who recalled wartime in their poetry were particularly popular – like Shefqet Musaraj (*The epic of the National Front*) and Kole Jakova (*The heroes of Vig*). Among satirical writers, Qamil Buxheli was very popular. A graduate of the Gorkii Institute in Moscow, he shone with his tale *The career of Mister Maksu* (Kariera e zotit Maksut), recalling the atmosphere of *The Government Inspector* by Nikolai Gogol, but with events taking place in pre-war Albania. Writers who did not use the socialist realism style, and those who in any way whatsoever opposed the regime, were deprived of the chance to publish their works, and were often repressed. In 1953, the writer Kasem Trebeshina, sent an open letter to Enver Hoxha in which he protested against the censorship of literature. He also warned that the continuation of such practices would lead to a catastrophe in Albanian culture. Trebeshina was sentenced to 17 years imprisonment, and his treatment was a warning to potential rebels.[17]

A key role in promoting the new pattern of literature was to be played by the theatre. Groups of actors, most commonly from school drama groups, created a partisan theatre during the war, and in 1944 formed a national stage from scratch. Initially, it was called the State Theatre (Teatri i Shtetit), and then the National Theatre (Teatri Kombetar).[18] The next stages were created in Shkoder (Migjeni Theatre, 1949), Kortcha (Andon Zako Çajupi Theatre, 1950), Durrës (Aleksander Moissi Theatre, 1953) and in Vlore (1962). By the 1960s, 25 permanent stages existed, which presented over 1,500 performances annually. The amateur theatre movement also developed intensively – in the whole country there were over 2,000 amateur groups,

---

16 Elsie, *Zarys historii literatury*, 130.

17 Pearson, *Albania*, vol. 3, 560.

18 Dorota Horodyska, "Przed szansą. O dramaturgii albańskiej," *Dialog* 11 (2004): 128.

competing with each other in countless competitions. In accordance with the new spirit, the professional groups were joined by workers who had previously acted in performances organized by workplaces. Dramatic works were dominated by two themes: partisan war and the construction of socialism, and models were taken from the works of Russian writers – Konstantin Trenyov, Boris Lavrenev and Nikolai Pogodin. A typical example of Albanian socialist realism drama was the work of *Our land* (Toka jone) by Kola Jakova in 1955.[19] The realistic picture of a mother fighting for the right to land ended happily after the agricultural reform in 1946.

Patronage over the majority of cultural events in the 1950s was the responsibility of the Association of Albanian-Soviet Friendship – during those times, an active and universally-present propaganda organisation. Every year, in September, a cycle of events within the Month of Albanian-Soviet Friendship were held. During the month, many events were organized, including a meeting presenting various aspects of daily life in the USSR, photographic exhibitions, concerts and theatre performances. For 8 hours per week, Radio Tirana broadcast retransmissions from Radio Moscow in Albanian.[20] The distribution of newspapers and books in Russian was handled by the Albanian branch of the Soviet Book enterprise.

Help of the Soviet Mosfilm allowed the creation of Albanian film-making from scratch. Cooperation lasting from the first months of independence was formalized by an agreement signed on 18 April 1946 by the Albanian Film Agency with representatives of Mosfilm.[21] In 1951, in the suburbs of Tirana, the New Albania Film Studio was established, which was until 1991 the only (besides television) centre of film production in Albania.[22] The history of Albanian feature films began with the historical epic – *Skanderbeg*, directed by Sergei Yutkevich and with the participation of Albanian actors, which was first shown in 1953. The first feature film solely produced by Albanians was *Tana*, made in 1958 by Kristaq Dhamo.

In Tirana's landscape of the 1950s, new cultural centres, unknown to the majority of Albanians, appeared. In 1950, the State Philharmonic, which became the main music culture centre, opened in Tirana. In 1953, the philharmonic team, with help from Soviet musicians, presented the first opera in Albanian history – *Rusallka* by Dargomyzhsky and the first ballet on the Albanian stage – *The Bakhchisarai Fountain,* with the libretto by Nikolai Volkov. On the ninth anniversary of liberation, November 29, 1953, the National Theatre of Opera and Ballet was opened. The Albanian team presented the works of Bizet and Puccini, and the first operas, mini-operas and ballets created by Albanian composers.[23] This stage became visible proof for Albanians of the development of high-level culture in a country still regarded

19 Horodyska, "Przed szansą," 129.

20 At the end of 1953 there were 3,200 local units active in Albania, and the number of members equalled 210 thousand. ASA, Committee of Culture and Art, 1949, d. 11.

21 ASA, Ministry of Finance, 1946, d. 223.

22 ASA, Prime Minister's Office, 1951, d. 1654.

23 Prifti, *Socialist Albania* 124.

by many foreigners as backward and primitive. The premiere of the first Albanian mini-opera, *The Dawn* (Agimi), composed by Kristo Kono, took place in 1954. The debut of Albanian opera was in 1959, with the piece *Mrika*, composed by Prenk Jakova. The story of a young girl sent by the party to work among the inhabitants of the Mirdit region was particularly popular due to its reference to contemporary life.[24]

In 1954 in Tirana, the Gallery of Fine Arts began its activity. Its mission was to collect the pictures and sculptures of Albanian artists, both from the past and contemporary ones. The Gallery organized a yearly exhibition of the new pictures, sculptures and graphics, as well as exhibitions of Albanian art outside the country. The Albanian impressionist painters, such as Vilson Kilica, Nexhmedin Zajmi and Agim Faja, or the older-generation Vangjush Mio mainly created landscape paintings and portraits. Among the works of Kilica, the portraits of Skanderbeg and his commanders were particularly outstanding, as was his portrait of a worker.[25]

The political turning point in 1961 came with a basic review of opinions towards Soviet contemporary culture. Albanian critics held the view that it had broken all the barriers dividing it from the West, and had therefore become "bourgeois, bureaucratic and degenerated."[26] The list of writers especially criticised in Albania included the "slave to imperialism" Yevtushenko, "falsifier of history" Solzhenitsyn, and the writer who discredited The Great Patriotic War, as Sholokhov was described. Among the criticised Soviet writers, there were also those whose works had been published in Albania in the 1950s, before the crisis in Soviet-Albanian relations. The stigmatization of foreign influence in culture meant the expulsion of all streams in literature and art which did not feature in the orthodox view of socialist reality. The categorization of culture did not solely concern Soviet artists. Works which encouraged the individualization of man, as well as those presenting life in comfort and in moral chaos, were also expelled. Targets of Albanian critics were representatives of "western decadence" – James Joyce, Marcel Proust and Franz Kafka. The works of artists such as Salvador Dali and Pablo Picasso were regarded as attempts to remove the qualities of aesthetic human form. The avant-garde theatre associated with Eugene Ionesco and Samuel Beckett was accused by Tirana of combining mysticism and pornography.[27]

The Palace of Culture in the capital was to be a statement of the greatness of Albanian culture in the 1960s. Initially built with Soviet help, but finished in 1966 without outside help, the building stood in the place of a former Ottoman building, representing an example of modern yet monumental Albanian architecture.[28] The building contained the headquarters of the Theatre of Opera and Ballet, and the

---

24 Vickers, *Albanians*, 200.

25 Arben Kuqali, "Realiteti shoqeror e historik në tematiken e kompozimit të piktures shqiptare të realizmit socialist gjate periudhes 1948–1973," *Studime historike* 4 (1977), 184–186.

26 Prifti, *Socialist Albania*, 139.

27 Prifti, *Socialist Albania*, 140.

28 Hamm, *Albania*, 34.

National Library. The Palace became the location of the most important cultural events, as well as the location of the next party congresses. Fascinated by the size of the building, journalists wrote about the 220 halls in the Palace, of which the largest could hold a thousand people, and about the distance of 4 kilometres necessary to walk through all the halls.[29]

The break in cooperation between Albania and the USSR in 1961 meant that the Soviet model was abandoned, but also created hope in artistic circles that the socialist realism methods would also be forsaken. In the 1960s, a group of writers appeared who dared to question the party dogmatism in art and tried to perform a "humanization" of literature through its partial movement away from politics and towards daily life. The new generation of artists who were "not burdened" by a partisan past, had not experienced the cruelties of war like the older generation. Their different view of war, communism and building of a new society caused particular suspicion among the party leadership. The weekly newspaper *Drita* (Light), first issued in 1962, became a forum for discussion about the future of Albanian culture.[30] The VI Congress of the Union of Albanian Writers and Artists (July 11, 1961) brought about a battle between the two generations of artists. The discussions did not lead to a breakthrough, but at least a few artists (I. Kadare, D. Agolli and F. Arapi) were tempted by the creation of more individual works.[31]

Among the writers who worked in accordance with the regime's expectations, but at the same time created original works, Ismail Kadare played the most prominent role. A graduate of the Gorkii Institute in Moscow, he became known as the greatest contemporary Albanian writer after publication of the cycle of historical stories – *The General of the Dead Army* (1963), *Doruntine* (1968) and *The Palace of Dreams* (1970). Although there were many references to the past, it was easy to find analogies to the contemporary world and fascination of Albanian folk culture. Kadare gained international fame thanks to the translation of his works into French. In addition to the tales set in the past, the writer's works also included the story of *The Wedding* (Dasma), which presented the efforts of communist activists, who had to struggle daily with the "destructive" influence of religion on society. Kadare presented a full range of examples of backward Albanian villages, from bloody revenge to circumcision of boys.[32]

A classic drama from the 1960s was the work of Ibrahim Uruci, *The Collapse* (Shembja), which criticised the tradition of arranged marriages. The question of female emancipation was also touched by the drama, *The house on the boulevard*

---

29 Luan Dibra, "Një dhurate e Re e Partise për popullin e rinine e kryeqytetit," *Zëri i Rinise*, September 14, 1966, 4.

30 Robert Elsie, "The National Role of the Albanian Literary Journals" in *History of the literary cultures of East-Central Europe: Junctures and Disjunctures in the 19th and 20th Centuries*, vol. II, ed. Marcel Cornis-Pope and John Neubauer (Amsterdam: J. Benjamins Pub., 2007), 93.

31 Elsie, *Zarys historii literatury*, 131–132.

32 Ismail Kadare, *Dasma: Roman* (Tirana: Shtëpia Botuese Naim Frashëri, 1968).

(Shtepia ne bulevard) by Fadil Paçrami about a young woman who was abandoned by a man during pregnancy and her fight to find place in society. Women also wrote about the problem of emancipation. The drama, *Quiet Lina* (Lina "e urta"), by Arsinoi Bino told the story of a young woman rebelling against her husband, who did not value his own wife as a partner for life, with equal rights in the family. Portraits of women at work dominated Albanian painting during the 1960s. Examples of such works are *Woman of Action* (Aksionistja) by Zef Shoshi and the cycle of portraits by Lumturi Dhrami, who concentrated on the presentation of women's role in the building of socialism in Albania, as well as in the fight for national liberation.

An interesting trend in Albanian drama of the 1960s were the "documentary" dramas, presenting scenes from the lives and work of socialist working heroes. The drama, *Diary of a Teacher* (Ditari i nje mesuesi) by Fadil Kraja, was based on the memoires of Sali Brucaj, a village teacher, who in 1968 died in a storm on her way to work. Brucaj became a model of socialist morality – shown not only through her sacrifices at work, but also her fight against ignorance and backwardness dominant in the village. In the theatre, the time of revolutionization had to include a place for comedy, generally taking the form of social satire. The most valued comedian was Spiro Comora, the author of *The Carnival of Kortcha* (Karnavalet e Korçes) and *Two to Nothing* (Dy me zero). By presenting the ethics of collectivism with old bourgeois habits, Comora laughed at the youth, infected by lower middle-class habits, who were leaving villages and small towns in search of a better life in Tirana.

In January 1965, the literature monthly *Nendori* attacked the writers, accusing them of leaving behind the principles of socialist realism and succumbing to the small-bourgeois and revisionist trend. The party stand as regards the role of literature in society was presented at the XV APL Central Committee Plenum, in October 1965. Ramiz Alia, who was considered to be the leading party cultural expert, gave a speech in which he defined the task of literature and art as to provide strong support for the Party in the mobilization of the working masses to build socialism, and to defend Marxist-Leninist ideology and the sovereignty of the socialist fatherland.[33] He advised artists to mix with the crowds of workers in factories and cooperatives in order to complete their task better. E. Hoxha sharply criticised the Union of Writers and Artists for their unsuccessful attempts to counter Anti-Marxist habits which still appeared in literature and art, especially if they were modelled on Soviet, and therefore "revisionist" culture. The strongest message of the XV Plenum was the conclusion that the Party would never tolerate any artistic experiments, but would consistently demand accordance with the obligatory lines in literature and art.[34] First on the list of those accused was Sterjo Spasse, who put himself in danger with the tale of *Unfinished symphony* (Simfoni e pambaruar). The story's heroine was not

---

33 Prifti, *Socialist Albania*, 178.

34 Enver Hoxha, *Raporte e Fjalime, 1965–1966* (Tirana: Shtëpia Botuese Naim Frashëri, 1971), 134–142.

well regarded in the eyes of the party experts, who considered her as fictitious and insulting to the socialist concept of a woman-heroine. The critics also attacked the tale of *Duel* (Dueli) by Qamil Buxheli for its ideological errors and its straying from historical reality. According to the *Nendori* monthly, some modern dramas posed an even greater ideological threat. *The White Encirclement* (Rrethimi i bardhe) by Naum Prifti, a tale of a group of workers who were cut off from the world by a snowstorm, showed, according to the critics, in an unacceptable way, the egoism of the heroes in a pessimistic manner instead of with full revolutionary heroism.

Naum Prifti described in his memoirs the specific atmosphere of pressure surrounding the writers of dramas, typical of the revolutionization period. The author of a drama had to be prepared for the Party leadership to declare his work as harmful, in other words, containing ideological mistakes.[35] This stigmatizing definition could destroy a drama and its author both before the premiere and after it. In such a situation, the author was expected to admit his error and to publicly analyse his own case. The Ministry of Culture was gradually less and less involved in this system, as it lost its influence on the shape of cultural life, becoming a bureaucratic machine, restricting itself to preparing reports and accounts.[36]

In October 1969 in Tirana, the IV National Festival of Dramatic Theatre took place. Among the dramas that won awards was the play *Grey Stains* (Njolla te murme) by Minush Jero, which presented the problem of the struggle with the bourgeois mentality in contemporary Albanian society. The party leaders, however, were not impressed by the play. On 18 November 1969, an article appeared in *Zëri i Popullit* which attacked Jero's play, as it showed an unreal portrait of the Albanian reality and was unable to consider the discussed problem from a Marxist-Leninist perspective. The *Nendori* monthly wrote about the drama writer Kole Jakova and the writer Fatmir Gjata in a similar vein. An article attacked a group from Kortcha for its play, the jury which gave it an award, and finally the Ministry of Culture and Education for not controlling the festival's program closely enough. The authors of *Grey Stains* had to return their prize, which was then given to Loni Papa – the author of *Marga* – a poorly written drama about the masses as a factor of progress[37]. The incident with Jero's play was a clear expression of the worrying appearance of the party leadership accepting the role of art connoisseur, judging artists in public.[38]

During the time of the revolutionization, writers and artists shared the fate of civil servants and underwent re-education through physical work. Thanks to this, they were supposed to learn the realities of the lives of workers and peasants, and then to create works based on the subject of production. Writers and artists were considered in the category of party helpers in the communist education of the

35 Naum Prifti, *Teatri ne kohen e krizës* (Tirana: Horizont, 2001), 47.

36 Prifti, *Teatri*, 79.

37 Prifti, *Socialist Albania*, 184.

38 In 1973, Minush Jero was arrested together with the play's director Mihallaq Luarasi and spent five years in prison. Dorota Horodyska, "Przed szansą," 130.

masses.[39] Their role can not be overestimated when talking about the development of amateur groups in the Albanian provinces. In the small town of Maliq, in the south-eastern part of the country, there was an unusually active cultural centre, in which a few music groups were formed, as well as a theatre group, helped by actors from the capital's State Theatre. The actor Jovan Bizhyti wrote about the dark side of "provincial culture" in 1967. While analysing the activity of the cultural centres in the Lushnje region, he defined them as buildings penetrated with the spirit of formalism, which could not be reshaped into cultural centres. The cultural centres active in agricultural cooperatives were attended by masses of youngsters only in Albanian films. In practice, as Bizhyti wrote, their activity was limited to the issuing of wall newspapers.[40] A dark picture of the cultural centre in Burrel was painted in an article by Luan Dibra. The collection of the local library was used only by school pupils, who borrowed compulsory reading books, in the only cinema hall there was a broken projector, and the music and theatre sections existed only on paper. In conversations with the journalist, the centre's director blamed the lack of talent in the town and the general drop in interest in cultural activity.[41]

The period of revolutionization also brought with it the development of various forms of commemorating heroes of the partisan wars and victims of World War II. In 1974 the party leadership appealed to artists to celebrate the 30th anniversary of the country's liberation. Within the framework of the great national creation of works, 2,200 works were created to commemorate the anniversary. The winners of the great artistic competition were announced on 27 November 1974, with 261 awards being given out. The opening of the next "martyrs cemeteries" (*varreze e deshmoreve*) in other towns was a matter of time. Both partisans who died during the war and those who died in the first few years after it were laid to rest there. These cemeteries became a place to commemorate the next anniversaries and served in the education of children and adolescents, by reference to the partisan model of behaviour.[42] The role of *lieux de mémoire* in towns were played by monumental sculptures. One example was the monument of the Mother of Albania, placed in the suburbs of Tirana and looking down on the cemetery of war victims. In November 1972, on the sixtieth anniversary of the proclamation of Albania's independence, a 17-metre-high statue by Kristaq Rama, Mumtaz Dhrami and Shaban Haderi was erected in Vlore. The statue, which expressed the permanency of the revolutionary idea and the fight for an independent Albania, presented a group of figures representing various parts of

39 Smirnova, *Istoriia Albani*, 333–334.

40 Jovan Bizhyti, "Perse ky formalizem në shtepite dhe vatrat e kulturës," *Zëri i Rinise*, March 11, 1967, 3. A picture of cultural engagement in cooperatives appears in the film *Woman from the Town* (Zonja nga qyteti), dir. Piro Milkani, Nowa Albania Film Studio 1976.

41 Luan Dibra, "Kjo nuk duhet lejuar. Shenime mbi jeten kulturalo-artistike në qytetin e Burrelit," *Zëri i Rinise*, April 12, 1967, 5.

42 Kastriot Dervishi, *Historia e shtetit shqiptar 1912–2005* (Tirana: Shtepia Botuese 55, 2006), 717.

the country and different professions, with the statue of Ismail Qemal, the architect of Albanian independence, in the centre.

The atmosphere in the time of revolutionization helped the development of the mass media. In 1976, 25 magazines were published in Albania, with an annual circulation of 47 million copies. The main party organ, *Zëri i Popullit*, was published daily with a circulation of one hundred thousand, and magazines for children and adolescents also had high circulation figures.[43] At the end of the 1960s, radio programs, and especially music programs, played an important role as a medium of information and culture.[44] The first experiments with television were conducted in Tirana in 1959 and 1960, but the break in cooperation with the Comecon countries delayed the process of creating permanent television transmissions. Technical help from China enabled the belated debut of Albanian television in November 1971, when it began regular transmissions.

The hope of modern forms of media and the abandonment of socialist realism patterns helped to create the new leadership of the Committee of Radio and Television, with Todi Lubonja as its leader.[45] The radio began to broadcast modern music from West Europe, as well as football matches from the Italian and German leagues. In December 1972, television broadcast the concerts of the XI Festival of Radio and Television Songs in Tirana, which were dominated by singers dressed "in a western style," singing love songs, far from the ideological patterns. The reaction of the party leadership to the "festival revolution" was similar to the political atmosphere which was dominant in 1967. Then, one of the magazines *Zëri i Rinise* (Voice of the Youth) warned against the moral downfall of the youth in the USSR, writing that the fashion for mini-skirts, American jazz orchestras and crazy dancing would unavoidably lead to the spread of hooliganism and attitudes typical of the bourgeois morality.[46]

The attack against the appearance of cosmopolitanism in Albanian culture dominated the proceedings of the party's IV Plenum on June 26, 1973, and ended the short episode of "small thawing." E. Hoxha accused the team of reformers of "liberalism," defining them as "worthless political dead corpses."[47] On 24 and 25 July 1973, there was a meeting of the leadership of the Union of Writers and Artists, with the participation of the Political Bureau member Ramiz Alia. The union's leaders declared their willingness to fight against ideological errors. During the proceedings, the leader of the Union, Dhimiter Shuteriqi, who had filled the position for 27 years, was dismissed. His place was taken by the poet Dritero Agolli.[48] The report from the

---

43 Fevziu, *Histori e shtypit shqiptar*, 67–74.

44 The first program of Radio Tirana was broadcast in 1938, using a low-power transmitter. The system was developed after the war, and in 1947 programs were broadcast for 7 hours every day. Józef Dyrlaga, "Prasa, radio i tv w Albanii," *Zeszyty Prasoznawcze* 2 (1988): 102.

45 Smirnova, *Istoriia Albanii*, 339.

46 "Aspekte nga jeta ne Bashkimin Sovietik," *Zëri i Rinise*, January 4, 1967, 4.

47 Todi Lubonja, *Ankthi pa Fund i Lirise* (Tirana: Albinform, 1994), 178.

48 Xhemal Gjecovi, ed., *Historia e Popullit Shqiptar në katër vellime*, vol. IV (Tirana: Toena, 2008), 296.

plenum was published on 28 July in *Zëri i Popullit* and informed of the cleansing action which had removed anti-party elements from the Union. The first victims of the purge were Fadil Paçrami and Todi Lubonja. Paçrami was described as an enemy of the party and people, while Lubonja was a "right-wing deviant," who "supported liberal-opportunist tendencies and had a modernistic aesthetic taste."[49] For a few years after the purge in 1973, it was difficult to notice any attempts to deviate from the official party line in artistic circles.

1973 turned out to be a turning point in Albanian film-making. The ban on foreign films being imported into the country, introduced in that year, also led to a significant increase in the budget of the New Albania Film Studio, which produced 25 films per year. Most films were created with a minimum of effort and funding. The directors officially did not receive any payment for the films, and soldiers and workers from nearby agricultural cooperatives were used as extras.[50] The film output of communist Albania equalled over 250 feature films, of which over half were made in the years 1981–1990.[51] Films about partisans, as well as the modern picture of working heroes, dominated. Audiences particularly liked the cinema comedies which appeared on screens in the 1970s. The most interesting of them (*Lady from the Town* from 1972, and *Kapedani* from 1976) presented the normal conflicts between the modernizing village, and entanglement in the behaviour of the lower middle-class trapped in urban life. Albanian cinema at the turn of the 1980s used topics previously absent in culture – family conflicts, alienation of the new generation, and the increasing problem of loneliness among old people.

A curiosity of Albanian culture in the 1980s was the huge number of new museums. In 1970 there were only seven, but by 1983 the number had risen to 2,034. The vast majority of them were small rural museums, which were equipped rather modestly and, as a rule, were limited to a few local costumes, photographs, and sometimes archaeological objects.[52]

49 Prifti, *Socialist Albania*, 189.

50 Juliusz Peltz, "'Nowa Albania' otwiera podwoje, " *Kultura* 13 (1988), 12.

51 Abaz T. Hoxha, *Enciklopedi e kinematografise shqiptare* (Tirana: Toena, 2002), 459–498.

52 *Zëri i Popullit*, May 15, 1988, 3–4.

Chapter VII: Confessional policy

Religion is the opium of the people. We must do everything to make each man understand this great truth, and we must treat those who are poisoned (and there are many of them). This is not easy work, but it is possible to carry it out. We can not stop this fight and be satisfied that the young generation have thrown away this opium, or live with the conviction that religion and its practices exist only among the elderly.[1]

In contrast with other Balkan nations, Albanians were a society with multiple religions, and one in which religion did not play a significant role in group identification. The process of Islamisation, which was particularly intensive from the 17th Century meant that the majority of inhabitants on Albanian soil recognised Islam. The Sunni Muslims were the largest group, but the Bektashi community, with almost 20% of Albanian followers of Islam, also played an important role (it was active mainly in the central and southern parts of the country). In the south and south-eastern part of the country, the Orthodox Church had considerable influence, while in the north and north-western parts, Catholicism was influential. Documents of a constitutional character, passed in the inter-war years, uniformly stated that in Albania there was no state religion. In the most important state bodies, the principle of religious equality applied.

A lasting tendency in the politics of the Albanian state were the attempts to control the communities, as well as to ensure independence from external influences. In March 1923, the Albanian Sunni Muslims broke off ties with Istanbul, establishing their own leadership, with the Great Mufti of Albania as its head. The intention of making the Church independent was also the guiding principle of the congress of Orthodox clergymen in Berat (September 1922), at which it was decided to create the Albanian Autocephalous Church. The Autocephaly, which was announced in a way that was not in accordance with Canon Law, wasn't recognized, despite diplomatic pressure, by the Ecumenical Patriarchate of Constantinople. Only on 12 April 1937, did Patriarch Benjamin I raise the Orthodox Church in Albania to the level of autocephaly. The third largest community – the Bektashi Sufis (consisting of about 15–20% of society) organized the first national congress in January 1921 in Skrapar. In 1925, after the Muslim monasteries were closed down in republican

[1] *Praktikat fetare t'and luftojme me frymen patriotike dhe revolucionare te masave* (We fight religious practices with the patriotic-revolutionary spirit of the masses), A letter from the APL CC to regional party committees about the fight against religion, superstitions and religious traditions, February 27, 1967, in: Enver Hoxha, *Vepra*, vol. 35 (Tirana: Shtëpia Botuese Naim Frashëri, 1985), 103.

Turkey, Tirana became the world centre of the Bektashi community, and the head of the community was Sali Niazi Dede with the title of World Leader of Bektashis (Kryegjush Botëror të Bektashinjve). From 1930 its headquarters were located in the new temple in Tirana.

Table 8. Structure of faith according to the census (September 1945)

Region	Population	Muslims %	Orthodox %	Catholics %
Berat	127,791	75.5	24.1	0.3
Durrës	106,220	83.3	8.4	8.2
Elbasan	109,906	93.5	6.3	0.1
Gjirokastra	125,580	57.2	42.3	0.4
Kortcha	151,794	71.0	28.6	0.3
Kukes	49,378	99.0	0.6	0.4
Peshkopi	84,043	98.1	1.2	0.6
Shkoder	157,994	36.3	2.4	61.3
Tirana	93,061	83.3	12.1	4.4
Vlore	116,182	71.3	28.0	0.6
Total	1,121,949	72.5	17.2	10.0

Source: *Vlast' i tserkov' w Vostochnoi Evrope 1944–1953*, vol. 2, 1127.

The census in 1945 showed that the vast majority of society (72.5%) were Muslims, 17.2% of the population declared themselves to be Orthodox, and 10% Catholics. In 1945, the Albanian leaders wanted religious organisations to maintain their influence over people, but on condition that they were politically subordinate. Religious issues were dealt with from 1945 by the Religious Section at the Council of Ministers. In the long-term, the policies of the communist government towards religion had two main aims: total separation of religious communities from the state and the removal of their influence on youth education. From 1945, spiritual leaders of all religions had to perform national military service, and applications for exemption from service for religious reasons were generally rejected.

The agricultural reforms passed on August 29, 1945, and extended in June 1946 deprived the religious institutions of most of their arable land, allowing churches to keep just 5 ha, and monasteries up to 20 ha. Protests against the reforms were most violent in Orthodox monasteries, as the reforms threatened the basis of their existence.[2] In a letter to the Minister of Justice, from December 1945, Kristofor Kissi

2 ASA, AAOC (Albanian Autocephalous Orthodox Church), 1945, d. 41.

stated that the land was mainly used by the church for grazing and would not be useful for *kolkhozes*. The Ministry's negative response of January 25, 1946, expressed the opinion that there could be no exceptions from the principles of the reforms.[3] By depriving the religious communities of their sources of income (including shops belonging to the communities), the state took the duty of subsidizing religious communities upon itself. In 1945, over 1 million francs were designated for this purpose. These funds were designated almost exclusively for salaries of the clergy, with the principle that the salaries of the church hierarchy were 4–5 times higher than that of an employed layman.[4] At the same time, the press condemned all attempts at increasing payments for spiritual services and described the encouragement of the congregation to donate money as the appearance of greed among the clergy, who did not understand the difficult material situation of the congregation.

The communist state accepted full responsibility for the education of the younger generation, which was confirmed by the act in August 1946 describing the "secular and communist character of upbringing and education." In April 1947, the party recommended the introduction of anti-religious propaganda into schools, and from November 1954 all social and political organisations were obliged to spread it.[5]

The communist relations with particular religious communities differed and depended on the degree of loyalty towards the new government. The Orthodox and Bektashis succeeded without difficulties in entering into agreements with the communist authorities, defining the acceptable range of clerical activity and declaring participation in propaganda campaigns organized by the communists. Many Orthodox clergymen fought against the occupants, and a large number of Albanian communists came from Orthodox families. The Bektashis were helped by the fact that, during wartime, 28 of the community's clergymen, as well as a few hundred of the faithful, were killed in fighting. The new government took a different position towards the Catholic clergy, who were accused of collaboration with the Italian occupants and of material gain from this collaboration. Until the first parliamentary elections, the new powers maintained a conciliatory attitude towards Catholics. The change in tactics came in May 1945. During talks with representatives of the communist rulers, the Church hierarchy and the Holy See's representative in Albania categorically rejected demands to create a "national church," independent of the Vatican, in exchange for security and subvention from the state. On May 24, after

[3] ASA, AAOC, 1945, d. 23.

[4] After the agricultural reforms, the state subsidies for the richest Orthodox Church amounted to 1 million francs in 1946, while other income – from donations, sales of books and others equalled 18 thousand francs. The head of the Church – archbishop Kristofor Kissi received 19,200 francs monthly (ASA, AAOC, 1945, d. 23).

[5] Circular letter from the APL Central Committee about widening atheist propaganda (ASA, AAOC, 1954, d. 674).

being recognized by the Albanian rulers as a persona non grata, the representative of the Holy See, Archbishop Giovanni B. Nigris, left the country.[6]

Pressure on the Catholic Church increased after the elections in December 1945. A group of Jesuits from Shkoder were sentenced to the death penalty and shot on charges of active collaboration with the occupants, including the Provincial Superior (January 30, 1946). The next wave of repression was caused by the Postribe Uprising, which took place in September 1946. In talks with the Soviet representative, D. Chuvakhin, the Minister of the Economy, Nako Spiru, recognized the participation of Catholics and Muslims in the uprising as significant.[7] The wave of repression in the years 1946–1949 affected almost half of the Catholic clergy. Among those murdered as enemies of the people were Bishop Frano Gjini, acting as the primate of Albania, and Bishop Gjergji Volaj. To a lesser degree, the repression also touched the Muslim community, as some of the clergy were accused of collaboration with the occupants. Among those imprisoned were the mufti of Durrës – Mustafa efendi Varoshi, Hafez Ibrahim Dibra – the former great mufti of Albania and sheh Xhemal Pazari from Tirana. In 1947, there were 44 Muslim clergymen, 36 Catholic priests, 16 Orthodox priests and one nun in Albanian prisons.[8]

Due to the close cooperation between Albania and Yugoslavia and the USSR, the Albanian Orthodox Church found itself in a privileged position. In accordance with government expectations, at the end of 1945, Archbishop Kristofor Kissi publicly condemned the activity of Bishop Pantelejmona Kotoko, previously the metropolitan bishop of Gjirokastra, who in Greece led the so-called Committee of Liberation for Northern Epirus, with the aim of separating it from Albania. This matter was particularly important in view of the Paris Peace Conference, where the Greek government renewed their demands to separate Northern Epirus from Albania.

The initiative to set up closer cooperation between the Russian Orthodox Church and the Albanian one appeared at the end of 1946. In a telegram of January 19, 1947, sent by Kristofor Kissi to the Russian patriarch Aleksei, the leader of the Albanian Church asked for a delegation of the Russian Church to visit. The preceding visit of Albanian Church representatives to Moscow was delayed by the case of Bishop Ireneo Banushi. Banushi was one of the few Orthodox clergymen to be accused of cooperation with the Italian occupants. The evidence of this was supposedly a few meetings between Banushi and the Italian governor in Albania – General Alberto Pariani. During the investigation, it came out that other clergymen had also met with Pariani, including Kristofor Kissi. The suspicions of collaboration directed at the Orthodox Church's hierarchy left the visit of Albanian clergymen to Moscow

6 Sabrina Ramet, *Nihil obstat: Religion, Politics and Social Change in East-Central Europe* (Durham, NC: Duke University Press, 1998), 213.

7 Tat'iana Volokitina, Grigorii Murashko, and Albina Noskova, *Moskva i vostochnaia Evropa. Vlast' i tserkov v period obshchestvennykh transformacii 40–50 godov XX veka* (Moscow: ROSSPÉN, 2008), 352.

8 Fehmi Sufaj, *Historia e burgjeve të Shqipërise gjate shekullit XX* (Tirana: Albin, 2000), 111.

under a question mark. On September 9, 1947, the Soviet Ministry of the Interior demanded the exclusion of all delegates whose wartime activities caused suspicion.[9] The Albanian delegation finally arrived in Moscow on January 10, 1948. Its leader was Archimandrite Pajsij (Pashko Vodica), a former partisan and member of the Anti-Fascist National Liberation Council. The aim of the visit to Moscow was to gain moral and economic help from the Russian Orthodox Church. The Russians were very positive about the fact that there were two bishops in the delegation who were not under any suspicion of collaboration, and who in the near future could replace the compromised Kissi to maintain the Orthodox Autocephalous Church of Albania (OACP).[10]

On April 14, 1948, the return visit of the Russian Church delegation, led by Bishop Nestor (Sidoruki), arrived in Albania. The program for the visit included trips to twelve Albanian monasteries and joint prayers.[11] Bishop Nestor took part in an ordination (*Cheirotonia*) by Bishop Pajsij Vodica. The visit made a good impression, as did the meeting with Enver Hoxha (19 April), which created the feeling that the Albanian government was interested in solving the community's problems.

Pajsij Vodica's ordination accelerated the changes in personnel in the Church. Soviet diplomatic relations with Tirana were dominated by the view that the compromised Kissi only had formal leadership, and for a few months the Church's issues had been directed by Archbishop Vodica, who enjoyed the greatest trust of the communist rulers.[12] On June 8, 1949, E. Hoxha informed Chuvakhin that Archbishop Vodica had presented a proposal to remove the Church's head so that the OACP leadership could obtain "democratic elements." On August 24–25, 1949, a meeting of the OACP Synod was organized in which, by a unanimous vote, Archbishop Pajsij Vodica was chosen as the new leader of the Church.[13]

The new Church head during his inauguration referred critically to the activity of "agents of imperialism," as he defined the new Ecumenical Patriarch Athenagoras, who he placed equally with "the Roman Pope, instigating war between nations."[14] Within the framework of the solidarity with the Albanian political leaders, the head of the Albanian Church made a speech on November 23, 1949 at a meeting in Tirana where he attacked the interference of "bandits from Belgrade," with Tito at their head, in Albania internal affairs.[15] In accordance with the Soviet model, Orthodox

---

9 Volokitina, Murashko, and Noskova, *Moskva i vostochnaia Evropa. Vlast' i tserkov*, 353.

10 In 1948, Kissi was also hindered by the case of Thoma Orologai, the former minister of justice during the pre-war period, who was reportedly found by the police hiding in Kissi's home. Volokitina, Murashko, and Noskova, *Moskva i vostochnaia Evropa, Vlast' i tserkov*, 210.

11 ASA, AAOC, 1948, d. 215.

12 Volokitina et al., *Vlast' i tserkov v Vostochnoi Evrope*, vol. 2, 76–77.

13 According to its statute, the Synod met once a year in October. In 1949, in the absence of Kissi, the Synod gathered on August 25, passing a resolution to remove the archbishop from his position "for anti-people and anti-church activities" (ASA, AAOC, 1949, d. 233).

14 Volokitina et al., *Vlast' i tserkov v Vostochnoi Evrope*, vol. 2, 357.

15 ASA, AAOC, 1949, d. 248.

clergymen were obliged to participate in peace campaigns organized by the APL leadership.[16] The Church actively supported Soviet and Albanian initiatives in the international arena. In 1952, the Church officially protested "against chemical and bacteriological war, as conducted by Americans in Korea."[17]

In June 1949 there was a meeting between Enver Hoxha and the leader of the Albanian Sunni Muslims – Hafis Musa Ali, who presented his requests to the Albanian government. The mufti's main postulates were to increase financial aid for the Muslim community, and to make those who wished in the future to become *hodjas* or *mullahs* exempt from military service. Hoxha reacted positively to the exemption of clergymen from military service, but did not support the idea of translating the Koran into Albanian, which the mufti requested.[18]

On November 26, 1949, the Presidium of the People's Assembly in Albania passed Act 743 on religious communities.[19] The act became the main regulator of religious activities and Church-State relations. All internal regulations inside communities, as well as the nomination of each leader and his deputy had to be approved by the government. The state controlled the educational plans and programs of religious schools. The Committee for Religion was to censure all religious publications if they were to be available to the public. The Council of Ministers had to approve community budgets, and state financial bodies systematically controlled the financial activity of communities. It was stated in the document that religious freedom meant the necessity for religious groups to obey the law and good customs.

Act 743 became the basis for negotiations concerning the legal status of religious communities. On May 4, 1950, a government decree accepted the new status of the Albanian Orthodox Church.[20] Article 3 of the statute declared that Albanian would remain the official language of the Church, which could in certain cases also use other languages. The Church hierarchy could only contain people with Albanian citizenship. On the same day, statutes concerning the Muslim communities were also approved. The highest power in the Sunni Muslim community was the Main Council, and the budget was to consist of income from property donations and budget subsidiaries. The statute also regulated the activity of the Community of Albanian Bektashis (Komuniteti Bektashian I Shqipërise). Owing to the fact that the leader of the community in Albania controlled the world community of Bektashis, he obtained the right to maintain contact with communities active outside the country (other community leaders did not obtain such rights).[21]

Act 743 also defined the position of the communist powers in discussions with the Catholic hierarchy. Enver Hoxha sent the Minister of the Interior, Tuk Jakova,

[16] Volokitina et al., *Vlast' i tserkov v Vostochnoi Evrope*, vol. 2, 529–530.

[17] ASA, AAOC, 1952, d. 466.

[18] ASA, Archdiocese of Shkoder, 1950, d. 2.

[19] *Dekretligji mbi komunitete fetare*, ASA, Prime Minister's Office, 1949, d. 561, p. 4.

[20] ASA, AAOC, 1950, d. 292.

[21] Dervishi, *Historia e shtetit*, 636.

to meet the Franciscan clergyman Marin Sirdani, at the time staying in the labour camp near Elbasan. In the discussions with Sirdani, Jakova convinced him that responsibility for the repression of the clergy in the past lay exclusively with Yugoslavia, who forced the policy upon the Albanian leadership, whereas the current government wished to have closer ties with the Church.[22] With Sirdani's help, talks were held between the government and the Catholic hierarchy, represented in 1949 by the bishop of Pulati, Bernardin Shllaku – the only member of the Catholic hierarchy who had survived the period of repression. The discussions were intended to define the principles of Church functioning in the state. The Catholic side did not accept the principles passed in the act of November 26, 1949. The main bone of contention was Article 13 of the statute – the matter of nominating bishops, who the government wanted to confirm before the Pope, and not after him.[23] One form of pressure on the Church leadership were the attempts to create a split among the clergy, some of whom were inclined to compromise and recognize the position of the government in the Church statute. A compromise was reached in July 1951. The Catholic Church kept the right to maintain contact with the Holy See, however, the communist government tried to restrict the contacts to a minimum. The Council of Ministers gained the right to confirm nominations for bishops, and the bishops had the duty to participate together with the faithful in propaganda meetings, such as the peace appeal. In August 1954, Bishop Bernardin Shllaku, on behalf of the Catholic Church, signed an appeal to the faithful about the participation in elections and support for candidates of the Democratic Front. This was a result of a clear government order.[24]

Complementary to the legal acts concerning the religious communities was the new Penal Code, passed in May 1952. Article 259 referred to crimes breaching the division of the Church from the state, and Article 261 defined the illegal performance of religious activities as a crime. Article 260 which defined the disturbance of religious ceremonies as a crime was, in reality, a dead letter.[25]

The 1950s came with a visible increase in the ideological conflict and an attempt to marginalize religious communities. The APL Central Commitee Plenum which was held in April 1955 debated the question of the strengthening scientific-materialistic views among workers. In his speech at the plenum, E. Hoxha claimed that the communist and religious worlds are not reconcilable in Albania, just as the exist-

---

22 Contents of E. Hoxha's discussions were given by the Soviet representative Chuvakhin. During the discussions with Sirdani, Jakova claimed that some clergymen were arrested as enemies of the nation, but this didn't affect the government's opinion of the Catholic Church leadership in Albania as a whole. (Volokitina et al., *Vlast' i tserkov v Vostochnoi Evrope*, vol. 2, 148–149.

23 In the opinion of Chuvakhin, there were two different positions in the APL leadership – Tuk Jakova was in favour of making concessions to Catholics, but the opposite position was taken by Enver Hoxha. (Volokitina et al., *Vlast' i tserkov v Vostochnoi Evrope*, vol. 2, 596, 828).

24 ASA, Arq. Shk., 1954, d. 6.

25 Michał Staszewski, *Państwo a związki wyznaniowe w europejskich państwach socjalistycznych* (Warsaw: Książka i Wiedza, 1976), 101.

ence of the two antagonistic worlds of capitalism and workers can not reconciled.[26] Ideological work and the systematic reduction in expenses for the still-active communities was to be a method to gradually close them. The inefficiency of the used methods accelerated the entry into the final phase of the elimination of religion, which was to deprive the religious communities of their places of worship.

In July 1960, the local government in Dhiver near Gjirokastra, with approval from the local party committee, decided to knock down the church which had been damaged in an earthquake and build a primary school in its place. The materials which had been gathered earlier to rebuild the church were used to construct the school.[27] In November 1960, three similar petitions arrived at the Bishop of Kortcha, from teachers of two secondary schools and residents of the district, requesting a change in use of the Church of St George into a museum which would be more useful for the residents of Kortcha. In January 1961, the cooperative in Peliçan took a decision to rebuild the temple which had been destroyed during the war and change it into a cultural centre.[28] Half a year later, despite the protests of clergymen, the church in Vuno was changed into a cinema.

A clear escalation of aggression occurred in 1964. During Pascha's liturgy, three police officers entered the church in Berat, with the intention of arresting the priest because the "sound of the church bells disturbed public order." In June 1964, congregations were not allowed to participate in religious ceremonies, as they were breaking the ban on organization of church celebrations.[29] The main role in the destruction of the Church of St Atanaz in Malasej near Cerrik was played by youths. A clergyman who protested against the barbarianism heard that a church in that place was not necessary, and the local party committee had allowed them to conduct such activity.[30]

The cases of destruction and liquidation of places of worship until the mid-1960s appeared to be separate isolated incidents, resulting from the over-zealousness of local party committees. During the process of revolutionization, conducted from the mid-1960s, one of the key tasks was considered to be the full atheisation of the country, also through the acquisition or destruction of "material bases" belonging to religious communities. Changes in the land plans introduced in the years 1965–1966 were often connected with sending dunning letters to parishes, to encourage them to destroy their own places of worship and make them available for the construction of dwellings or cultural centres. Youth organisations most frequently used the postulate of reshaping places of worship into cultural centres. On May 14, 1966,

26 Prifti, *Socialist Albania*, 154.

27 ASA, AAOC, 1960, d. 1056.

28 ASA, AAOC, 1960, d. 1059.

29 Bans on organising festivals were issued by local party committees based on sanitary-health concerns. ASA, AAOC, 1964, d. 1228.

30 Correspondence between Vodica and Shehu. ASA, AAOC, 1965, d. 1281.

a youth organisation carried out the liquidation of mosques in Belsh and Muriqan. On June 10, 1966, the Catholic church in Theth was adapted into a cultural centre.[31]

Throughout 1966 there was a dramatic fight by the communities to stop the process of eliminating places of worship. Letters from the head of the Catholic Church, Bishop Ernest Çoba, to the government were generally unanswered. The intervention of the Orthodox hierarchy also had little effect. The death of Pajsij Vodica in March 1966 additionally weakened the position of the Church against the communist rulers. His successor, Bishop Damian Kokoneshi, did not have such influence on the party as his predecessor, and the party leaders were irritated by his good relations with the Russians before 1961.[32] The decision of the Main Council of the Bektashi Community to give away four places of worship, in which the congregation was small, may be considered as an act of desperation.[33]

On February 6, 1967, Enver Hoxha, in a speech to the Albanian youth, stated that a real revolutionary attitude demands the rejection of all backward customs and ceremonies.[34] Particular information concerning the new strategy against religion was found in the APL Central Committee's letter of February 27, sent to local party structures. The party leadership investigated the course of atheization actions to date, and expressed concern that places of worship with large congregations still existed and were active. This was to be the best proof that the ability of religious communities to grow again should not be disregarded. In the context of the events of 1967, the following fragment of the document seems to be key:

> "The destruction of churches, mosques and monasteries creates certain difficulties due to the fact that open conflict with the part of the nation that still believes should be avoided. Due to this, caution and tact should be maintained. However, many of these sacral objects have already been destroyed by the masses and did not bring about any reaction."[35]

The mass movement to close churches and mosques in the whole country was started by students of the Naim Frashëri Higher School of Education in Durrës. The choice of town in which the campaign began was not a coincidence. Durrës, which had the largest Albanian port, played host to the most foreigners, both sailors from units sailing into port, and tourists. The Secretary of the local party committee, Rita Marko, regarded the atheization of Durrës, a flagship of "revolutionary Albania," as a priority.[36]

---

31 Dervishi, *Historia e shtetit*, 704.

32 Chosen on March 7, 1966, the new head of the Orthodox Church was already the Metropolitan of the diocese of Gjirokastra, and from March occupied both positions (ASA, AAOC, 1966, d. 1334).

33 Dervishi, *Historia e shtetit*, 705.

34 The main object of this attack was the principles of customary law (i.e. *Kanun*), but formally it was not expressed and Kanun was not formally forbidden by law (see also: Brandon Doll, "The Relationship between the Clan System and Other Institutions in Northern Albania," *Southeast European and Black Sea Studies* 3/2 (May 2003), 160–162).

35 *Praktikat fetare t'i luftojme*, 105.

36 Letter from Rita Marko to the APL Central Commitee Political Bureau, September 1, 1967. ASA, APL Central Committee, 1967, d. 14, p. 12.

In the opinion of Luan Dibra, the model of atheism was created in Durrës, and was copied by other youth organisations. The Committee for youth organisations set up a team to coordinate anti-religious activity, and it divided the propaganda tasks between three groups. The connection to the partisan model was even more visible in Elbasan, where the 15th Cultural Brigade, which was to fight backward customs and superstitions, was established.[37] Praising the acts of Albanian youths, Hamit Beqja emphasised in one of his articles that in the fight against religion, academic discussion was insufficient, but definite action was necessary.[38] Personal attacks on clergymen and religious communities became a common subject of the flete rrufe – wall newspapers hung on town streets, in schools and government offices. The party organ *Zëri i Popullit* inspired atheization activities, counting the clergymen who acted against the Albanian state, as well as criticising "the Roman Pope," who in the encyclical *Populorum Progressio* issued in March 1967 supposedly confirmed his support for capitalism.[39] The daily press provided numerous examples of the inappropriate behaviour of clergymen – backward, greedy and irresponsible. Ilinden Spasse's column in the youth magazine *Religion against science* emphasised the particular role of doctors, who stood on the front line in the fight against the clergy who profited from the cultivation of "people medicine."[40]

The religious fight was not just of a propaganda character. Albanian documentary films, recorded in February and March 1967 and stored in archives, captured scenes of youths destroying churches and the profanation of religious objects. Documents of the Orthodox Church provide numerous examples of "direct action" in the first months of 1967. Youths in Lezhe initiated the campaign of collecting all religious items (crosses, icons and religious literature) found in private homes, in order to place them in the local museum.[41]

Until April 1967 the anti-religious activity appeared to be social action rising from the ranks, organised by local party committees and youth organisations, which enjoyed the quiet support of the state. From a formal perspective, this meant a breach of the constitutional principles guaranteeing freedom of religion, as well as statutes defining the principles of religious community activity. The official stand of the state, after a few months of silence, was expressed by the Act of April 29, 1967, with which the People's Assembly proclaimed Albania as "the first atheist country in the world." Decree 4263 of July 11, 1967 from the Presidium of the People's Assembly decided to transfer all religious property to kolkhozes or local party committees.

---

37 Luan Dibra, "Lufta kunder zakoneve prapanike dje paragjykimeve fetare eshte lufta klasash," *Zëri i Rinise*, February 8, 1967, 1; *Zëri i Rinise*, June 7, 1967, 2.

38 Hamit Beqja, "Vale e fuqishme e revolucionit ideologjik," *Zëri i Popullit*, April 21, 1967, 3.

39 "Vatikani dhe veprimtaria e tij diallezore," *Zëri i Popullit*, January 18, 1967, 4.

40 Ilinden Spasse, "Feja përballe shkences," *Zëri i Rinise*, February 8, 1967, 3. Also: Myzejen Rama, "Forca e shkences dhe feja," *Zëri i Rinise*, March 8, 1967, 1.

41 ASA, AAOC, 1967, d. 1371.

The balance of the "direct action" was discussed widely during the congress of the Union of Working Youths in Albania (the largest youth organisation), which was held in June 1967. The place of honour in the presidium (beside Enver Hoxha) was taken by Martina Ndou from the Mirdita region. This region had for centuries been connected with Catholicism and common law and the young activist was a model of the radical changes: "Youths in Mirdita don't go to church, they don't get married in church and don't christen their children. Great work has been carried out. One of the village elders in Kacinari stated that he did not believe in the Pope and Jesus Christ any more, but in the Party and Comrade Enver."[42]

The legal sanctioning of the practice of destroying sacral objects meant that the duty of continuing the act of destruction was taken on by the local party structures, and the demolition of sacral buildings often took place as part of social events, under the supervision of experienced party activists, who travelled from Tirana. The demolition of village temples was usually conducted in the framework of social actions or as part of the plan carried out by cooperatives.[43] Reports from the field usually painted a picture of cooperation with the aim of eliminating "religious remnants." The afore-mentioned Rita Marko quotes just one example of "the influence of hostile elements." The workers of cooperatives in Gose halted the destruction of temples, demanding a pay rise for such hard work.[44]

One of the most important places for Albanian Catholics, the abbey in Orosh, was blown up.[45] Its fate was shared by a range of buildings which were regarded as useless, including tens of village churches, as well as the Orthodox Cathedral in Tirana. The saved buildings were used for various purposes. The Ministry of Culture and Education defined the criteria according to which some buildings, mainly mosques, were to be maintained as an element of cultural inheritance and treated as a monument. The capital's Et'hem Bey Mosque was recognized as a monument. This place later served as a place of prayer for diplomats working in Tirana, but Albanians were forbidden from praying in this place. A few Bektashi temples, including the main *tekke* in Tirana were changed into retirement homes for the aged. Some of the sacral buildings were changed into cultural centres, warehouses and restaurants. The Roman Catholic Cathedral in Shkoder was transformed into a sports hall, and one of the monasteries became the headquarters of the Sigurimi.[46]

---

42 *Zëri i Rinise*, June 26, 1967, 2.

43 The report published in 1990 by the *Albanian Catholic Bulletin* was unusual in this sense. Inhabitants of the village of Kastrat near Shkoder described the closure of the church as a joint action of the local party structure and the army. A few women tried to stop the closure of the temple and the arrest of the clergymen. The encouragement of the locals to join in the destruction of the church bell turned into a fiasco.

44 Letter from Rita Marko to the APL Central Commitee, 14.

45 De Waal, *Albania Today*, 79.

46 Janice Broun, "The Catholic Church in Albania" in *Catholicism and Politics in Communist Societies*, ed. Pedro Ramet (Durham, NC: Duke University Press, 1990), 423.

The continuation of the destruction of temples were mass rallies in work places and cooperatives. The scenario of such rallies consisted of speeches calling for the judgement of the Church by the people and the condemnation of its actions. At some rallies, alleged sons of clergymen appeared, accusing their fathers of hostile action against the state. The instructors who appeared at the mass rallies drew attention to the necessity of removing references to God and religion from the language, and also answered questions about the sense of the coming changes.

On November 13, 1967, the People's Assembly passed a law annulling the statutes concerning religious communities from 1949–1951, which defined the rights of religions and the status of the congregations. In the November issue of the monthly magazine *Nendori*, there was information about the closure of 2,169 religious buildings previously active in the country.[47]

The closure of the temples was accompanied by an intensive propaganda campaign, which was intended to strengthen the materialistic and anti-religious view of society. In the years 1967–1968 the Naim Frasheri publishing house printed over a dozen works (some of which were brochures) designated for atheist educational aims, but also representing initial material for the preparation of press articles, reports etc. These included the work of Mina Qirici *The Miracle of Faith*, with a series of caricatures of clergymen; *Mental Illness, and Religion* (Ulvi Vehbiu) and *The Damage of Rites and the Religious World* (Sotir Melka). A group of Albanian ethnologists (Edlira Çela, Mark Tirtja and Zihni Sako) dealt with the problem of non-religiousness in Albanian folk culture.[48] The satirical book *Naked Religion* by Bik Pepa accused all believers of naivety and the tendency to conduct servile behaviour, described using caricatures of people with the heads of donkeys, listening to instructions from a fat clergyman.[49]

Historians played a specific role in the anti-religion campaign. Their task was to prove the non-religiousness of the Albanian nationalist movement, and in connection with this to reinterpret the history of the Albanian nation. The Institute of History in Tirana created the two-volume *History of Albania* in 1965–1967, regarded until the end of the 1980s as one of the greatest achievements of Albanian human scientists.[50] Both this synthesis, and the monograph issued later reaching back to the nationalist uprising in the 19th Century highlighted the working character of the Albanian nationalist movement. Albanians were to be the only nation who had rejected religion for nationalism, with the belief that enemies used religion to divide their nation and to hinder its free development. The presentation of religion as

47 In 1967, 608 churches and monasteries as well as 327 catholic churches were closed. The Jewish community lost the synagogue which functioned in Tirana. Ramet, *Nihil obstat*, 217.

48 Markus W. Peters, *Geschichte der Katolischen Kirche in Albanien 1919–1993* (Wiesbaden: Harrasowitz, 2003), 211–212.

49 Bik Pepa, *Feja lakuriq. Vjersha satirike* (Tirana: Shtëpia Botuese Naim Frashëri), 1967.

50 Skender Islami and Kristo Frasheri, eds., *Historia e Shqipërise* (Tirana: Shtëpia Botuese Naim Frashëri, 1965–1967).

a way of foreign infiltration constantly appeared in accusations directed at the Church from the beginning of the communist rule. At the end of the 1960s, the theories of the Illyrian origin of Albanians and the conquering of Illyrian land by the Romans were enriched with an element of "forced Christianity", carried out by the invaders. In this context, it was easy to find analogies between the political-religious invasions conducted by the Romans and the similar one carried out by the Italians in the years 1939–1943.

Religious issues were willingly dealt with by historians who looked into economic history. A particularly strong argument, directed against the Church was the definition of it as a hindrance to development. Figures showing the under development of Albanian industry in the inter-war years were frequently shown in tandem with the material state of religious communities. The Church was accused of hindering the social advance of young people, encouraging them to leave their family home. Religion as a factor of the social-economic inequality of women was written about by Hulusi Hako, in the work *We Accuse Religion*, published in 1968.[51] His attack was aimed mainly at Muslims, who kept women almost as slaves and were opposed to them earning money outside the home. The scientific research centre into atheism was created in Shkoder, where in 1970, in one of the closed Catholic churches, the "Exhibition of Atheism" opened, and five years later became a museum. The majority of the exhibits collected in the museum were posters with anti-religious themes.[52]

In the 1970s, the next stage of desacralization was attempted with the renaming of towns or villages whose names referred to Christianity. In September 1975, the government decided to change the names of 90 places, with the village of Shenkoll (Saint Nicholas) given the name of Ylli i Kuq (Red Star). The removal of religious elements from public life was also helped by Act 5354 from September 1975, which contained the following sentence: "Citizens with names inappropriate from the political, ideological and moral perspective are obliged to change them." The Act assumed that those people which were affected by the law would willingly change their names, and those that didn't do so by themselves would receive a name from a social organisation in their place of residency.[53]

After closing the religious buildings, the clergymen who had been "released" from their liturgical service returned to their family homes or were given shelter by friends, in order to "return" to society in a new role. The places of re-education for former clergymen were most frequently agricultural cooperatives. Those who decided to continue their religious activities in secret were sentenced and placed in labour camps. Some of them paid for their activity with their lives. On March 28, 1973, *New*

---

51 Hulusi Hako, *Akuzojme fene* (Tirana: Shtëpia Botuese Naim Frashëri, 1968).

52 Clariss Brubaker-Smith, *The Song of Unsung Heroes. Chronicles from God's Messengers Who Helped Bring Down Those Iron Curtain Walls* (New York: WestBow Press, 2011), 78–79.

53 *Gazeta Zyrtare*, September 11, 1975, 2.

York Times published information about the execution of the priest Shtjefën Kurti, who had been found guilty of illegally baptising a child.[54]

Criticism from the Western press was ignored by the Albanian press, who applied the tactic of the religion problem not existing. In November 1976, in his report for the VII APL Congress, Hoxha did not mention religion, while at the VI Congress in November 1971 two pages had been sacrificed to the influence of religion in Albanian society, describing the removal of religious community leaderships as a "decisive victory, which prepared the ground for the total emancipation of people from religious superstitions." The constitution which was passed in 1976 contained a formal ban on the creation of religious institutions and the rejection of their existence by the state.[55] In the Penal Code from 1977, the issue of "religious crimes" was covered by Article 55. Any form of religious propaganda, including the "publication, distribution and sale of literature of this type" was threatened with imprisonment from three to ten years. In order to be sentenced for breaking Article 55, it was sufficient to illegally possess a copy of the Bible. The article contained the warning that, during wartime, or if the court recognized the high social damage of the act, the term of imprisonment could not be less than ten years, but could even be punished by the death penalty. In the same year, the Franciscan Fran Mark Gjini from Shkoder stood in front of the court for illegal possession of the Bible and religious literature. Although he claimed that he had found the Bible in the park where foreign tourists spent time, he received a punishment of imprisonment for 12 years.

At the end of the 1960s, the press anxiously reported that many people, mainly the elderly, but also partially communist youngsters continued to practise religion. The religious practices which had transferred to the domestic arena turned out to be almost impossible to control by the security services. Just as in the Ottoman times, the most common form of resistance were the figures concerning Crypto-Christianity. Declaring themselves as atheists in public, Albanians often conducted domestic religious services, left their work place during religious holidays, or also observed fasts. In 1972 the Bashkimi newspaper wrote about a Muslim healer, who had created a very profitable business out of healing until the government took an interest. In the public trial, it was emphasised that the threat of poisonous religious ideology could not be ignored and underestimated.[56] In 1985 *Bashkimi* wrote about the case of a private house in the Partizani district of Vlora, where a "small chapel" was set up. People of an advanced age met there, and the service was conducted by the owner's son. At the IX APL Congress in November 1986, one of the party ideologists, Hulusi Hako, delivered a speech in which he pained over the fact that, despite

---

54 The official version presented by the Albanians described Kurti as a long-term agent of the British secret services. Jacques, *Albanians*, 495.

55 William Simmons, ed., *The Constitutions of the Communist World* (Leiden: Sjithoff & Noordhoff, 1980), 17, 19.

56 Sabrina Bowers, "Stalinism in Albania: Domestic Affairs under Enver Hoxha," *East European Quarterly* (January 1989): 448.

activities taken by the "powerful revolutionary movement directed against religion and backward customs," there was proof that "there remained some religious practices and their accompanying superstitions."[57]

After the death of Enver Hoxha, a slow liberalization of the government's anti-religious policy took place. In 1988, the ban issued on the naming of newborns with Christian and Muslim names was practically the last anti-religious act of the government. In the same year, the last surviving Catholic bishop, Nikola Troshani, left prison. The conference of ministers of foreign affairs of the Balkan states in February 1988 began by placing diplomatic pressure on Hoxha's successor, Ramiz Alia, to change the policy against religion. The Greek government declared on a few occasions that the lack of spiritual services for Orthodox Greeks should be understood as an expression of political repression against minorities by the Albania government.[58]

In the same year, some of religious buildings were renovated; however, this mainly concerned mosques. A sign of the changes in religious policy was the agreement of the government in 1988 to allow clergymen from other countries to visit Albania. In the summer of 1988, Tirana was visited by Orthodox clergymen, as well as imam Vehbi, working in the Albanian Sunni Muslim community in Detroit. In August, Mother Teresa of Calcutta travelled to Tirana for the first time on a three-day visit. She met with Hoxha's widow, Nexhmije, as well as with directors of scientific and cultural institutions. The liberalization of government policy began to gain speed. Repression against secret religious services was no longer used, but was even tolerated with the granting of holidays for workers during religious holidays.

Of the 1,050 mosques active before 1967, over two hundred had been completely destroyed, and the others remained in a state of disrepair. Only a few buildings were kept in good condition as cultural monuments. In the Bektashi community, among two hundred teachers – *baba* (father), only five survived the period of atheism. Out of the 60 Bektashi temples (*tekke*) open before 1967, at the beginning of the 1990s only six were successfully reopened. The losses of the second largest religious community in Albania, in other words the Orthodox community, turned out to be even more harmful. The majority of churches were destroyed or closed. The main Orthodox Cathedral in Tirana was destroyed, and a hotel was built in its place. The last head of the Orthodox Church, Archbishop Damian Kokoneshi, died in prison in November 1973.[59]

---

57 Ramet, *Nihil obstat*, 218.

58 "Travelling in an Atheist State," *Albanian Catholic Bulletin* (1990): 54.

59 Ramet, *Nihil obstat*, 217.

Chapter VIII: First steps to de-communisation

The essence of Albanian government is the drive towards leaving the state in the hands of clans possessing absolute power, who will wipe other clans off the surface of the earth and decide exclusively about the fate of the nation, taking advantage of all privileges given by political power. Only in this way can the paradox which surprises all be explained: the combination in the only ruling party of former communists with former political prisoners and former Sigurimi members.[1]

When, in 1989, communist regimes in Eastern Europe were collapsing, Albania tried to distance itself from the transformations. Speaking at the congress of trade unions in December 1989, the head of the state, Ramiz Alia, said the following words: "There are those abroad who ask: Are the same processes taking place in Albania as in other countries of Eastern Europe? We answer that question decidedly and categorically: No, in Albania there is no such process..."[2]

The purges in personnel consistently conducted for forty years by the government of Enver Hoxha meant that all the best individuals from the dictator's environment had been eliminated. At the end of the 1980s in the APL Political Bureau there was a lack of fully independent politicians, and even more of someone who could be associated with the myth of a political hero and a necessity for the nation. Such authority was out of reach of "Hoxha's pupil" Ramiz Alia, known for his opportunism, or "the Commandant's companion for life" – Nexhmije Hoxha. During the times when the next communist regimes were falling like a house of cards, the Albanian party leadership was absorbed by disputes about how to best continue the work of the Commandant. The disputes in the leadership had a domino effect and led to the gradually increasing slackness of the state, which until recently had worked effectively and followed orders. Discussions concerning the political future of Albania stopped being the sole property of the central government, but spread to the lower levels of administration, to the army and the police. The sixty-something politicians dominating in the party failed to recognize the real power which the Albanian youths, who at the beginning of the nineties were entering their adult lives, had at their disposal. This generation, which had not experienced the traumatic times of revolutionization, in 1989 utilized the gradually weaker information blockade, learning about the events which were taking place in Eastern Europe.

---

[1] Fatos Lubonja, "Wolność wciąż zagrożona" in: *Albania – wolność zagrożona*, 258.

[2] Elez Biberaj, *Shqipëria në tranzicion. Rruga e veshtire drejt Demokracise* (Tirana: ORA, 2001), 63.

An important impulse for events taking place in Albania was the overthrow of N. Ceaușescu in December 1989. The dictator of Romania was firstly "betrayed" by his own nation, and soon afterwards by the Albanian leadership. The fall of the Romanian leader, who had been regarded in Tirana as a powerful socialist politician, could be seen on television screens. During the time of the events in Romania, western news agencies informed of the distribution of leaflets in Tirana and Vlora by young people, which were quickly removed from the streets by the police. In his New Year's speech to the nation, the leader of the state, Ramiz Alia, ensured that Albania would still follow the road of socialism. Continuing this theme in January 1990, he publicly stated that Albania was a democratic country, and having only one party did not hinder democracy in any way.

The lessons from Romania did affect the situation in Albania. The first large-scale social protests took place on January 14 in Shkoder. A crowd tried to destroy a statue of Stalin.[3] The police succeeded in restoring order, but a few days later the statue was discretely removed. Two weeks later, students entered the streets of Tirana, demanding a reduction in repression and the removal of E. Hoxha's name from the name of the university. On January 22, 1990, the IX Central Commitee Plenum of the Albanian Labour Party was held. On the day before the proceedings, the daily *Zëri i Popullit* convinced readers about the inevitability of changes taking place in the world, to which Albania must adapt, because it doesn't want to be isolated. The proceedings of the IX Plenum took place under the motto: "Our duty today – is the revolutionization of the party and country." In a statement which was placed in the press after the plenum, the following words were found: "We have fought against revisionism for 30 years, but we must draw conclusions from what is happening in other countries of Eastern Europe. We did not want isolation before and we still don't want it now."[4]

Between the IX plenum, and the May visit of the UN Secretary General, Javier Perez de Cuellar, the ruling party daily *Zëri i Popullit* radically changed its views. "Human rights," which had previously been projected as a banal idea, began to gain a positive context, whereas the idea of political pluralism slowly became accepted as a necessary condition for Albania to adapt to standards in other countries.[5] In April 1990, the Albanian government allowed its citizens to telephone relatives living in other countries. As the majority of citizens did not possess their own telephones, the conversations took place in government offices, but it was the first chance for decades to contact family living abroad.[6] On May 13, 1990, the People's Assembly (parliament) met. On behalf of the Council of Ministers, the deputy prime minister, Manush Myftiu, delivered the key speech in which he stated that an opportunity

---

3 Biberaj, *Shqipëria në tranzicion*, 65.

4 "Thellimi i revolucionizmit të jetës se partise e të vendit – detyre e perhershme," *Zëri i Popullit*, January 21, 1990, 1–2.

5 Shaban Demiraj, "Ne rastin e 435-vjetorit të botimit e Mesharit," *Zëri i Popullit* 23 (1990): 3.

6 Biberaj, *Shqipëria në tranzicion*, 70–71.

for people who had earlier been convicted to return to society should be created.[7] Parliament passed an act which was designed to rebuild the law in the country. The Ministry of Justice was recreated, as were the professions of lawyer and solicitor, which were formally banned in 1967.[8] As a result of the changes in the Penal Code, it was possible to issue the death penalty in 11 cases (the Penal Code from 1977 included 34 cases).

After border controls were sharpened in the middle of 1990, attacks on embassies began – thousands of people besieged the headquarters of diplomatic representatives, attempting to enter their grounds and gain the chance to leave the country. In July, the "Battle of Kavaje" took place. Initially, demonstrations there had an exclusively economic nature, and above all concerned the fair division of the property of kolkhozes. Special police units pacified the town with extreme brutality. One of the young workers died, while over a dozen people with heavy wounds ended up in hospital. The funeral of the victim was attended by 30 thousand people, the same as the population of Kavaje. The funeral procession passed from the cemetery to the party building, which was torched and demolished. Before reinforcements arrived, the inhabitants of the town ruled for one whole day. The events in Kavaje were just part of the visible examples of disintegration of the state and greater and greater impotence of the government against social protests.

Spontaneous acts of protest were initially void of any coordination. Through the forty years of Enver Hoxha's government, no real opposition camp could form, or even rebel political groups, which had not been subjected to repression. The lack of any opposition meant that the first groups fighting against the dominating party were created by its activists who had previously not played a significant role, but saw an opportunity in the coming changes. A new political power was formed during the students' strike, lasting from November 1990, at the capital's university. The demonstrators named it the Independent Organisation of Democratic Students and Young Intellectuals. To the postulates concerning the increased social care for students and the right to establish organisations, other postulates demanding the widening of and guarantee of citizens' rights, as well as changes in economic policies were added in December.[9] The case of the students' strike became a basic problem discussed by the APL Central Commitee Political Bureau (December 11, 1990). In the report opening the meeting, Ramiz Alia admitted that the situation had an extraordinary character, and the ferment of the student environment could move to the workers' and military environment. This led to the necessity of entering into conversations with the protesters, before the demonstrations spread throughout the whole country.[10] On the same day, in the capital's Brigade Palace, a meeting of the leader of the Albanian state, Ramiz Alia, with a group of students and scientific workers of the

---

7 *Zëri i Popullit*, May 14, 1990, 2.

8 Smirnova, *Istoria Albanii*, 357.

9 Aleksander Meksi, ed., *Dhjetor '90. Dokumente & Materiale* (Tirana: UET Press, 2010), 11.

10 Meksi, *Dhjetor '90*, 12–14.

University of Tirana, took place. During the conversations, which were broadcast on state television, there was a declaration to build state law (shteti ligjor), as well as to hold new elections in which independent political organisations could take place.[11] A day later, in the student town in Tirana, a meeting was held in which participants of the meeting with Alia presented the project to establish the first independent political party, which was to be named the Democratic Party (Partia Demokratike).

In just a few days, the party statute and program were created. The latter emphasised the postulate of making the country democratic and of conducting free parliamentary elections.[12] The founding declaration was signed by 285 people, and a charismatic doctor, Sali Berisha, was chosen as the party leader. The support of R. Alia allowed him to publish a few articles about "state law" and "the freedom of speech," which appeared in the magazines: *Bashkimi* and *Drita*.[13] His influence grew dramatically when he participated in negotiations between the government and the students bodies. The party was registered on December 19, 1990, on the basis of a decree passed two days earlier by the presidium of the People's Assembly "concerning the establishment of political organisations and societies."[14] Soon afterwards, three more parties were established: the Agrarian Party, the Ecology Party, and the Republican Party, as well as the Omonia organisation which represented the Greek minority.

Information passed on 16 December 1990 through the newspaper of the ruling party *Zëri i Popullit* concerning the registration of the first opposition parties, was purposefully placed next to reports of demonstrations on the streets of Elbasan and Durrës. Doubts as to the social results of political pluralism were expressed in the article "Sphere of tolerance" by Sedat Braja. In the author's opinion, modern Albania stood in front of two threats: radical de-communism and total dismissal of atheist views. The text appeared a few days after the meeting between Ramiz Alia and the Democratic Party of Albania leadership and clearly referred to the postulates of punishing those responsible, which appeared in the opposition press.[15] A few days later, Pandeli Korçari wrote in a similar spirit, warning of the threat connected with excluding the socially present atheists.[16] The newly-established political parties announced their priorities of guaranteeing freedom of gatherings and the release of all political prisoners. Also important for the elimination of the remnants of the previous epoch was Decree 7449 of January 1991, which restricted the freedom of weapon usage by the security bodies and border guards to life-threatening cases.[17]

---

[11] Meksi, *Dhjetor '90*, 28–59.

[12] "Platforma elektorale e Partise Demokratike," *Rilindja Demokratike* 9 (1991): 1–2.

[13] On September 17, 1990, in *Bashkimi* was a Berisha's article. *Democracy and Humanism – An Inseparable Pair* (p. 2–3). Biberaj, *Shqipëria në tranzicion*, 57.

[14] *Zëri i Popullit* 302 (1990): 1–2.

[15] Sedat Braja, "Hapesirat e tolerancës," *Zëri i Popullit* 13 (1991): 2.

[16] Pandeli Korçari, "E kerkoi populli kete kuvend," *Zëri i Popullit* 23 (1991): 2.

[17] *Gazeta Zyrtare* 1 (1991): 11–14.

The border guards, who stopped shooting at escapees, as they had done during the times of Hoxha, were unable to stop the exodus of countrymen fleeing through the mountains to Greece and Macedonia. In the spring of 1991, 563 political prisoners were released. In March 1991, the government stated that, although it had released all political prisoners, there were still 64 people in prison who had been sentenced for such serious crimes as: sabotage, abduction, terrorism and espionage.

While preparing for the parliamentary elections, the main political forces fought for the votes of society, whose political preferences remained a great unknown. The Democratic Party leadership was faced in 1991 with the difficult problem of how to widen their range of activity and conduct an effective election campaign in a society which for tens of years had not experienced such a campaign. The main party organ, *Rilindja Demokratike*, was issued twice a week, with a circulation of 60 thousand and could not compete with the APL newspaper – *Zëri i Popullit*, issued 6 days per week with a circulation of hundreds of thousands.[18] The opposition press practically did not reach rural areas. Besides a few towns where there were spontaneous anti-communist demonstrations (Shkoder, Kavaja and Tirana), in other towns there was a problem with even organizing rallies for the Democrats. The southern part of the country in 1991 was hostile towards the growing democratic opposition, and its leaders were regarded as "outsiders" – representatives of the northern part of the country. In Tirana itself, where the fight for the greatest number of seats took place, the range of activities for the Democrats was limited. The vast majority of demonstrations and rallies were held in the student town and near the university.

The pre-election atmosphere was marked by the destruction of monuments. On December 21, 1990, in Tirana, the statue of Joseph Stalin was destroyed, and his name was removed from the names of state institutions. Further destruction of monuments (including ones in memory of E. Hoxha) was to be prevented by Decree 7459 from February 1991. Monuments were regarded as symbols of the state, connected with the history of Albania, and their damage was to be punished by imprisonment of up to 3 years. With respect to the mass demonstrations, the decree turned out to be a dead letter. In February 1991 a crowd gathered in the centre of Tirana and knocked over a statue of Hoxha, but the police response was limited to warning shots fired in the air. The idea of freedom was more frequently associated with anarchy. The passion for destruction, providing a release of the emotions built up over years, encouraged people to perform acts of vandalism and to destroy everything identified with the hated state.

The date of the first multi-party elections was chosen as March 31, 1991. This was the first such experience for Albanians since the beginning of the 1920s. The elections were won by the communist Albanian Party of Labour. The Democrats dominated the large towns: Tirana, Shkoder and Durrës, but were represented in

---

[18] Vickers and Pettifier, *Albania* 40.

parliament by only 75 deputies as compared to 169 seats for the communists.[19] The mainstay of the communists remained the southern and north-eastern parts of the country. Demonstrations accusing the election results of being falsified began in Shkoder on April 2. When the demonstrators set fire to the APL headquarters, the police opened fire on them. Among those killed was one of the leaders of the DPA in Shkoder – Arben Broçi, who had tried to pacify the demonstrating crowd.

Without the participation of the opposition deputies, who protested against the events in Shkoder, the first session of the new parliament took place on April 29. The deputies voted on a change of the country's name to the Republic of Albania. Its first President was Ramiz Alia, although the opposition boycotted the election of the head of state. The nightmarish constitution from 1976 was updated, with the introduction of a wider range of rights for citizens and a division of power. The formal end of the Sigurimi's activities took place on July 12, 1991. In its place, the National Information Service ShIK was created, in which only a small part of the communist political police officers found employment.[20] The government formed after the elections, led by Fatos Nano, lasted just two months. Representatives of the democratic opposition were successfully incorporated in the new government, known as a stabilizing government, led by Ylli Bufi. The exposé of the new premier contained a dramatic appeal for foreign help to protect the country against a humanitarian disaster and destabilisation. At the same time, the prediction of a shock therapy was announced, with the intention of entrusting the fate of the country and the budget to the new owners of the national property.[21]

The two largest political groups seemed at first to follow the plan of "restoration of normality" and liquidation of the remains of Hoxha's era. Passed in September 1991, the act concerning trade unions guaranteed the possibility of negotiating workers' rights for every union with over 300 members. On September 30, 1991, the People's Assembly passed an act recognising all former political prisoners as innocent, with the exception of those who had carried out acts of terrorism and murder.

The cooperation between the democrats and the socialists in the government ended in November 1991. The growing popularity of the democrats pushed S. Berisha into a political offensive. The unwillingness to cooperate between the main political powers and the economic differences led to the dissolution of parliament and the setting of the date for the next elections in March 1992. In these elections, the competition for the Democratic Party of Albania was to be a "new" political force. On June 13, 1991, the tenth and last APL Congress began. The party was renamed the Socialist Party of Albania (Partia Socialiste e Shqipërise, PSSh).[22] The renaming of the party was, in the reality of 1991, a rather risky step. The place of a known

19 Dervishi, *Historia e shtetit*, 802–805.

20 Sabrina Ramet, *Eastern Europe: Politics, Culture, and Society since 1939* (Bloomington: Indiana University Press, 1998), 271.

21 Vickers and Pettifier, *Albania*, 67.

22 Afrim Krasniqi, *Partite politike në Shqipëri (1920–2006)* (Tirana: Eurolindja, 2006), 327.

party which was “familiar” in the Albanian mentality was taken by an unpredictable political group, which was led by little known medium-level activists. At its head was the economist and journalist – Fatos Nano.

On December 4, 1991, parliament agreed on a new election ordinance, combining the majority system, used in the previous elections, with elements of the proportional representation system. The number of 250 seats was reduced to 140, of which 40 represented a bonus for the strongest parties. The right to nominate candidates was gained by all existing party and social organisations.[23]

The growing economic-social crisis convinced Albanians to choose a new political option. The March elections in 1992 brought a victory for the Democratic Party of Albania, which won 92 seats in the new parliament (to 38 for the socialists). The previous opposition took full responsibility for the state, which for many Albanians signified the end of communism in the country. At the press conference after the election victory, Sali Berisha told the nation and the gathered journalists that Albanian communism had ended. On April 8, 1992, Berisha reached the peak of the political ladder, replacing R. Alia as the President of Albania. The head of the government was a representative of the Democratic Party – Aleksander Meksi, and the function of parliament leader was taken on by the former political prisoner and leader of the Democrats in Shkoder – Pjeter Arbnori. The Democratic majority in parliament forced through an increase in the President's competencies, explaining this due to the country's particular situation. The first months of the government's rule showed a clear tendency of the party's leaders to centralize the government and to limit the independence of the media, which led to the definition of this system of government as “Berisha's dictatorship.”

To maintain political influence, the governing party placed particular emphasis on strengthening its “hard-core electorate,” who consisted of former political prisoners and their families. Representing their interests, the Association of Former Political Prisoners contained over 70 thousand people in its ranks. In order to make it possible for them to integrate with society, a three-month legal course was organized so that prisoners could obtain work in administrations. The old problem for Albania – the lack of qualified staff – returned not only in regards to the Justice Department. The civil servants who were hurriedly educated were to replace the old communist staff. In the first months of the DPA government a large part of the procurators and judges were changed, which left the idea of removing political influence from the area of justice under a question mark. The easiest and most obvious way of “repairing the harm of the communist period” was to punish the former decision makers. The first signal of de-communism was the removal of symbols of the previous period from the national emblems and flags, as well as the banning of communist party activity. Using charges of fraud and excessive use of power, the government imprisoned most of the former APL leadership. The wave of cases led to the impris-

[23] *Zëri i Popullit*, December 5, 1990, 1–2.

onment in 1993 of Nexhmije Hoxha for 11 years and Ramiz Alia for 8 years.[24] The break from communism was also a pretext for purges in the army, police and courts.

In parallel with the political changes, the mechanics of a free market appeared in the Albanian economy. The XI Central Commitee Plenum, which met on February 6–7, 1990, agreed to the establishment of private firms for trade and crafts, but on condition that only members of the family could be employed. This meant the acceptance of private economic activity in trading, services and production on a small scale. The acceptable prices and charges were also defined, as was the level of taxation. The parliamentary presidium in 1990 also broke another fundamental principle – foreign capital was allowed into the Albanian market, permitting investment and economic activity inside Albania by foreigners, as well as Albanians living abroad.[25] The legislative changes which opened the road to a free market took place slowly. The government unwillingly and slowly introduced in 1990 the independence of economic organisations which were still in state hands. Enterprises gained the possibility of independently selling their own products on the market. The local communist party structures retained control over the distribution of just stable products until 1991. In June 1991, a table of maximum prices and charges for services was introduced with the aim of halting the spiral of inflation. Ministerial civil servants were to control the market and monitor possible shortages in supplies. However, on November 1, 1991, prices were freed (with the exception of a few basic food products).[26] The full liberalization of prices was introduced in August 1992 and brought about a violent increase in prices for basic food products of 300–400%.[27]

The year 1991 came with the first phase of privatisation of property which had in the past been gathered by the communists. Even before the parliamentary elections in March 1992, over 20 thousand shops and small craft workshops had moved into private hands.[28] The privatisation also concerned most of the land belonging to cooperatives, together with their assets. The act concerning land removed the collective ownership right and restored individual ownership. By June 1992 this had covered 86% of the land previously owned by cooperatives. Each farming family which had previously tended the land received part of it depending on the size of the family. The movable assets of the cooperatives were generally stolen or destroyed, and the new owners lacked funds necessary to start production. Even in 1999, the sight of tilling the land with a wooden plough, tied to oxen, was a common appearance in Albanian villages. The inefficiency of agriculture and the lack of funds for investment inevitably led to shortages of food supplies in the market.

---

24 Robert Bideleux and Ian Jeffries, *The Balkans: A Post-communist History* (London: Taylor & Francis, 2007), 45–46.

25 Kaser, "Economic System", 294.

26 *Zëri i Popullit*, November 3, 1991, 2.

27 Bideleux and Jeffries, *Balkans*, 51.

28 Biberaj, *Shqipëria në tranzicion*, 292.

With an income of 200 dollars per inhabitant, at the turn of the nineties, Albania belonged to the poorest countries in Europe. The state of the economy in 1991 was most often defined by the catastrophic indicator of the 40% drop in value of industrial production in just one year. Thanks to the lifting of the constitutional ban on foreign loans, in 1993 it was possible to significantly reduce the huge budget deficit, and to lower inflation to the level of 40% per year. At the end of 1992 the country's debt equalled 600 million dollars. The average salary, which in 1992 equalled 20–25 dollars monthly, rose by very little in the next two years. Official data about unemployment showed the level of 35%, however, western experts gave the number at 50–55%.[29]

The economic policies of the Democratic Party were a combination of impotence and improvisation. Although privatisation was introduced on a wide scale, it mainly concerned trading and transport. The privatisation of large firms from key sectors (transport, telecommunications, the exploration industry) was delayed due to the lack of suitable offers or political problems. The impressive growth in the number of firms active in the market was mainly due to one-person firms dealing in retail trade. The scale of investment of foreign capital was much lower than expected, and the investment that did appear did not help the country's economic growth. Any attempt to limit the level of unemployment was especially difficult in the situation where any vacations were applied for by people without suitable qualifications. Changes in the exchange rate between the Albanian currency (lek) and the US dollar did not reflect the state of the Albanian economy, but were mainly connected with the inflow of currency from Albanian guest workers abroad. The income of those people working "on the black market" in Greece equalled 800 million–1 billion USD. The state was financed to a large extent thanks to the help of hundreds of thousands countrymen working abroad and began to come out of its deep crisis. The country had one of the highest in Europe increases in GDP per year (5%) and inflation dropped to 10%. The guest workers solved the problem of overcrowding in the country. In reality, being able to maintain a large family in free market conditions was extremely difficult and those who had no family members abroad were sentenced to poverty. Leaving the country and sending money back for family members became not just a chance for survival, but also the most important source of income for the nation.

The specifics of the Albanian experience during the transformation was the parallel return to the public forum of political pluralism, the multi-party system, as well as religion and religious practices. For the vast majority of Albanian society, the appearance of religious ceremonies and proceedings in public was something they had never experienced before. In 1990, Albania signed the Declaration of Human Rights, which included a clause about the freedom of religion, annulling the anti-religious legislation of Hoxha's times. On 1 November, 1999, in Shkoder, the recently released Catholic priest Simon Jubani conducted the first government-approved public mass,

---

[29] Ian Jeffries, *Socialist Economies and the Transition to the Market: A Guide* (New York: Routledge, 1993), 418.

with the participation of a few thousand believers.[30] The next mass was attended by about 50–60 thousand people. Two months later, mufti Ibrahim Bala, who had been working as a teacher, inaugurated the activity of the Et'hem Bey Mosque in Tirana. In November 1990, the Lead Mosque in Shkoder opened for worshippers, and soon afterwards the mosques in Berat and Shijak followed suit. Within the framework of cooperation between the largest religious communities an Inter-religion Commission was established, thanks to which delegates of all active groups participated in the following religious ceremonies.[31]

The rebuilding of the religious communities was mainly conducted by clergymen released from the labour camps and ad hoc committees. The Muslim community was led by mufti Hafiz Sabri Koçi, who returned to clerical activity after 20 years spent in prison. The process, which is defined in modern Albanian works as the return to normality, did not take place without some disturbances. The first attempt to conduct a mass in the Franciscan church in Tirana, which took place on 6 January 1991, finished unsuccessfully, and the closed church was protected by law and order forces from the crowd. A similar situation was seen in 1991 during the first attempts to open Orthodox churches in the south of the country.[32]

The opening of the first Orthodox Cathedral in Tirana on March 31, 1991, had a special significance. The ceremony was attended by, besides members of the diplomatic corps, the leadership of the DPA with Sali Berisha at its head. With regard to the upcoming elections, *Rilindja Demokratike* published a number of interviews with clergymen working in Albania, which convinced readers that there was no antagonism between Islam and democracy, and that Muslim clergymen remained apolitical.[33] Particular controversy was created by the fact that the Albanian Autocephalous Orthodox Church was led by Greek clergymen. Among the 22 surviving clergymen none could lead the church in accordance with the Canon. An initiative to select its head was taken on by the Ecumenical Patriarch. On August 2, 1992, the Greek bishop, Anastasios Jannulatos, was inaugurated as the Archbishop of Tirana and Albania. This step, which was seen as a threat to the sovereignty of Albania, united the nationalist and anti-Greek communities in a joint protest and led to hostility in Albanian-Greek relations. The Albanian government's objections to the appointment of a Greek national to the position of Church's head blocked the normal functioning of the Orthodox Church until 1997.

The new government of Albania, dominated by politicians from the Democratic Party of Albania hesitated between the choice of the westernization option, signifying an openness to West Europe, and the Albanian-Islam option. Albania was one of the first post-communist countries to apply for membership of NATO, empha-

[30] Peters, *Geschichte der Katholischen Kirche in Albanien*, 233.

[31] Agim Musaj, "Miting i madh fetar në Kavajë," *Rilindja Demokratike* 4 (1991): 4; Ivah Mehilli, "Pas çerek shekulli në xhaminë e Tiranës," *Rilindja Demokratike* 5 (1991): 1.

[32] Ridvan Peshkepia, "Devocion besimtaresh," *Rilindja Demokratike* 3 (1991): 6.

[33] Emin Barçi, "Sherbesa fetare nuk ka asgje, vec shpirti," *Rilindja Demokratike* 20 (1991): 4; N. Mahmudi, "Demokracia dhe islamizmi," *Rilindja Demokratike* 29 (1991): 4.

sising that, as opposed to other candidate countries, there were no foreign armies stationed in its territory. The long attempts to renew relations with the USA led to a happy result in 1991. The Americans recognized that, after the legalization of opposition political parties and the first free elections in Albania, it had met the basic requirements of a democratic country.[34] The visit of Sali Berisha to the White House (June 1992) confirmed the desire of Albania to become a strategic partner of the United States in the Balkan region and to gain American support in its process of political-economic transformation.[35]

In 1990, Albania recognised its responsibility for the Corfu Incident, and on May 22, 1991, the British Foreign Office agreed to restore diplomatic relations between the two countries.[36] The matter of returning Albanian gold was positively viewed by London. The request of Albania to obtain membership of the OSCE was met in June 1991. Doubts concerning the future of Albania were created by the controversial decision in December 1992 to join the Organization of Islamic Cooperation. This decision, taken without consultation with parliament, was a purely pragmatic one, however it created the opinion in the world's press that Albania was an Islamic country, inclined to cooperate more with Arab countries than Western Europe. With hindsight, the decision from December 1992 seems to be fully understandable with respect to Albania's international situation at the time. Fears of the Bosnian conflict spreading to Kosovo, as well as the growing pressure from its southern neighbour meant that Berisha's team also looked for allies in the Middle East. This was connected with the hope of Albanians concerned with potential economic aid from the Arab states and Turkey.[37]

After the first five years of the transformation, the press connected with Sali Berisha's party presented Albania as an oasis of peace in the restless Balkans. However, this peace seemed to be superficial. In the political life of a country described as "democratic," there was a systematic increase in the role of people raised in the reality of common law and the dark practices of the communist regime. For them "conquering the capital" was connected with the belief that power once gained is not given away voluntarily. They described their political mission as the necessity to defend the country against the return of communism. The new generation of politicians were unable to and did not want to demarcate the borders between politics and business. In a world of unclear interests which was difficult to foreigners to understand, the financial disproportion of Albanian society grew. For people who had been taught the principles of egalitarianism for their whole lives, this was an extremely frustrating experience.

---

34 Hall, *Albania and the Albanians* (London: Pinter Reference, 1994), 194.

35 Biberaj, *Shqipëria në tranzicion*, 352–353.

36 Vickers and Pettifier, *Albania*, 224.

37 Besides the extreme National Rebirth Party, led by Abdi Baleta, the remaining parties were not connected solely with Islam – Natalie Clayer, "Zoti në vendin e mercedesëve," *Përpjekja*, vol. 11, no. 20 (2005): 17.

The new history of Albanian communism? Instead of an epilogue

On September 6, 2011, a special session of the Albanian parliament took place, with the intention of commemorating the 65th anniversary of the Postribe Uprising, as it was described by Albanian historians. The Speaker of the Assembly, Jozefina Topalli, while describing the historic role of the events in Postribe, sharply criticised the previous activity of Albanian historians: "The Postribe Uprising was the first anti-communist uprising in Europe, and I have one question for the historians: where are you? Why do you not write about it, why do you not say the truth? It wouldn't hurt anyone. I invite you to reopen this new chapter."[1]

Topalli's speech from September 6, 2011, is part of the rhetoric which, since the victorious parliamentary elections in 2009, Sali Berisha's ruling Democratic Party of Albania has used. The idea of *rishikimi i historise* (literally: a revision of history) seems to be a new idea in Albanian public discourse, but it is also a clear reference to the propaganda of Berisha's party between 1992 and 1997. Following the works of Albanian historians during those years, it is easy to observe a clear tendency to discredit the communist leaders. Accusations of treason against nationalist interests, the inability to govern and the repression of its own nation may be interpreted not only from monographs saturated with emotions and scientific articles, but also from official sources. These included shorthand notes from trials and selected statements of betrayal of nationalist interests on behalf of Yugoslavia or the USSR. The tendency to eliminate officers of the communist system from political life was especially visible in the years 1995–1997, when it gained clear support from the historians. This situation changed after the collapse of the so-called pyramid funds and anarchization of the Albanian state which took place in the spring of 1997. After the socialist party regained control of the government, people who had been discredited in the previous years returned to the public forum, and the history of communism became a subject of secondary importance and did not create such interest or emotions as during the first years of the transformation.

After eight years of socialist party rule, the next elections in 2005 brought a return to power of the Democratic Party of Albania (DPA). Still led by Sali Berisha, the party had clearly rejuvenated its membership, announcing the ideas of modernizing and Europeanizing Albania, while stopping its anti-communist rhetoric. Evidence

[1] "Levizja e Postribes, Topalli: Historiane, ku jeni?," *Standard*, September 6, 2011.

that the change was not a lasting one could be seen in their participation in disputes, which divided the historians, as well as the still active veterans of World War II. The seemingly unimportant question of the date of Albanian liberation from the German occupation blocked for a few years the publication of a new edition of the *History of the Albanian People*, but also created a previously unknown polarization of Albanian historians.[2] The date of November 28, 1944, which was accepted during the communist times, coincided with the date of the Declaration of Independence in 1912, and in this way legitimized the new Albanian government in 1944. The "revisionist" environment, sympathising with the DPA gave the date of November 29 as the day the communists came into power, explaining the unlawful use of independence symbols connected with the previous date. The dispute over the date reached a peak of absurdity when, based on German sources, there was an attempt to find out, with efforts worthy of a much greater cause, when the last German soldier left the territory of Albania.

The debate in progress in parliament in October 2006 over the resolution condemning the communist crimes led to the presentation of two differing projects. The resolution of the socialist party was practically limited to the motto of punishing people guilty of communist crimes. The resolution of the DPA considered the changing of school course-books as one of the key tasks for the future, as they needed a "revision of the historical dates contained in them."[3]

The continuation of the revisionist "political history" of the ruling party could be found in one of the "programmed" answers of Sali Berisha, who in 2010 demanded historians to subject the figure of Enver Hoxha to fair criticism so that the place of nostalgia for the time of his rule was taken by awareness of the crimes which he allowed during his regime. The dynamics of discussions concerning the *rishikimi i historise* clearly grew in 2011. Plans for a new act concerning compensation for those politically repressed represent a return to the political slogans of the years 1992–1997, when the DPA's "iron electorate" was built on the repressed environment and their families. However, other proposals seem to be closely connected with the new politics of remembrance. The idea of opening a museum of national memory in the grounds of a former labour camp in Spaç seemed to be a mistake when it was set up. The ruined buildings of the former camp are surrounded by land rich in ore, and plans to renew the exploration of pyrite ore left a question mark over the possibility of opening a museum in this place. More binding seems to be Berisha's declaration that the rewritten Albanian history can not just include the days of praise, but should also contain the darker days of the Albanian past.[4] The

---

2 The fourth volume of *History of Albanian People*, covering the period between 1939 and 1990 was published only in 2008 – Xhelal Gjecovi, ed., *Historia e Popullit Shqiptar ne kater vellime*, vol. 4 (Tirana: Botimet Toena, 2008).

3 Rozeta Rapushi, "PS dorezon ne Kuvend projekt-rezoluten e saj per krimet e komunizmit. Opozita kunder ndryshimit te historise," *Gazeta Shqiptare*, October 27, 2006.

4 "Berisha: Rishikim historise se komunizmit," *Panorama*, July 31, 2011.

idea of *rishikimi i historise* was used in one of her speeches in June 2011 by Jozefina Topalli, when speaking about the preparation of a new history to the Albanian parliament. Within the framework of *rishikimi i historise* the case of the postulate to remove the "episode" of the People's Assembly, which according to the constitutions of 1946 and 1976 played the role of parliament in the years 1946–1991, seems to be different. One of the historians who was engaged in the work on a new history of the Albanian parliament highlighted in the press that the "role of parliament during the period of communism was fictitious, and was not subject to verification through free elections, and it is impossible to talk about pluralism."[5] The annihilation of over 40 years of parliament-non-parliament activity also foresees a change in the numbering of successive tenures, according to which the beginning of the new era is regarded as 1991.

If it weren't for a few surviving, but devastated, memorial plates referring to the partisan communists from the years 1939–1944, it could be possible to feel that, as opposed to other towns in Albania, Tirana was never touched by the adversity of communism. Besides symbolic statues to the victims of communism and information plates with the numbers of victims of the system, there is no idea to commemorate the suffering and persecution whose scale seems to have been much greater than in other Soviet Bloc countries. Other places of commemoration, defining the specifics of Albanian communism, are also disappearing from the awareness of the residents of Tirana. This happened with the *Blok* – a separate district for the people of the government, which until 1990 was not accessible for the average mortal. The *Blok* represented a substitute of the Forbidden City for Albanians living in Tirana, and at the same time was a symbol of the isolation of the group of leaders. In one of his essays, Fatos Lubonja wrote about the residents of Tirana that "on the streets of the Blok half a century of history could be found, history written in reverse, starting from the most recent events".[6] Access to the streets of the Blok after tens of years allowed ordinary people to experience the widening of the margins of freedom with all their senses. The *Blok* soon stopped being an attraction, especially as its description by the opposition press as an "island of luxury" was unconvincing. Against the background of descriptions of N. Ceaușescu's palace in Romania, the list of televisions and CD players found in the villas printed by the Albanian press only created pitiful smiles. Today, the *Blok* has become part of the trading district and, apart from the second-hand booksellers selling classic works of communism on its streets, it is difficult to find any trace of the previous period.

One of Tirana's most characteristic buildings remains until today the Pyramid, standing between Skanderbeg Square and the University. Planned initially as the mausoleum of Enver Hoxha, after its opening in 1988 it filled the role of a museum.

---

5 Nevila Perndoj, "Topalli, rishikim historisë së Parlamentit para '91," *MAPO*, June 29, 2011.

6 Fatos Lubonja, "Blok (bez nostalgii)" in: *Znikająca Europa*, ed. Katharina Raabe, Monika Sznajderman (Wołowiec: Wydawnictwo Czarne, 2006), 295.

The museum was closed in December 1990, and the Pyramid began to function as a cultural-conference centre. The park surrounding it became a favourite place for Tirana's inhabitants. Both the building itself, with its distinguishing shape, as well as its surroundings gradually began to lose its significance as a symbol of communism, becoming an increasingly important symbol of Tirana and one of the most original Albanian architectural works of the 1980s.

In 2006, the building most closely associated with communism in Tirana – the Pyramid received the new name of "the Pjeter Arbnori International Centre." The choice of a politician regarded as a moral authority, but also as a victim of communist repression, seemed to testify to the symbolic "de-communism" of Hoxha's museum. Two years later, the next projects concerning the Pyramid appeared, including the idea of locating the headquarters of the National Theatre there. Until that time the main theatre in Albania had been located in an old building, constructed in 1939, whose size and form left a lot to be desired when compared with similar buildings in neighbouring countries. The idea of changing the function of the Pyramid was not realized for the next three years. In 2011, the DPA deputies, realizing the second "decommunisation offensive" proposed the destruction of the Pyramid as a symbol of communism and to replace it with a new parliament building. The ceremony of transferring the members of parliament to the new headquarters was to take place during the one-hundredth anniversary celebrations of the modern Albanian state. The plans to build a complex of parliament buildings in one of the most attractive points of the capital have the aim of finally and irreversibly depriving the town of the "last monument" to Enver Hoxha, which in the opinion of DPA activists still blemishes the town centre. The well-known Albanian publicist Blendi Fevziu defines the Pyramid as a gigantic and useless building blemishing today's Tirana. In addition, as the building can not be viewed separately from its original meaning, it can "serve only as part of the cult for the most negative figure in the history of Albania".[7]

The Pyramid became a test of the relations to communism in the Albanian media, and its defence represented a classic example of anachronical identity destroyed by communism. The decision of the Albanian parliament in 2011 to destroy the Pyramid caused widespread social protests, identified by the pro-government press as a clear example of the identification of some of society identifying with communism. Followers of the theory that the Pyramid represents part of Albanian inheritance were usually informed that a building with a thirty-year-long history could not represent part of its heritage, and could not be treated as a monument. The comparisons between the Pyramid and other symbols of the communist dictatorship, the statue of Enver Hoxha, destroyed by a crowd in February 1991, or the buildings associated with the Communist Party of Albania, which were destroyed in the 1990s, seem to be quite curious. It is difficult today to even find the location of the building

7 Blendi Fevziu, "Piramide apo parlamenti?" in: Ardian Klosi, ed., *Piramida e Tiranës e hijshme, e braktisur, e rrezikuar* (Tirana: Botimet Dudaj 2011), 11.

in Tirana in which "the party was born," but which represented for over forty years a place of pilgrimage for school children and pioneers.[8]

The well-known Albanian publicist Mero Baze considers the destruction of the Pyramid as an example of a lack of the "culture of remembrance."[9] The idea of removing the symbol of communism represents, in his opinion, an attempt to wipe out the communist crimes from the memory of Albanians, on behalf of party interests more than as an attempt to condemn the actions of Enver Hoxha. Baze also recalls the numerous unsuccessful attempts to create a museum of communism in Albania, or just a state-financed institution dealing with the souvenirs of communism. Diana Ndrenika draws attention to the consequences of the Pyramid's destruction in her essay "We are (not) communists."[10] The publicist regards the destruction of Tirana as a result of its old Ottoman part being destroyed, which was carried out in the 1950s by the communist government. If it is difficult for tourists to find traces of the Ottoman past in Tirana, then, as Ndrenika states, the last signs of communism will also disappear from the town. Tourists who are interested in the period of Enver Hoxha's rule are left with a visit to his reconstructed family home in Gjirokastra, in which the only elements of equipment, besides old furniture, are communist brochures which are kept in storage rooms and are not accessible.

In the debate concerning the fate of the Pyramid, Klement Kolaneci, who in the 1980s belonged to the team of architects who prepared the controversial building, has also spoken out. Without disguising his opposition to the idea of destroying the Pyramid, Kolaneci referred to the example of Hagi Sophia in Istanbul, which even though it was a symbol of the destroyed state was not knocked down, but transformed. Explaining his view, Kolaneci recalled the great cost of constructing the Pyramid ("which in the past was born by the Albanian people"), as well as the necessity of keeping it as a statement of the previous period.[11]

The conflict concerning communism and its place in Albanian history represents just part of the modern conflict about the identity and evolution of the Albanian nation. History is treated as a medicine for damage and the frustration of a "nation in a suitcase" (chosing emigration as a path out of poverty and deprivation) is an inevitable creation which has undergone mythologization and mystification. Against a backdrop of a "heroic" five-century-long struggle with Ottoman rule, the communist times seem to be a short episode. The Albanian paradox of (no)memory of communism is for casual observers a case of two factors: conviction of the uniqueness

---

8 Tadeusz Czekalski, "(Nie)pamięć o komunizmie. Przypadek albański," *Rocznik Antropologii Historii* 1–2 (2012), 170.

9 Mero Baze, *Per nje kultur te kujteses kunder komunizmit*, http://www.fjala.info/arkiv/fjala1/?p=4540 (accessed: March 25, 2013).

10 Diana Ndrenika, "Ne (s) jemi komuniste!," *Shekulli*, July 30, 2011.

11 Literally: "it's not people who should judge times, but time should judge people" – Arjola Hekurani, Oliverta Lila, *Kolaneci: Piramida s'eshte e Enverit, eshte ndertuar me leket e popullit*, www.shqip.dk (accessed: October 1, 2011).

of the communist system in Albania (for the majority of those who witnessed the period), as well as the escape from communism as a social experiment with limited value, serving only political, or even party, aims. The public debate, connected with plans to destroy the statues or the Pyramid, does not change the fact that the theme of life under communism, punishment of those guilty of crimes during that time, or commemorating victims, remains on the edge of current social-political problems.

Bibliography

Archival sources

Albanian State's Archive (Tirana)

Collections

Albanian Autocephalous Orthodox Church (Kisha Ortodokse Autoqefale ë Shqipërise)
Archdiocesy of Durres (Arqipeshkvia e Durresit)
Archdiocesy of Shkoder (Arqipeshkvia e Shkodres)
Ministry of Foreign Affairs (Ministria Puneve te Jashtme)
Prime Minister's Office (Kryeministria)

Published documents

Anuari Statistikor i RPSH. Tirana: Drejtoria e Statistikës, 1960.

Borodziej, Włodzimierz, ed. *Polskie Dokumenty Dyplomatyczne 1972*. Warsaw: Polski Instytut Spraw Międzynarodowych, 2005.

Dallin, Alexander, Jonathan Harris, and Grey Hodnett, eds. *Diversity in International Communism: A Documentary Record 1961–1963*. New York: Columbia University Press, 1963.

Dedi, Veli, Shavit Struga, Fane Veizi, and Mediha Shuteriqi, eds. *Dokumenta e materiale historike nga lufta e popullit shqiptar për liri e demokraci 1917–1941*. Tirana: Botim i Drejtorisë së Arkivave Shtetërore të R.P.Sh, 1959.

Fishta, Iljaz and Theodhor Kareco, eds. *Prona private në Shqipëri 1924–1944 (permes burimeve arkivore e bibliografike)*. Tirana: Dituria, 1996.

Góra, Władysław, ed. *Reformy agrarne w socjalistycznych państwach Europy (1944–1948)*. Wrocław: Zakład Narodowy im. Ossolińskich, 1987.

Górowska, Beata, ed. "Nowa Konstytucja Ludowej Socjalistycznej Republiki Albanii," *Zeszyty Naukowe Instytutu Nauk Politycznych Uniwersytetu Warszawskiego* 7 (1980).

Grishina, Ritta, ed. *Natsional'nyi vopros na Balkanakh cherez prizmu mirovoi revoliucii: v dokumentakh tsentral'nykh rossiiskikh arkhivov nachala – serediny 1920-kh godov*, vol. 2. Moscow: ROSSPÉN, 2003.

Hoxha, Enver. *Mbi problemin e gruas pjesë nga fjalime, raporte e biseda*. Tirana: Shtëpia Botuese Naim Frashëri, 1967.

——. *Our Policy is an Open Policy: The Policy of Proletarian Principles*. Tirana: Shtëpia Botuese 8 Nëntori, 1974.
——. *Report Announced at the VII Congress of the Albanian Party of Labour*. Tirana: Shtëpia Botuese Naim Frashëri, 1978.
——. *Vepra*, vol. 35. Tirana: Shtëpia Botuese Naim Frashëri, 1985.
Kochański, Aleksander and Mikołaj Mokrzycki-Markowski, eds. Polskie Dokumenty Dyplomatyczne 1974. Warsaw: Polski Instytut Spraw Międzynarodowych, 2007.
"Kodi Penal i Republikes Popullore Socialiste të Shqipërise." *Drejtesia Popullore* 3 (1977).
Kondis, Basil, Eleutheria Manta, eds. *The Greek Minority in Albania: A Documentary Record (1921–1993)*. Thessaloniki: Institute for Balkan Studies, 1994.
Kongresi i I-re i Partise Komuniste të Shqipërise (8–22 nentor 1948). Tirana: Botim i Partisë Punës se Shqipërisë, 1950.
Kupric, Nikolai, ed. *Konstituciia i osnovnye zakonodatelnye akty Narodnoi Respubliki Albaniia*. Moscow: Izdatel'stvo inostrannoi literatury, 1951.
Letter from the APL CC and the Albanian Government to the Chinese CP CC and the Chinese Government. Tirana: Shtëpia Botuese Naim Frashëri, 1978.
Plasari Ndreçi and Luan Malltezi, eds. *Marrëdhëniet shqiptaro-jugosllave 1945–1948. Dokumente*. Tirana: Drejtoria e Përgjitshme e Arkivave, 1996.
Pravda o sovetsko-albanskikh otnosheniiakh, Tirana: Shtepia Botuese Naim Frashëri, 1961.
Report Concerning the Activity of the APL CC Announced at the IV Congress of APL by Enver Hoxha on 13 February 1961. Tirana: Shtëpia Botuese Naim Frashëri, 1961.
Ruchniewicz, Krzysztof and Tadeusz Szumowski, eds. *Polskie Dokumenty Dyplomatyczne 1957*. Warsaw: Polski Instytut Spraw Międzynarodowych, 2006.
Simmons, William, ed. *The Constitutions of the Communist World*. Leiden: Sjithoff & Noordhoff, 1980.
Volokitina, Tat'iana, Galina Murashko, Albina Noskova, and Dina Novokhotovich, eds. *Vlast' i tserkov' v Vostochnoi Evrope, 1944–1953: Dokumenty rossijskikh arkhivov*. Vol. 1–2. Moscow: ROSSPÉN, 2009.

Diaries and memoirs

Alia, Ramiz. *Jeta ime. Kujtime*. Tirana: Botimet Toena, 2010.
Allkja, Osman. *...fije nga Ditari i Kryeministrisë*. Tirana: O. Allkja, 2000.
Chuvakhin, Dmitrii. "S diplomaticheskoi missiei v Albanii 1946–1952 gg." *Novaia i noveishaia istoriia* 1 (1995).
Djilas, Milovan. *Conversations with Stalin*. New York: Harcourt, Brace & World, 1962.
Lubonja, Todi. *Ankthi pa Fund i Lirise. Shenime*. Tirana: Albinform, 1994.
Pllumi, Zef. *Rrno vetem per me tregue*. Tirana: Shtëpia Botuese 55, 2006.
Prifti, Naum. *Teatri ne kohen e krizës*. Horizont: Tirana, 2001.

Monographs and articles (most important used in text)

Abazi, Halim and Kolasi Klevis, "Reformimi i Akademise Ushtarake të Shtabit e Pergjitshem." *Revista Ushtarake* 2 (1993).
Antoszek, Jadwiga, "Problemy narodowościowe i religijne na Półwyspie Bałkańskim." *Czasopismo Geograficzne* 3–4 (1995).

Balliu, Fahri. *The Ghoulish Lady Nexhmije Hoxha*. Tirana: Shtëpia Botuese 55, 2005.
Bendza, Marian. "Albański Autokefaliczny Kościół Prawosławny." *Rocznik Teologiczny* 2 (1981).
Biberaj, Elez. *Shqipëria në tranzicion: Rruga veshtire drejt Demokracise*. Tirana: ORA Botime, 2001.
Bihiku, Koço. *Kratkaia istoriia albanskoi literatury*. Tirana: Shtëpia Botuese Naim Frashëri, 1964.
Blajer, Mario. *Albania, from Isolation toward Reform*. Washington: International Monetary Fund, 1992.
Bland, William and Ian Price, *A Tangled Web: A History of Anglo-American Relations with Albania (1912–1955)*. Ilford: Albanian Society, 1986.
Blumi, Isa. "Hoxha's Class War: The Cultural Revolution and State Reformation, 1961–1971." *East European Quarterly* 33 (September 1999).
Bowers, Stephen. "Stalinism in Albania: Domestic Affairs under Enver Hoxha." *East European Quarterly* (January 1989).
Butka, Uran. *Ringjallje*. Tetovo: Botues Phoenix, 1996.
Capps, Edward. *Greece, Albania and Northern Epirus*. Chicago: Argonaut, 1963.
Chmielewski, Paweł. *Dyplomacja sowiecka w Radzie Bezpieczeństwa ONZ wobec zadań utrzymania pokoju i bezpieczeństwa międzynarodowego u progu zimnej wojny*. Łódź: Wydawnictwo Uniwersytetu Łódzkiego, 2005.
Clayer, Natalie. "Islam, State and Society in Post-Communist Albania." In: *Muslim Identity and the Balkan State*. Edited by Hugh Poulton and Suha Taji-Farouki. London: New York University Press, 1997.
Cook, Steve and Marash Rakaj. "Social Changes in the Albanian Alps during Communism." *Middle States Geographer* 28 (1995).
Cygański, Mirosław. "Polityka wschodnia RFN wobec Bułgarii i Albanii w latach 1964–1982." *Przegląd Stosunków Międzynarodowych* 1–2 (1984).
Czekalski, Tadeusz. "Długi powrót do Europy. Albańska polityka zagraniczna w latach 80. XX wieku." In: *Tantum historiae. Księga ofiarowana prof. Mieczysławowi Tantemu w osiemdziesiątą rocznicę urodzin*. Edited by Piotr Żurek. Bielsko-Biała, 2008.
——. "Historyczne uwarunkowania państwa bezwyznaniowego. Przypadek Albanii." In: *Religia wobec historii, historia wobec religii*. Edited by Elżbieta Przybył. Kraków: Nomos, 2006.
——. "(Nie)pamięć o komunizmie. Przypadek albański." *Rocznik Antropologii Historii* 1–2 (2012).
——. "Północny Epir i Czamuria – współczesne oblicze sporu grecko-albańskiego." In: *Naród – Państwo – Europa Środkowa*. Edited by Artur Patek and Wojciech Rojek, Kraków: Wydawnictwo Uniwersytetu Jagiellońskiego, 2006.
——. *Zarys dziejów chrześcijaństwa albańskiego 1912–1993*. Kraków: Nomos, 1996.
Czekalski, Tadeusz, Jerzy Hauziński, and Jan Leśny, *Historia Albanii*. Wrocław: Zakład Narodowy im. Ossolińskich, 2009.
Çaushi, Shpëtim. *Diplomacia shqiptare në normalizimin e marrëdvhënieve me Gjermanine*. Tirana: Ombra GVG, 2002.
Çollaku, Shaban "Zhvillime te demokracise socialiste në vitet 60." *Studime Historike* 1 (1988).
Dawson, Andrew H. *Planning in Eastern Europe*. New York: St. Martin's Press, 1987.
Dedijer, Vladimir. *Jugoslovensko-albanski odnosi (1939–1948)*, Belgrade: Borba, 1949.

Dervishi, Kastriot. *Historia e shtetit shqiptar 1912–2005: organizimi shtetëror, jeta politike, ngjarjet kryesore, të gjithë ligjvënësit, ministrat dhe kryetarët e shtetit shqiptar në historinë 93-vjeçare të tij*. Tirana: Shtëpia Botuese 55, 2006.

Deszczyński, Marek Piotr. "Wykluczenie Komunistycznej Partii Jugosławii z Biura Informacyjnego Partii Komunistycznych i Robotniczych. Zarys dziejów konfliktu jugosłowiańsko-sowieckiego w 1948 roku." *Studia z Dziejów Rosji i Europy Środkowowo-Wschodniej* 28 (1993).

Dezhgiu, Muharrem. *Veprimtaria e Shtetit te Ri te Demokracise Popullore (maj–nentor 1944)*. Tirana: Akademia e Shkencave e RPS të Shqipërisë, Instituti i Historisë, 1982.

Doll, Brandon. "The Relationship between the Clan System and Other Institutions in Northern Albania." *Southeast European and Black Sea Studies* 3, no. 2 (May 2003).

Dostatni, Bronisław. "Rozwój gospodarczy Albanii." *Sprawy Międzynarodowe* 9 (1960).

Dyrmishi, Demir. "Arsimi dhe shkenca në vitet 1949–1960." *Studime Historike* 1–2 (2001).

——. "Goditjet e organeve te drejtësisë dhe denimi i Tuk Jakovës dhe Bedri Spahiut (1949–1952)." *Studime Historike* 1–2 (2007).

——. "Krijimi i organizatës opozitare ilegale 'Bashkimi demokratik' dhe veprimtaria e saj në vitin 1945." *Studime Demokratike* 1–2 (1998).

——. "Krijimi i organizatës opozitare nacjonaldemokratike dhe veprimtaria e saj në asamblene kushtetuese (1944–mars 1946)." *Studime Historike* 1 (1995).

——. "Lufta politike në udhëheqjen e PKSh në vitet 1947–1948 dhe mënjanimi i ndërhyrjes Jugosllave." *Studime Historike* 3–4 (2000).

——. "Plenumi i 2-te te KQ te PKSh, rrjedhoje e nderhyrjes se PKJ (nentor 1944)." *Studime Historike* 1–2 (2003).

Dziak, Waldemar. *Albania między Belgradem, Moskwą i Pekinem*. Warsaw: Instytut Studiów Politycznych Polskiej Akademii Nauk, 1991.

Eberhardt, Piotr. "Problematyka ludnościowa Albanii." *Czasopismo Geograficzne* 1 (1992).

Elezi, Ismet. "Sur la vendetta en Albanie," *Studia Albanica* 1 (1966).

——. *Zhvillimi historik legislacjonit penal në Shqiperi*. Tirana: Albin, 1997.

Elsie, Robert. *A Dictionary of Albanian Religion, Mythology and Folk Culture*. New York: New York University Press, 2001.

——. *Zarys historii literatury albańskiej. Współczesna literatura albańska*. Toruń: Wydawnictwo Uniwersytetu Mikołaja Kopernika, 2005.

Estrefi, Diana, ed. "Republika e Shqipërise. Kuvendi." *Ligjvenesit Shqiptare 1920–2005*. Tirana: Kuvendi i Shqipërise, 2005.

Falkingham, Jane and Arjan Gjonca. "Fertility Transition in Communist Albania 1950–1990." *Population Studies* 55 (2001).

Fevziu, Blendi. *Histori e shtypit shqiptar 1848–1996*. Tirana: Grupimi "Brezi 22" / Shtëpia Botuese Marin Barleti, 1996.

Fischer, Bernd J., *Albania at War 1939–1945*. London: Hurst, 1999.

——. *King Zog and the Struggle for Stability in Albania*. Boulder, CO: East European Monographs, 1984. Distributed by the Columbia University Press.

Fishta, Iljaz. "Kolektivizimi në mase i prodhuesve te vegjel te fshatit (1956–1960)." *Studime Historike* 3 (1990).

Fishta, Iljaz and Veniamin Toçi, *Ekonomia e Shqipërise në Vitet e para te ndertimit socialist (nentor 1944–nentor 1948)*. Tirana: Akademia e Shkencave e RPS të Shqipërisë, Instituti i Historisë, 1984.

Frashëri, Kristo. *Historia e levizjes se majte ne Shqiperi dhe e themelimit te PKSh-se 1878–1941 (veshtrim historik me nje shtojce dokumentare).* Tirana: Akademia e Shkencave e Shqiperise, 2006.

——. *The History of Albania: Brief Survey.* Tirana: Shtëpia Botuese Naim Frashëri, 1964.

Frashëri, Xhemal. *Pushteti Popullor ne Vitet e Luftes Antifashiste Nacionalçlirimtare.* Tirana: Akademia e Shkencave e RPS të Shqipërisë, Instituti i Historisë, 1983.

Geço, Pandi. "Aspekte te rritjes se popullsise se qytetit te Tiranës pas clirimit." *Studime Historike* 1 (1971).

——. "Rritja e popullsise qytetare ne RPSh dhe shperndarja e re gjeografike." *Studime Historike* 2 (1970).

Gjecovi, Xhelal, ed. *Historia e Popullit Shqiptar ne kater vellime*, vol. 4. Tirana: Toena, 2008.

——. *Marredheniet shqiptaro-jugosllave ne Vitet e Luftes Antifashiste Nacionalçlirimtare (nentor 1941–nentor 1944).* Tirana: Shtëpia Botuese Naim Frashëri, 1986.

Gjilani, Feti. "Rruga historie e lindjes dhe e zhvillimit te legislacjonit te punës ne RPSh." *Studime Historike* 4 (1971).

Griffith, William E. *Albania and the Sino-Soviet Rift.* Cambridge, MA: MIT Press, 1963.

Halimarski, Andrzej. "Polityka zagraniczna Chińskiej Republiki Ludowej (1949-1984)." In: *Polityka zagraniczna socjalistycznych państw Azji.* Edited by Jerzy Muszyński. Warsaw: PISM, 1985.

Hall, Derek. *Albania and the Albanians*, London: Pinter Reference, 1994.

——. *Tourism and Economic Development in Eastern Europe and the Soviet Union.* London: Belhaven Press, 1991.

Hamm, Henry. *Albania – China's Beachhead in Europe.* New York: Praeger, 1963.

Hasani, Proleter. *Histori e pashkruar. Historia e organizimit te UNCSh-se.* Tirana: Fllad, 1999.

Hauziński, Jerzy. "Muzułmanie w Albanii." In: *Muzułmanie w Europie.* Edited by Anna Parzymies. Warsaw: Dialog, 2005.

Horodyska, Dorota. "Przed szansą. O dramaturgii albańskiej." *Dialog* 11 (2004).

Jacques, Edwin E. *The Albanians: An Ethnic History from Pre-Historic Times to the Present.* Jefferson, NC: McFarland, 1995.

Jano, Ariste. *Forcimi dhe demokratizimi i pushtetit popullor në Shqipëri (nentor 1944–nentor 1948).* Tirana: Akademia e Shkencave e RPS të Shqipërisë, Instituti i Historisë, 1986.

Kaba, Hamit. "Demshperblimet Italiane te Luftes se Dyte Botërore per Shqipërine (1945–1960)." *Studime Historike* 1–2 (2003).

Kastory, Andrzej. "Problem granicy albańsko-greckiej w obradach paryskiej konferencji pokojowej." *Prace Naukowe Uniwersytetu Śląskiego. Historia* 1 (1977).

Kerçiku, Kadri. *Zhvillimi i shendetsise në Shkodër gjate shek. XVIII–XX.* Tirana, 1962.

Klosi, Ardian, ed. *Piramida e Tiranës e hijshme, e braktisur, e rrezikuar.* Tirana: Botimet Dudaj, 2011.

Kola, Paulin. *The Search for Greater Albania.* London: Hurst & Co., 2003.

Koseski, Adam. *Albania. Krótki zarys dziejów.* Warsaw: Książka i Wiedza, 1988.

Krzepkowski, Stanisław. "Islam w krajach bałkańskich w przeszłości i współcześnie – zarys ogólny." In: *Bałkany – Bułgaria – Polska. Studium z historii powszechnej XIX i XX w.*, Kielce: Bog & Art, 1998.

Lalaj, Ana. "Konferenca e Partise e Tiranës, nje pranvere e deshtuar e se majtës ne Shqipëri (14–19 prill 1956)." *Studime Historike* 1–2 (2009).

——. "Shqipëria dhe Informbyroja." *Studime Historike* 3–4 (2009).

Leci, Elmas. *Eliminimit i lidershipit ushtarak*. Tirana: Instituti i Sigurimit dhe Mbrojtjes, 2002.

Logoreci, Anton. *The Albanians: Europe's Forgotten Survivors*. London: V. Gollancz, 1977.

Luarasi, Skender. *Ne Brigadat Internacionale në Spanje*. Tirana: Toena 1996.

Lubonja, Fatos. *Albania – wolność zagrożona*. Translated by Dorota Horodyska. Sejny: Pogranicze, 2005.

Luthi, Lorenz. *Chiny-ZSRR. Zimna wojna w świecie komunistycznym*. Translated by Józef Pawłowski and Katarzyna Urban-Pawłowska. Warsaw: Dialog, 2011.

Mejdiaj, Bajram. "Mbi te drejten e gruas për te kerkuar zgjidhen e marteses." *Studime Historike* 1 (1970).

Meta, Beqir. "Raportet Midis Greqise dhe Shqipërise në vitet 1950–1953." *Studime Historike* 3–4 (2002).

Mičunović, Veljko. *Dziennik moskiewski – 1956*. Warsaw: Niezależna Oficyna Wydawnicza, 1988.

Milo, Paskal. "Incidenti i Kanalit te Korfuzit (1945–1946)." *Studime Historike* 3–4 (2000).

Misja, Vladimir. "Aspekte te zhvillimit te arsimit te larte në RPS te Shqipërise." *Studime Historike* 3 (1986).

Musta, Agim. *The Prisons of the Prison State*, Tirana: Shtëpia Botuese Bilal Xhaferri, 2000.

Myzyri, Hysni, ed. *Historia e Shqipërise dhe e Shqiptareve*, Prizren: Siprint, 2001.

Nova, Koço. "Aspekte nga veprimtaria gjyqesore revolucionare gjate luftes N.Cl." *Studime Historike* 4 (1971).

Nowak, Jerzy Robert. "Albania 1944–1948. Terror wobec sił niekomunistycznych i walki frakcyjne." In: *Czy Europa Środkowo-Wschodnia mogła się wybić na wolność*. Edited by Tadeusz Kisielewski and Norbert Kasparek. Olsztyn: Wyższa Szkoła Pedagogiczna, 1996.

——. "Polityka zagraniczna Albanii w latach 1944–1980." *Sprawy Międzynarodowe* 10 (1982).

——. *Powstanie Ludowej Republiki Albanii 1944–1949*, Warsaw: Instytut Krajów Socjalistycznych PAN, 1983.

O'Donnell, James. *A Coming of Age: Albania under Enver Hoxha*. Boulder, CO: East European Monographs, 1999. Distributed by the Columbia University Press.

Omari, Luan. "Mbi funksionet e brendshme te shtetit tone socialist." *Studime Historike* 4 (1971).

Pano, Nicholas. "The Albanian Cultural Revolution." *Problems of Communism* (July–August 1974).

——. *The People's Republic of Albania*, Baltimore: Johns Hopkins Press, 1968.

Pearson, Owen. *Albania in the Twentieth Century*, vol. 2: *Albania in Occupation and War: From Fascism to Communism 1940–1945*. London: Centre for Albanian Studies / I.B. Tauris, 2005.

——. *Albania in the Twentieth Century*, vol. 3: *Albania as a Dictatorship and Democracy: From Isolation to the Kosovo War*. London: Centre for Albanian Studies / I.B. Tauris, 2007.

Pepa, Bik. *Feja lakuriq. Vjersha satirike*. Tirana: Shtëpia Botuese Naim Frashëri, 1967.

Pepa, Pjetër. *Dosja e diktaturës*. Tirana: n.p., 1995.

Peters, Markus W. *Geschichte der Katolischen Kirche in Albanien 1919–1993*. Wiesbaden: Harrasowitz, 2003.

Pipa, Arshi. *Albanian Stalinism: Ideo-Political Aspects*. Boulder, CO: East European Monographs, 1990. Distributed by the Columbia University Press.

Plasari, Ndreçi. "Kongresi Antifashist Nacionalclirimtar i Permetit – Themelimi i Shtetit te ri shqiptar te Demokracise popullore." *Studime Historike* 4 (1975).

——. "Krijimi i Ushtrise Nacional-çlirimtare shqiptare (1941–1943)." *Buletin i Universitetit Shteteror te Tiranes. Seria Shkencat Shoqerore* 4 (1958).

Plasari, Ndreçi and Shyqyri Ballvora, "Politika dhe strategija e luftes antifashiste nacionalclirimtare te popullit shqiptar." *Studime Historike* 3 (1975).

Pollo, Stefanaq et al. *The History of Albania (from its Origin to the Present Days)*. London & Boston: Routledge & Kegan Paul, 1981.

Post, Susan, E. Pritchett. *Woman in Modern Albania*. London: McFarland, 1998.

Prifti, Peter. *Remote Albania: The Politics of Isolation*, Tirana: Onufri, 1999.

——. *Socialist Albania since 1944: Domestic and Foreign Developments*, Cambridge, MA: MIT Press, 1978.

Protas, Teresa. "System społeczno-ekonomiczny Ludowej Socjalistycznej Republiki Albanii w latach 1945–1985." *Balcanica Posnanensia* 9/10 (1999).

Przedpełski, Borys. "Sytuacja religijna w Albanii." *Rocznik Teologiczny* 33, no. 1 (1991).

Ramet, Sabrina. *Nihil obstat: Religion, Politics and Social Change in East-Central Europe*. Durham, NC: Duke University Press, 1998.

Ressuli, Namik. *Albanian Literature*. Boston: Pan-Albanian Federation of America Vatra, 1987.

Roszkowski, Wojciech. *Land Reforms in East Central Europe after World War One*, Warsaw: Institute of Political Studies, Polish Academy of Sciences, 1995.

Różański, Henryk. *Spojrzenie na RWPG. Wspomnienia, dokumenty, refleksje 1949–1988*. Warsaw: PWN, 1990.

Rychlik, Jan. "Następstwa XX Zjazdu KPZR w krajach Europy Środkowej i Wschodniej. Podobieństwa i specyficzne różnice." In: *Rok 1956 w Polsce i jego rezonans w Europie*. Edited by Joanna Szymoniczek and Eugeniusz Król. Warsaw: ISP PAN, 2009.

Sadikaj, Dilaver. "Kufizimi i prones private dhe krijimi i ekonomise se centralizuar në qytet (dhjetor 1944–1948)." *Studime Historike* 1–2 (2001).

——. "Levizja revolucionare kunder fese në vitet gjashtedhjete." *Studime Historike* 4 (1981).

——. "Politika e jashtme e shtetit shqiptar në vitet 80." *Studime Historike* 1–2 (1999).

——. "Rindertimi i industries në vitet 1945–46." *Studime Historike* 3 (1975).

Sandström, Per and Örjan Sjöberg. "Albanian Economic Performance: Stagnation in the 1980s." *Soviet Studies* 5 (1991).

Sawicka, Irena, ed. *Albanistyka polska*. Toruń: Wydawnictwo Uniwersytetu Mikołaja Kopernika, 2007.

Schnytzer, Adi. *Stalinist Economic Strategy in Practice: The Case of Albania*. New York: Oxford University Press, 1982.

Schwandner-Sievers, Stephanie and Bernd J. Fischer, eds. *Albanian Identities. Myth and History*. London: Hurst, 2002.

Seddon, David and Ruth Davey. "The Politics of Economic Reform in Albania." In: *Political and Economic Liberalization: Dynamic and Linkages in Comparative Perspective*. Edited by Gerd Nonneman. New York: Lynne Rienner Publishers, 1996.

Sjöberg, Örjan. *Rural Change and Development in Albania*. Boulder: Westview Press, 1991.

Skarżyński, Michał. *Rozwój gospodarczy Ludowej Republiki Albanii 1944–1970*. Warsaw: Polski Instytut Spraw Międzynarodowych, 1971.

Skendi, Stavro. *Albania*. New York: Free Europe Committee, 1956.

Skobelski, Robert. *Polityka PRL wobec państw socjalistycznych w latach 1956–1970. Współpraca – napięcia – konflikty*. Poznań: Wydawnictwo Poznańskie, 2010.

——. "Stosunki polsko-albańskie w latach 1956–1970." *Limes. Studia i materiały z dziejów Europy Środkowo-Wschodniej* 1 (2008).

Smirnova, Nina D. *Istoriia Albanii w XX veke.* Moscow: Nauka, 2003.

Stahl, Johannes. *Rent from the Land: A Political Ecology of Postsocialist Rural Transformation.* London: Anthem Press, 2010.

Stamova, Marijana. *Albanskijat vopros na Balkanite (1945–1981).* Sofia: Faber, 2005.

Staszewski, Michał, *Państwo a związki wyznaniowe w europejskich państwach socjalistycznych.* Warsaw: Książka i Wiedza, 1976.

Stępniak, Władysław. "Albania a konflikt Tity ze Stalinem." *Balcanica Posnanensia* 9/10 (1999).

Sufaj, Fehmi. *Historia e burgjeve te Shqipërise gjate shekullit XX.* Tirana: Albin, 2000.

Tase, Alfreda. "Aspekte te luftes per emancipimin e plote te gruas ne rrethin e Tiranes ne vitet 1961–1970." *Studime Historike* 3 (1984).

Tebinka, Jacek. *Uzależnienie czy suwerenność? Odwilż październikowa w dyplomacji Polskiej Rzeczypospolitej Ludowej 1956–1961.* Warsaw: Wydawnictwo Neriton, 2010.

Tirtja, Mark. "Mbi martesat e bera mbas clirimit midis personazh nga besime te ndryshme." *Studime Historike* 2 (1970).

Titani, Gjergj and Hasani Proleter. *Personalitete ushtarake shqiptare në vitet 1912–1997.* Vol. 1. Tirana: Toena, 1997.

Tomaszewski, J. *Europa Środkowo-Wschodnia 1944–1968. Powstanie, ewolucja i kryzys realnego socjalizmu.* Warsaw: Wydawnictwo Uniwersytetu Warszawskiego, 1992.

Trenova, Bashkim. "Marredheniet shqiptaro-jugosllave ne fushen ekonomike ne viten 1944–1946." *Studime Historike* 3 (1990).

Trix, Frances "The Resurfacing of Islam in Albania," *East European Quarterly* 28, no. 4 (January 1995).

Omari, Luan, Stefanaq Pollo, and Bardhyl Golemi, eds. *Universiteti Shteteror i Tiranes 1957–1967.* Tirana: N.I.SH.Shtypshkronjave „Mihal Duri", 1967.

Vankovska, Biljana and Håkan Wiberg. *Between Past and Future: Civil-Military Relations in the Post-communist Balkans.* London: I.B. Tauris, 2003.

Vickers, Miranda. *The Albanians: A Modern History.* London: I.B. Tauris, 1999.

——. *Between Serb and Albanian: A History of Kosovo*, New York: Columbia University Press, 1998.

Vickers, Miranda and James Pettifier, *Albania: From Anarchy to a Balkan Identity.* 2nd ed. London: Hurst, 1999.

Waal, Clarissa de. *Albania Today: A Portrait of Post-communist Turbulence.* London: I.B. Tauris, 2005.

Wojnicki, Jacek. *System konstytucyjny Albanii.* Warsaw: Wydawnictwo Sejmowe, 2007.

——. *Zgromadzenie - Parlament Albanii.* Warsaw: Wydawnictwo Sejmowe, 2005.

Volokitina, Tat'iana, Galina Murashko, Albina Noskova, and Tat'iana Pokivailova, eds.. *Moskva i Vostochnaia Evropa. Stanovlenie politicheskikh rezhimov sovietskogo tipa 1949–1953.* Moscow: ROSSPÉN, 2002.

Volokitina, Tat'iana, Galina Murashko, and Albina Noskova. *Moskva i Vostochnaia Evropa. Vlast' i tserkov' v period obshchestvennykh transformacii 40–50 godov XX veka*, Moscow: ROSSPÉN, 2008.

List of tables

Personal index

Geographical index

TECHNICAL EDITOR
Jadwiga Makowiec

PROOFREADER
Małgorzata Szul

TYPESETTER
Katarzyna Mróz-Jaskuła

Jagiellonian University Press
Editorial Offices: Michałowskiego St. 9/2, 31-126 Cracow
Phone: +48 12 631 18 81, +48 12 631 18 82, Fax: +48 12 631 18 83